Judith Wolfe is Tutor in Theology at St John's
College, and teaches systematic and philosophical
theology at the University of Oxford.

HEIDEGGER'S ESCHATOLOGY

DIVINE PRODUCTION IN LATE MEDIEVAL TRINITARIAN THEOLOGY
Henry of Ghent, Duns Scotus, and William Ockham
JT Paasch (2012)

THE SALVATION OF ATHEISTS AND CATHOLIC DOGMATIC
THEOLOGY
Stephen Bullivant (2012)

COMEDY AND FEMINIST INTERPRETATION OF THE HEBREW BIBLE
A Subversive Collaboration
Melissa A. Jackson (2012)

THE STORY OF ISRAEL IN THE BOOK OF QOHELET
Ecclesiastes as Cultural Memory
Jennie Barbour (2012)

THE ANTI-PELAGIAN CHRISTOLOGY OF AUGUSTINE OF HIPPO,
396–430
Dominic Keech (2012)

VISIONARY RELIGION AND RADICALISM IN EARLY INDUSTRIAL
ENGLAND
From Southcott to Socialism
Philip Lockley (2012)

REPENTANCE IN LATE ANTIQUITY
Eastern Asceticism and the Framing of the Christian Life c.400–650 CE
Alexis C. Torrance (2012)

SCHELLING'S THEORY OF SYMBOLIC LANGUAGE
Forming the System of Identity
Daniel Whistler (2013)

PATMOS IN THE RECEPTION HISTORY OF THE APOCALYPSE
Ian Boxall (2013)

THE THEOLOGICAL VISION OF NIEBUHR'S *THE IRONY OF AMERICAN
HISTORY*
'In the Battle and Above It'
Scott R. Erwin (2013)

Heidegger's Eschatology

Theological Horizons in Martin Heidegger's Early Work

JUDITH WOLFE

OXFORD
UNIVERSITY PRESS

OXFORD
UNIVERSITY PRESS

Great Clarendon Street, Oxford, OX2 6DP,
United Kingdom

Oxford University Press is a department of the University of Oxford.
It furthers the University's objective of excellence in research, scholarship,
and education by publishing worldwide. Oxford is a registered trade mark of
Oxford University Press in the UK and in certain other countries

First Edition published in 2013

Impression: 1

British Library Cataloguing in Publication Data
Data available

ISBN 978–0–19–968051–1

Printed and bound in Great Britain by
CPI Group (UK) Ltd, Croydon, CR0 4YY

Acknowledgements

I would like to thank the following:

For making this book possible, the Arts and Humanities Research Council, the Oxford Centre for Christianity and Culture, and the Trustees of the Squire & Marriott Fund. For providing an academic home during the last years of its completion, the European College of Liberal Arts, Berlin, and St John's College, Oxford.

For their patience and help throughout its long gestation, the staff at the Bodleian and Taylorian Libraries, Oxford, and the Staatsbibliothek and Humboldt University Library, Berlin.

For answering various enquiries, Ulrich v. Bülow (Deutsches Literatur-Archiv Marbach), Prof. Theodore Kisiel, Prof. Dr Raimund Lachner, Dr Sean McGrath, and Dr Holger Zaborowski. For generously providing offprints of articles, Johannes Schaber OP and Thomas Sheehan. For offering valuable feedback, seminar audiences at Oxford, Cambridge, Nottingham, and Bonn, especially Prof. Daphne Hampson, Prof. Karen Kilby, Dr Ben Morgan, and Dr Joel Rasmussen.

Above all, Dr Mark Edwards, Prof. Paul S. Fiddes, Prof. Stephen Mulhall, and Dr Johannes Zachhuber for their guidance, and Profs. John Milbank and George Pattison for acting as examiners of the thesis as which this book began. The knowledge, wisdom, generosity and courtesy of these men have taught me—however slow a student I may have been—what it is to be a scholar.

Contents

List of Abbreviations

WORKS

ESGA 4   E. Stein, *Selbstbildnis in Briefen III: Briefe an Roman Ingarden* (1917–38)

ESGA 11   E. Stein, *Endliches und Ewiges Sein: Versuch eines Aufstiegs zum Sinn des Seins* (1938)

GA 1   M. Heidegger, *Frühe Schriften* (1912–16)

GA 4   M. Heidegger, *Erläuterungen zu Hölderlins Dichtung* (1936–68)

GA 5   M. Heidegger, *Holzwege* (1935–46)

GA 9   M. Heidegger, *Wegmarken* (1919–61)

GA 12   M. Heidegger, *Unterwegs zur Sprache* (1950–9)

GA 13   M. Heidegger, *Aus der Erfahrung des Denkens, 1910–1976* (1910–76)

GA 14   M. Heidegger, *Zur Sache des Denkens* (1962–64)

GA 16   M. Heidegger, *Reden und andere Zeugnisse eines Lebensweges* (1910–76)

GA 18   M. Heidegger, *Grundbegriffe der aristotelischen Philosophie* (SS 1924)

GA 20   M. Heidegger, *Prolegomena zur Geschichte des Zeitbegriffs* (SS 1925)

GA 21   M. Heidegger, *Logik: Die Frage nach der Wahrheit* (WS 1925/6)

GA 29/30 M. Heidegger, *Die Grundbegriffe der Metaphysik: Welt–Endlichkeit–Einsamkeit* (WS 1929/30)

GA 39   M. Heidegger, *Hölderlins Hymnen 'Germanien' und 'Der Rhein'* (WS 1934/5)

GA 40   M. Heidegger, *Einführung in die Metaphysik* (SS 1935)

GA 56/57 M. Heidegger, *Zur Bestimmung der Philosophie* (KNS 1919 and SS 1919)

GA 58   M. Heidegger, *Grundprobleme der Phänomenologie* (WS 1919/20)

GA 60   M. Heidegger, *Phänomenologie des religiösen Lebens* (1918/19, WS 1920/1 and SS 1921)

GA 61	M. Heidegger, *Phänomenologische Interpretationen zu Aristoteles: Einführung in die phänomenologische Forschung* (WS 1921/2)
GA 62	M. Heidegger, *Phänomenologische Interpretationen ausgewählter Abhandlungen des Aristoteles zu Ontologie und Logik* (1922 and SS 1922)
GA 63	M. Heidegger, *Ontologie. Hermeneutik der Faktizität* (SS 1923)
GA 64	M. Heidegger, *Der Begriff der Zeit* (1924)
GA 66	M. Heidegger, *Besinnung* (1938–9)
HJB	A. Denker, H. H. Gander, and H. Zaborowski (eds.), *Heidegger-Jahrbuch 1* (2004)
SZ	M. Heidegger, *Sein und Zeit* (1927)
WA	D. *Martin Luthers Werke*, Weimar Ausgabe

OTHER ABBREVIATIONS

KNS	Kriegsnotsemester (War Emergency Semester)
SS	Summer Semester
WS	Winter Semester

Note on the Text

All translations are my own unless otherwise indicated. In the first citation of each text, I have provided the date of its first (original language) publication in parentheses.

All biblical quotations are from the *New Revised Standard Version* unless otherwise noted.

Introduction

Using newly available German texts of Heidegger's earliest letters and lectures (1909–), contextualized within the church-political and theological debates of his early university career, this book evaluates Martin Heidegger's continued debt to theological sources after his renunciation of academic theology and his turn towards the a-theistic[1] philosophical method epitomized in *Being and Time* (1927). The result, I hope, stakes out new ground in providing a theological genealogy of Heidegger's early thought—a genealogy that centres on an eschatological vision, derived from theological sources but reshaped into a central resource for the development of an a-theistic phenomenological account of human existence.

In the years 1909 to 1915, Heidegger, originally immersed in an anti-Modernist Roman Catholic milieu, gradually dissociated himself from post-Vatican I Catholicism against the background of his growing sense of the importance of philosophical questions '*as questions*'. By this he chiefly meant two things: one, the epistemological questions about metaphysics posed first by Kant and now by Husserlian phenomenology; and two, the problem of 'historicity' for an understanding both of individual human existence (as inherently temporal) and of Christianity (as a historically situated and developing religion). Searching for a theological method capable of doing justice to lived experience rather than remaining entrenched in a statically conceived *philosophia perennis*, Heidegger, after 1915, began to develop a synthesis of Schleiermacher's and the medieval mystics' 'proto-phenomenology' with an emphasis on the basic religious experience of affliction—suffering our own finitude—which he found in the early Luther, Friedrich Hölderlin, Fyodor Dostoevsky, Søren Kierkegaard, and Franz Overbeck.

These concerns converged on a reappropriation of early Christian eschatology in Heidegger's thought of the early 1920s, within the context of similar but competing appropriations by other theological thinkers

[1] A-theistic here refers to a philosophical methodology that brackets God from its analyses, rather than to a more definitive world-view (atheistic).

of the time, especially Karl Barth and Eduard Thurneysen. Following a dominant interpretation in early 20th-century Protestant scholarship, Heidegger posited, in the early 1920s, a profound irreconcilability of earliest ('authentic') Christian experience—centrally characterized by eschatological expectation—on the one hand, and the subsequent development—when this expectation failed to materialize—of a Christian 'philosophy' on the other. Building on his phenomenological analysis of affliction with our own finitude as the basic religious experience, Heidegger now found in early Christian eschatological expectation an instantiation *par excellence* of authentic religious existence. His description of this expectant restlessness, however, is fundamentally at odds with its original Christian context, for Heidegger's commitment to a phenomenological description of the human situation—that is, a description of that situation solely from within—leads him to divorce the 'existential' experience of expectation from its (from this perspective merely 'existentiell' or derivatively postulated) object, the 'blessed hope' of the coming Kingdom of God. As a consequence, that hope no longer appears as constitutive of, but rather as fundamentally inimical to, 'eschatological' unrest as Heidegger understands it, because it projects an end to that unrest, and so a cancellation of the nexus of authentic existence.

Against the Christian vision, Heidegger thus developed, in the mid-1920s, an eschatology without eschaton that found paradigmatic expression in his account of being-unto-death, and underlay both his critique of theology (*Phenomenology and Theology*, 1927) and his re-conception of metaphysics (*What is Metaphysics?*, 1929). On this account, its own being is, at the deepest level, a *question* for each person (or 'Dasein'[2]). This question cannot be answered or resolved in any traditional sense, because the consummation of Dasein—death—is at the same time its negation. Authentic existence is the resolute anticipation of this perpetual, inavertible, and inescapably personal possibility—it is being-unto-death.

---

[2] In *Being and Time* and other important texts, Heidegger uses the term *Dasein* (lit.: 'being-there') both in its conventional meaning of '(human) existence' and in the idiosyncratic sense of 'human being'/'person'. The elision is not accidental, but implies that the human being is determined by his/her existence rather than a pre-defined 'essence'. English-language Heidegger scholarship has, for the most part, adopted the term 'Dasein' (not italicized) rather than attempting a translation. I have followed that practice when discussing *Being and Time* and Heidegger's phenomenology in general. In a book of intellectual history like this one, however, it is important to remember that until 1927, Heidegger used *Dasein* in its conventional sense as 'human existence', and I have translated it as such in the relevant contexts.

The burden of this book is to lay out and substantiate this biographical-intellectual account, and analyse some of its implications. Before doing so, it is important to clarify a matter of likely controversy. It is well known that Heidegger first encountered many of the concepts that became distinctive of his phenomenology (including 'hermeneutics', 'falling', and 'guilt') in theological contexts.[3] Consequently, a key question within Heideggerian philosophy and, even more so, in theological engagements with Heidegger is whether his phenomenological concepts parasitically 'secularize' theological ideas, or whether they uncover the existential ground—itself more basic than the 'existentiell' or life-choice between faith and non-belief—of all human existence, including Christian thought and practice. The secularization critique was advanced in various forms from earliest days by both theologians (including Emil Brunner, Erich Przywara, and Edith Stein) and philosophers (including Heidegger's student Löwith and his teacher Husserl).[4] Heidegger consistently repudiated it, most fully in his 1947 'Letter on Humanism'.

This debate remains as entrenched as it always was. And because the intended force of Heidegger's phenomenological approach is precisely to uncover those existential structures (such as relationality, situatedness, and temporality) which underlie and make possible any particular life-choice or interpretation of the world—in other words, because he purports to argue at an ontological depth which most religious (and other) thinkers have not reached—the current debate proceeds along similar lines: The opposing position is generally regarded not as a reasonable disagreement, but as a failure to grasp the depth of one's own arguments. Consequently, the change demanded of the other side is typically not so much the assimilation of new information or the admission of a logical fallacy, but a Gestalt shift, or the realization of a depth against which contrary arguments fall flat.

But such rhetoric conceals the particularity of Heidegger's theological-philosophical development, as well as of any singular

---

[3] For his own acknowledgement of this fact, see, among many other places, *Ontologie. Hermeneutik der Faktizität* (SS 1923), ed. Käte Bröcker-Oltmanns (Frankfurt: Klostermann, 2nd edn., 1995), 5 [hereafter cited as GA 63], and 'Aus einem Gespräch von der Sprache: Zwischen einem Japaner und einem Fragenden', in *Unterwegs zur Sprache* (1950–9), ed. Friedrich-Wilhelm von Herrmann (Frankfurt: Klostermann, 1985), 79–146; especially p. 91 [hereafter cited as GA 12].

[4] See Brunner's summary note on this question in his 'Theologie und Ontologie, oder: Die Theologie am Scheidewege', *Zeitschrift für Theologie und Kirche* 12 (1931), 111–22; p. 120.

theological image of the world. Primary sources, particularly German materials only recently made available, make it possible—now more than ever before—to follow out the complexity and volatility of Heidegger's early engagement with Christian sources. Doing so, this book hopes to make clear both that Heidegger mounts a formidable case against certain basic assumptions of the neo-Scholastic and dialectical theologies of his time, and that he cannot sustain his own claim to conceptual priority in its fullness, or not without serious sacrifices. It is considerably more interesting to find and test the pressure points that each exposes in the other than to cover up those pressure points by dismissing opposing claims out of hand.

The progression of this book, therefore, encompasses four steps. The first is to establish a position of empirical strength by describing, in some detail, Heidegger's earliest religious milieu, education, and reading. The second is to present Heidegger's interpretations of key religious thinkers, including St Paul, St Augustine, Luther, Schleiermacher, and Kierkegaard, as 'strong misreadings'[5]—in other words, to analyse both how Heidegger reinterprets his theological sources, and in what ways the sources themselves enable his 'misreadings', both in their substance and their tacit critique (or 'phenomenological reduction'[6]) of the source material. The result is a clearer understanding not only of Heidegger's concepts themselves, but also of the pressure points in the theological tradition to which Heidegger critically and creatively responds. The third step is to test Heidegger's eschatology without eschaton from within by means of a close reading of the relevant sections of *Being and Time*, to determine its analytical strengths and limits.

These last two steps lead to a dual conclusion. On one hand, Heidegger's de-theologized eschatology effectively challenges both the 'dialectical' and the neo-Scholastic theologies dominant at the time of the publication of *Being and Time*. Against neo-Scholasticism, Heidegger objects that the God's-eye view of history implicit in a Vatican I *philosophia perennia* is not in fact ever available to human beings; worse, that to arrogate such a view to oneself is not merely a mistake but a consequential human failing, since any analysis of man as part of a timeless metaphysical system inherently distorts his nature,

---

[5] See Harold Bloom, *The Anxiety of Influence* (Oxford: Oxford University Press, 1997 [1973]), xxiii and *passim*.

[6] I do not here use this term in its technical Husserlian sense, but in that dictated by the *lex parsimoniae*.

and so programmes those who live by it for an inauthentic existence. Against Protestantism, Heidegger implicitly objects that any theological account of a fallen humanity which appeals (as theologians from Luther to Emil Brunner do) to 'phenomenological' evidence for this fallenness, but also insists on setting it in the context of salvation, is guilty of obfuscating the boundary between phenomenology and dogmatics, and therefore undermines its own epistemic method (whether that method is heuristic or represents a deep ontological commitment).

On the other hand, Heidegger's eschatology, by positing death or Nothing rather than eternal life or God as the horizon of an eschatological (and therefore authentic) existence, itself runs into problems that may best be explained as consequences of attempting to eradicate the religious foundations of an irreducibly religious concept. This book does not attempt to assess the severity of these problems for Heidegger's own project: whether they represent lacunae that could in principle be filled, or whether they undermine basic premises of that project. My interest here is, rather, how such pressure points may be creatively engaged by theology.

Among other things, then, I argue that while Heidegger's analysis is a virtuoso *plaidoyer* for the ineluctable finitude of human existence, its pathos depends on the assumption of a desire to transcend finitude which the analysis itself cannot and does not attempt to account for. The passionate acts of 'shattering oneself against death' or bearing its 'affliction' which characterize authentic human existence are predicated on a contrary longing which is as consistently assumed as it is obfuscated by Heidegger's analysis. If—as Heidegger's analysis itself shows—human existence teaches us that we can never attain fulfilment but also that we seek it, that we can never find our ground but also that we crave it, then the phenomenological conclusion cannot *simply* be a denial of the object. C. S. Lewis offers a competing phenomenological analysis, gesturing back to Christian eschatology:

> [I]f a man diligently follow[s] ... desire, pursuing the false objects until their falsity appear[s] and then resolutely abandoning them, he must come out at last into the clear knowledge that the human soul was made to enjoy some object that is never fully given—nay, cannot even be imagined as given—in our present mode of subjective and spatio-temporal experience.[7]

---

[7] C. S. Lewis, *The Pilgrim's Regress* (London: J. M. Dent, 3rd edn., 1943), preface.

A fourth step, therefore, is to bring Heidegger's analysis back into dialogue with theology. The final chapter recapitulates the mutual criticism of Heidegger and his theological contemporaries, and concludes by suggesting how a theology informed by his phenomenological critique might in turn respond to the pressures to which Heidegger's treatment of theological sources exposes his own system.

Two further notes of guidance may be useful. First, this is a book about Heidegger's early intellectual development, culminating in *Being and Time*. In confining itself to this period, the book deliberately abstains from assessing Heidegger's subsequent development, including his involvement in National Socialism and his later writings. My thoughts about these are recorded elsewhere.[8] Conversely, the book also refrains from following Heidegger's own later re-evaluation of his early work. It is clear that from his earliest university career onward, Heidegger habitually reinterpreted his own earlier thought and writings, either by offering 'authoritative' interpretations (as in his 'Letter on Humanism') or by editing the texts themselves (as for the 1944 publication of his lectures on Hölderlin).[9] Heidegger's relationship to Christianity was fraught and changeable, and his own interpretation of his earlier work changed accordingly throughout the 1930s and 1940s. It seemed most fruitful, in the context of this book, to let his early work speak in its own voice, rather than to mute it by overlaying it with his later thought.

Secondly, one of the aims of this book is to demonstrate that eschatology is a key category for understanding Heidegger's early theological-philosophical development, as well as for a fruitful

[8] See Judith Wolfe, 'Messianism', in Nick Adams, George Pattison, and Graham Ward (eds.), *Oxford Handbook of Theology and Modern European Thought* (Oxford: Oxford University Press, 2013), and Judith Wolfe, *Heidegger and Theology* (London: Continuum, 2013).

[9] *Erläuterungen zu Hölderlins Dichtung* (Frankfurt: Klostermann, 1944). The subsequent publication history of this collection is somewhat complicated, but the point to note here, made by Kathleen Wright, is simple: Heidegger attempts to downplay the political dimension of his 1936 lecture 'Hölderlin and the Essence of Poetry' by positioning it, in the 1944 published version, *after* the apolitical 1943 lecture 'Homecoming/ To his Relatives', and so encouraging an interpretation of the earlier lecture through the lens of the later. See Wright, 'Heidegger and the Authorization of Hölderlin's Poetry', in Karsten Harries and Christoph Jamme (eds.), *Martin Heidegger: Politics, Art, Technology* (New York: Holmes and Meier, 1994), 164–74; esp. pp. 164–5. The publication of Heidegger's Collected Works in German (*Gesamtausgabe*) has caused scholarly frustration partly for following his own demand for 'last hand' rather than critical editions—i.e. for publishing texts only in the form in which he last revised or authorized them, often decades after their original publication.

dialogue between his phenomenology and theology. This also means that the book is, among other things, an implicit argument for a particular understanding of 'eschatology'—an understanding strongly informed by Heidegger's eschatological critique of theology and phenomenological re-reading of eschatology. The explicitly theological work of the book is to argue that this critique is to be brought back into theology rather than simply constituting a way out of it.

A brief word, therefore, about 'eschatology' as that term is used in this book. Eschatology was formalized in the Middle Ages as the study of the *eschata* or last things: death, judgement, heaven, and hell. After a period of change and reconstitution in the Reformation, these formalized, strongly metaphysically committed doctrines came under attack by the metaphysical critique of the Enlightenment, and soon became the province of a- or anti-philosophical theologies, whether Protestant (with its strong emphasis on depravity and judgement, counterpoised by irrupting grace) or Roman Catholic (with its assertive and complex map of the afterworld, including not only a lavishly imagined heaven and hell, but also limbo and purgatory). In the nineteenth and early twentieth centuries, however, theologians became increasingly aware of the gap, even contrast, between these formalized eschatological doctrines and their source material—the pervasive but often unsystematic references to and discussions of the end of life and world in the Old and New Testaments and the non-canonical texts surrounding them. The key point of this contrast was not primarily one of content but of form: Eschatology in the New Testament (argued Franz Overbeck, Albert Schweitzer, Rudolf Bultmann, and others) was not so much a system of beliefs as an attitude to the future. In the most general terms, an eschatological attitude, in the earliest Christian community as described by these thinkers, was an orientation towards an envisioned end as determinative of the present: the hope of future communion with God vouchsafed by Christ's own incarnation and resurrection. Present life in its transience is therefore lived in anticipation of an eternal future which can be neither anticipated nor controlled, but which nevertheless inflects the present, both through a particular contextualization of human hopes and desires and through moral imperatives.

Heidegger's early work adapts this formal understanding of eschatology and rigorously tests its scope and implications, both ontological and methodological. As such, Heidegger's work is indispensable for any further serious work on the relation between eschatology and ordinary existence. His own early work, in turn, is misunderstood if this dimension of it is not grasped. This book's aim is to demonstrate the latter and prepare the ground for the former; if it succeeds in doing so, it will also have contributed to a more general valorization of 'eschatology' as a vital category in the interpretation of modern European thought more generally.

1

Heidegger's Religious Provenance: *Kulturkampf* and the Modernist Crisis

Und wer wollte verkennen, daß auf diesem ganzen bisherigen
Weg verschwiegen die Auseinandersetzung mit dem Christentum mitging—eine Auseinandersetzung, die kein auf-
gegriffenes 'Problem' war und ist, sondern Wahrung der eigensten
Herkunft—des Elternhauses, der Heimat und der Jugend—und
schmerzliche Ablösung davon in *einem*. Nur wer so verwurzelt
war in einer wirklichen gelebten katholischen Welt, mag etwas
von den Notwendigkeiten ahnen, die auf dem bisherigen Weg
meines Fragens wie unterirdische Erdstöße wirkten.

—Martin Heidegger (1937/8)[1]

This and the following two chapters will prepare the way for a more
specific genealogy of the 'eschatology' of *Being and Time* by analysing
Heidegger's theological development in the decade leading up to the
announcement of his break with Catholicism in early 1919. The first
chapter will outline the main developments of Catholic ecclesiastical
history during the German *Kulturkampf* and the more wide-ranging
Modernismusstreit, and discuss Heidegger's initial response to these
developments by way of his earliest articles and reviews (published
between 1909 and 1913, mostly in the conservative Catholic organs

---

[1] 'And who should fail to recognize that my entire path hitherto has been accompa-
nied by a silent engagement with Christianity: an engagement that has never taken the
form of an explicitly raised "problem", but was rather *at once* the preservation of my
ownmost provenance—the childhood house, home, and youth—and a painful emancipation from it. Only someone similarly rooted in a truly lived Catholic world can
fathom some of the necessities that have affected the whole path of my questioning
like subterranean, seismic shocks.' *Besinnung*, ed. Friedrich-Wilhelm von Herrmann
(Frankfurt: Klostermann, 1997), 415. [Hereafter cited as GA 66.]

Heuberger Volksblatt, Der Akademiker, and *Allgemeine Rundschau).*
The second chapter will analyse the increasing tension between his
own developing commitments and the consequences of Pius X's
Anti-Modernist Oath, pivoting on Heidegger's consequential change of
subjects after the third term of his theological course. The main sources
for this account will be Heidegger's own (diverging) evaluations of
this period in two academic curricula vitae, written in 1915 and 1922,
information about his course selections at Freiburg University between
1909 and 1913, his private correspondence, and his qualifying thesis
(particularly the conclusion added in late 1915 for its 1916 publication). The third chapter will give a critical account of Heidegger's continuing reading in Protestant theology and philosophy—particularly
Luther and Schleiermacher—and its creative impact on his developing understanding of Husserlian phenomenology. In addition, it will
argue that Heidegger's developing Protestantism was itself inflected by
his reading (and writing) of Romantic poetry, particularly Hölderlin.
The primary texts for this analysis will be Heidegger's notes towards an
ultimately cancelled lecture course on the philosophical foundations
of medieval mysticism (planned for WS 1919/20), his own published
poetry and correspondence, and student transcripts of his 1920/1
lecture series *Introduction to the Phenomenology of Religion.*

Because many of the actors and texts relevant to these developments
are here presented to an English-speaking academic audience for the
first time, historical/biographical documentation of their influence
on Heidegger and conceptual analysis are necessarily interwoven.
The slow-down of argumentative flow entailed by this dual task is
balanced, in my opinion, by its vital contribution to a fuller and more
nuanced account of Heidegger's theological development than hitherto presented.

Martin Heidegger was born in 1889 in the small town Meßkirch
in Baden as the oldest son of the local Catholic sexton and cooper.
For the Archdiocese of Freiburg (to which Meßkirch belongs), this
was a decisive period in the reception of the First Vatican Council.
Almost immediately after the adjournment of the Council in October
1870, Chancellor Bismarck, aided by the National Liberal Party, had
launched the *Kulturkampf,* a large-scale anti-Catholic campaign trig-
gered by Pope Pius IX's controversial documents *Syllabus Errorum*
(1864) and *Pastor Aeternus* (1870), whose open condemnation of lib-
eralism and declaration of papal infallibility had given strong impetus to the formation of Catholic political parties. Beside the national

Centre Party (formed in 1870), there were a number of local parties, among which the Catholic People's Party of Baden (formed in 1867), a traditionally Catholic county, was a particularly strong supporter of the cause of the Church during the *Kulturkampf*.

After the official resolution of the *Kulturkampf* in 1878, the ultramontanist impetus in Baden faded slightly, but was renewed in 1888, when—Bismarck's 1872 prohibition against the settlement of Jesuit orders in the entire Reich still in force—the Catholic People's Party re-formed as the Baden Centre Party with the aim of revoking this law and, more generally, promoting an ultramontanist renewal based on adherence to papal supremacy and the more general anti-Modernist position outlined in Pius IX's *Syllabus Errorum*. This renewal was encouraged in the educational sector by the reopening, in the same year, of the archiepiscopal boys' boarding schools which, under the direction of the ultramontanist Archbishop Johannes Christian Roos of Freiburg and his successors, became the main recruitment centres for the priesthood.[2]

In Meßkirch, and especially in the sexton's family, the ultramontanist cause had a particularly high profile. In the decades before Martin's birth, a majority of the Meßkirch population had, for a time, joined the Old Catholic movement, rejecting strict adherence to Rome in favour of a more autonomous and local Catholic life. From the 1870s to 1895, when the Roman Catholic cause finally triumphed, Martin's father was among a small minority of ultramontanists, a commitment which incurred discrimination and even, for a while, the loss of the home (which belonged to the parish church). Martin could not fail to imbibe some of this entrenched religious commitment.[3]

Martin, intended for the priesthood from an early age, was sent to the episcopal schools in Constance and then in Freiburg from 1903 to 1909. The local community, newly rallied around Rome, also encouraged support for the ultramontanist cause by founding the Meßkirch *Heuberger Volksblatt* (1899), a Catholic daily associated with the Baden Centre

---

[2] See Johannes Schaber, 'Martin Heideggers "Herkunft" im Spiegel der Theologie- und Kirchengeschichte des 19. und beginnenden 20. Jahrhunderts', in Alfred Denker, Hans-Helmuth Gander, and Holger Zaborowski (eds.), *Heidegger und die Anfänge seines Denkens (Heidegger-Jahrbuch I)* (Freiburg: Karl Alber Verlag, 2004), 159–84; pp. 159–60. [This volume is hereafter cited as *HJB*.]

[3] See Rüdiger Safranski, *Ein Meister aus Deutschland: Heidegger und seine Zeit* (Frankfurt am Main: Fischer Verlag, 2001), 19–20. I am grateful to Laurence Paul Hemming for drawing my attention to this context.

12   *Heidegger's Religious Provenance*

Party and publicly opposing the liberal daily *Oberbadischer Grenzbote* (founded 1872). The foundation of this paper provoked the so-called *Meßkircher Zeitungskrieg* (Meßkirch Newspaper War), which continued until the demise of the Weimar Republic and became the main local vehicle for carrying out the *Modernismusstreit* (Modernist crisis) in Baden.[4] As such, we shall see, it became Heidegger's first organ.

During Heidegger's school years, the Modernist controversy sparked by Pius IX reached a new level of intensity with the publication of Pius X's decree *Lamentabili sane exitu* (July 1907), closely followed by the encyclical *Pascendi dominici gregis* (September 1907). The decree was a formal condemnation of sixty-five theological theses seen to undermine points of Catholic Tradition. The encyclical following it proposed a systematic grouping of these positions under the term 'Modernism', which it described summarily as 'the synthesis of all heresies'.[5] The term 'Modernism' remained notoriously multivalent throughout the so-called *Modernismusstreit* (Modernist crisis) ensuing from these publications, but was by both parties agreed to include methodical agnosticism (the use of secular methods in theology), vital immanentism (an understanding of religion as primarily a matter of feeling and experience), symbolism (the view that doctrines are only symbols of inner beliefs), and evolutionism (the view that authority and dogma undergo historical development).[6]

At home and in school, Heidegger imbibed a distinctly anti-Modernist attitude. In Constance (as he remembered in 1915), he received 'decisive spiritual influence' from the rector Dr Conrad Gröber, an ultramontanist

---

[4] See Markus Vonberg, 'Der Meßkircher Zeitungskrieg: "Oberbadischer Grenzbote" und "Heuberger Volksblatt" im liberal-ultramontanen Streit', in Edwin Ernst Weber (ed.), *Renitenz und Genie: Meßkirch und der badische Seekreis zwischen 1848/49 und dem Kulturkampf* (Konstanz: Gesellschaft Oberschwaben, 2003), 153–87.

[5] On the history of the ensuing Modernist crisis in the Catholic Church, see Hubert Wolf (ed.), *Antimodernismus und Modernismus in der katholischen Kirche: Beiträge zum theologiegeschichtlichen Vorfeld des II. Vatikanums* (Paderborn: Schöningh, 1998); Otto Weiß, *Der Modernismus in Deutschland: Ein Beitrag zur Theologiegeschichte* (Regensburg: Pustet, 2001).

[6] See Schaber, 'Herkunft', *HJB* 162–3. The most prominent contemporary defence of 'Modernism' is the Modernist tract *Il programma dei modernisti: Riposta all' Enciclica di Pio X, 'Pascendi Dominici gregis'* (Rome: Soc. Interna Scientifico-Religiosi, 1908), especially p. 5. A representative anti-Catholic description can be found in A. Vermeersch, 'Modernism', in *The Catholic Encyclopedia*, 15 vols., gen. ed. C. G. Herbermann (New York: Robert Appleton, 1907–14); vol. x (1911), 415–21; especially p. 416.

and later Archbishop of Freiburg.[7] In Freiburg (according to his head-master's graduation report of September 1909), he grew 'confirmed in his choice of the theological profession', and formed the intention to 'seek admittance to the Society of Jesus' after completing grammar school.[8]

Immediately after his graduation in August 1909, Heidegger began to defend the anti-Modernist position publicly. Earlier that year, the *Heuberger Volksblatt* had called for the erection of a monument in hon-our of the 200th anniversary of the death of Abraham a Sancta Clara (1644–1709). Abraham, an Augustinian priest-orator from the nearby Kreenheinstetten, was revered as a patron by the literary circle surround-ing the anti-Modernist historian and writer Richard von Kralik of Vienna, whose endeavour of a cultural renewal based on Catholic principles strongly attracted the young Heidegger.[9] Martin, who (as his friend Ernst Laslowski recalls in 1911[10]) already showed a marked passion for apolo-getics, presided over a preliminary celebration in honour of Abraham on 6 September 1909. In his 'president's speech' (reported in enthusiastic detail by the *Heuberger Volksblatt*), he commented on the public contro-versy between Richard von Kralik's journal *Gral* and the rival Catholic journal *Hochland*, which he accused of 'sailing more and more in the fair-way of Modernism'.[11] Heidegger concluded by calling upon the attending youth to subscribe to *Gral* and 'become its disciples'.[12]

From 1909 to 1910, Heidegger also contributed enthusiastically to the 'newspaper war', writing polemical pieces for the *Volksblatt* as well as two conservative Catholic journals, the *Allgemeine Rundschau* and

---

[7] Heidegger, 'Lebenslauf' (1915), first published in *Reden und andere Zeugnisse eines Lebensweges* (1910–76), ed. Hermann Heidegger (Frankfurt: Klostermann, 2000), 37. [Hereafter cited as GA 16.] On Gröber, see Wilhelm Friedrich Bautz, 'Gröber, Conrad', in Bautz (ed.), *Biographisch-Bibliographisches Kirchenlexikon*, 18 vols. (Hamm: Traugott Bautz Verlag, 1990); vol. ii, cols. 353–4.

[8] 'Rektoratszeugnisse für die Abiturienten', 10 September 1909; quoted in Hugo Ott, *Martin Heidegger: Unterwegs zu seiner Biographie* (Frankfurt: Campus, 1988), 59.

[9] See Judith Beniston, *Welttheater: Hofmannsthal, Richard von Kralik, and the Revival of Catholic Drama in Austria, 1890–1934* (London: Maney & Son, 1998). Abraham a Sancta Clara was widely known in the German-speaking world for his rhetorical and literary work. Schiller praised him in a letter to Goethe as 'wonderful [in] originality' and 'not at all easy…to approach or surpass…in mad wit and cleverness' (quoted in N. Scheid, 'Abraham a Sancta Clara', *Catholic Encyclopedia*, vol. i (1907), 57).

[10] Letter from Laslowski to Heidegger dated 20 April 1911; rpt. in *HJB* 28–30; p. 29.

[11] *Hochland* was a Catholic monthly founded in 1903 and edited by Karl Muth for Kösel Verlag in Munich. Its contributors included Heinrich Finke and Herman Schell, who later became influential for Heidegger's own development (see Chapter 2).

[12] *Heuberger Volksblatt*, 10 September 1909; cited in Víctor Farías, *Heidegger und der Nationalsozialismus* (Frankfurt am Main: Fischer, 1989), 76.

Der Akademiker.[13] Though the rhetoric of these essays is typical of the anti-Modernist literature of the period, their emphases are sufficiently distinctive to indicate Heidegger's developing commitments and concerns.

Modernist attitudes, in these short pieces, incur Heidegger's contempt because they both promote and are promoted by weakness, delusion, and enslavement to the superficial, ephemeral, and 'low'. His earliest known publication, a lyrical short story about the dramatic conversion of a young atheist on All Souls' Morning ('Allerseelenstimmungen', November 1909), opens with a description of the urban 'Moderns' as unable to hear God's judgement call, sounded by the church bells on All Souls' morning. This inability is rooted in their 'desire [for] lust', which they willingly mistake for 'intelligence' and 'freedom', turning (in an inimical and remarkably early allusion to Nietzsche) 'into "blonde beasts" when you dare to doubt the logic of their passions'.[14] The result of this denial is self-delusion (they mistake the 'dark, agonising night' for the sun) and weakness: 'In heavy chains—whose clangour they no longer hear—they drag a tired, overwrought body through existence.'[15] What these people run away from, according to Heidegger, is 'seriousness', which 'only befits the strong': 'The feeble soul, the dull, creeping soul flees from the redemptive seriousness of life which is eager to overcome, it shirks the self-reflection which is glad to make sacrifices.'[16]

In a near-contemporaneous review of Johannes Jørgensen's 1903 autobiography *Lebenslüge und Lebenswahrheit* (published March 1910), Heidegger assimilates this contrast between spiritual 'strength'

---

[13] *Der Akademiker* acted as the official organ of student association 'Catholic German Academics' (Katholischer Deutscher Akademikerverband). It strongly supported Pius X's interpretation of Vatican I and also attracted such contributors as Romano Guardini and Oswald von Nell-Breuning (see Ott, *Martin Heidegger*, 63). The *Allgemeine Rundschau* was a 'weekly for politics and culture' edited by the controversial Catholic intellectual Dr Armin Kausen. It continued from 1904 to the eve of the accession of the National Socialist German Workers' Party, and was directed particularly against what the editor perceived as Modernist 'immorality in life and art'; see Klemens Löffler, 'Periodical Literature (Germany)', trans. Douglas J. Potter, in *Catholic Encyclopedia*, vol. xi (1911), 677–80; p. 679.

Heidegger continued to write for these journals until 1913, but the tenor of his contributions (as we shall see) changed after 1910.

[14] *Heuberger Volksblatt*, 5 November 1909; rpt. *HJB* 18–21; pp. 18–19. Heidegger also gave a highly critical lecture on Nietzsche at the *Katholische Gesellen- und Jünglingsverein* (Catholic Men's and Boys' Club) of Meßkirch in October 1912. The event was reported by the Heuberger Volksblatt 14, no. 124 (21 October 1912); the report is reprinted in Alfred Denker and Elsbeth Büchin, *Martin Heidegger und seine Heimat* (Stuttgart: Klett-Cotta, 2005), 127–8.

[15] *HJB* 18.

[16] *HJB* 18.

and passion-enslaved 'weakness' to Darwinist biology, which, during this period, he regarded as a particularly fascinating corroboration of Christian belief.[17] Just as all 'higher life is predicated on the demise of the lower forms', he argues in the review, so the higher, 'spiritual life' requires the 'killing' of 'what is low' in oneself. Rather than being a cause of suffering, such self-mortification or 'carrying [the] cross' naturally brings joy. Extending his earlier biological analogy, Heidegger expounds: "'Happiness is only possible through the life-lie.' Will Ibsen prove to be right with this statement? No; it contradicts a fundamental biological law. The truth must *naturaliter* lead to happiness, the lie to downfall.'[18]

In a May 1910 review of the moral philosopher Friedrich Wilhelm Foerster's essay *Autorität und Freiheit: Betrachtungen zum Kulturproblem der Kirche* (1910), Heidegger gives a more philosophical account of the same conflict. Here, he argues that both dominant tendencies of contemporary thought, the 'naturalist' (with its 'reality fanaticism' [*Wirklichkeitsfanatismus*]) and the 'immanentist' (with its invention of new 'values of existence' [*Daseinswerte*][19]), are the result of an 'unbounded autonomism'.[20] As such, neither is capable of solving the 'deepest problems of religious-ethical life': the former because 'the fundamental truths of life cannot be constructed in a priori scientific terms', the latter because 'most people, left to themselves, do not find the truth' because they 'do not want to fight for it'.[21] 'Rich life-experience' and a 'spiritual freedom from the world of drives' are necessary—and

---

[17] '*Per mortem ad vitam*: Gedanken über Jörgensens "Lebenslüge und Lebenswahrheit"', *Der Akademiker* 2, no. 5 (March 1910), 72–3; rpt. in GA 16, 3–6; p. 3. Cf. Heidegger's statement in a curriculum vitae of 1915: 'Things said in RE classes...suggested to me a more extensive study of the biological theory of evolution'; GA 16, 37. Heidegger also gave a talk entitled 'Die tierische Abstammung des Menschen und das Urteil der Wissenschaft' ['The animal origins of man and the verdict of science'] at the *Katholische Gesellen- und Jünglingsverein* in Meßkirch on 21 April 1912. The event was reported by the Heuberger Volksblatt 14, no. 47 (22 April 1912); the report is reprinted in Denker and Büchin, *Martin Heidegger und seine Heimat*, 126–7.

[18] '*Per mortem ad vitam*', GA 16, 5. The Ibsen reference is to *The Wild Duck*, Act V: 'Rob the average man of his life-lie, and you rob him of his happiness at the same stroke.'

[19] '*Per mortem ad vitam*', too, attacks this 'invention of new value terms', especially that of 'personality value', that is, the ascription of intrinsic worth to 'self-realisation' or the development of an 'interesting personality'. This, he there argues, leads to the idolization of dissolute characters such as Wilde, Paul Verlaine, Gorky, or Nietzsche; see GA 16, 3.

[20] 'Foerster, Fr. W. *Autorität und Freiheit*' (review), *Der Akademiker* 2, no. 7 (May 1910), 109–10; rpt. GA 16, 7–8; p. 7.

[21] GA 16, 7.

these can be achieved only by 'intimate contact with' the Church, the 'richest and deepest source of religious-ethical authority'.[22]

In other words, while the Modernists demand free scientific enquiry and free thought, true freedom of thought and joy of life require a habit of self-discipline: 'Truly *free* thinking', Foerster writes, 'presupposes an heroic act of moral self-liberation'.[23] Heidegger echoes this conviction almost *verbatim* in an essay entitled 'Philosophical Orientation for Academics' the following March:

> Strict logical thinking that hermetically seals itself off from all affective influences of the emotions, all *truly* presupposition-less scholarly work, requires a certain fund of ethical power, the art of self-collection and self-emptying.[24]

Such self-liberation, however, according to Foerster, can only be achieved through obedience to the Catholic tradition:

> Not *I* should judge the highest tradition from my perspective, but I should learn to evaluate myself in a wholly new way from *its* perspective: That is true emancipation, that is the service which firm objective authority can render the personal life.[25]

Intellectual honesty or objectivity is here coextensive with personal truthfulness or '*Wahrhaftigkeit*' (authenticity). Church doctrine is authoritative precisely because it contains not only factual truth but also the 'light of truth' that enables an authentic life. Heidegger echoes this idea in the conclusion of his Foerster review, borrowing the language of the Judaeo-Christian Wisdom tradition—a genre that inflects the classical ideal of knowledge with a specifically moral and spiritual emphasis culminating, for the Christian, in the Incarnation of the 'Wisdom of God' (1 Cor. 1: 24):

> To him who has never set foot on straying paths [cf. Ps. 1: 1; Prov. 1: 15, 2: 18, 4: 14] and has not been blinded by the deceptive dazzle of the modern spirit; who can dare to walk through life in the radiance of truth, in true, deep, well-grounded offering-up of self [cf. Wis. 9: 11]; to him, this

---

[22] GA 16, 7.

[23] Foerster, *Autorität und Freiheit: Betrachtungen zum Kulturproblem der Kirche* (Kempten-Munich: Kösel, 1910) 28; quoted in Denker, 'Denkweg', *HJB* 104.

[24] 'Zur philosophischen Orientierung für Akademiker', *Der Akademiker* 3, no. 5 (March 1911), 66–7; rpt. in GA 16, 11–14; p. 11.

[25] Foerster, *Autorität und Freiheit*, 58; quoted in Denker, 'Denkweg', *HJB* 104.

book bears tidings of great joy [cf. Luke 2: 10], and conveys again with startling clarity the high joy of possessing the truth.[26]

Several themes familiar from Heidegger's later work emerge from this brief review of his earliest writings. The terms of his denunciation of 'the Moderns' are cognate with those he later develops in relation to 'the crowd'[27] or *das Man*.[28] Similarly, his call to overcome this inauthentic mode of existence by opening oneself to the light of truth within which humans live and know anticipates his development, in the 1915 qualifying thesis (and more radically in later writings), of the Scholastic doctrine of the convertibility of *ens* and *verum*, which implies (for Heidegger in 1915) that beings are 'true' (i.e. are capable of *manifestativa sui*) because they participate in Being (associated with God), whose essence includes *communicabilitas sui*.[29] At the same time, these earliest texts present radically different requisites from Heidegger's later writings for the achievement of 'authenticity', or an existence true to one's 'essence'—differences signalled by the fact that 'authenticity' is not here characterized as '*Eigentlichkeit*' (mine-ness) but as '*Entselbstung*' (offering-up of self).

---

[26] GA 16, 8.

[27] This is Hubert L. Dreyfus's translation for 'das Man'; see his 'Foreword' to Carol White, *Time and Death: Heidegger's Analysis of Finitude* (London: Ashgate, 2005), ix–xxxvi.

[28] This emerges even more succinctly in the following passage from an August 1910 article: 'Daß unsere Zeit der Außenkultur und Schnellebigkeit doch mehr rückwärtsblickend vorwärtsschaute! Die grundstürzende Neuerungswut, das tolle Hinwegspringen über den tieferen seelischen Gehalt des Lebens und der Kunst, der auf fortwährend sich ablösende Augenblicksreize gerichtete moderne Lebenssinn, die zuweilen erstickend wirkende Schwüle, in der sich die heutige Kunst jeder Art bewegt, das sind Momente, die auf eine Dekadenz hinzeigen, auf einen traurigen Abfall von der Gesundheit und dem Jenseitswert des Lebens'; 'Abraham a Sankta Clara: Zur Enthüllung seines Denkmals in Kreenheinstetten am 15. August 1910', *Allgemeine Rundschau*, August 1910; rpt. Heidegger, *Aus der Erfahrung des Denkens* (1910–76), ed. Hermann Heidegger (Frankfurt: Klostermann, 2nd edn., 2002), 1–3; p. 3. [Hereafter cited as GA 13.]

[29] See *Die Kategorien- und Bedeutungslehre des Duns Scotus* (Tübingen: J. C. B. Mohr, 1916); rpt. Heidegger, *Frühe Schriften* (1912–16), ed. Friedrich-Wilhelm von Herrmann (Frankfurt: Klostermann, 1978), 189–411; esp. p. 222. [Hereafter cited as GA 1.] Cf. Richard Schaeffler, *Frömmigkeit des Denkens? Martin Heidegger und die katholische Theologie* (Darmstadt: Wissenschaftliche Buchgesellschaft, 1978), 22–8; esp. pp. 27–8.

2

The Developing Critique of 'Scholasticism', 1911–15

On 30 September 1909, Martin entered the novitiate house of the Jesuits, which was then located in Vorarlberg, Austria, on account of Bismarck's Jesuit laws. He completed a two-week candidacy for the novitiate, but was dismissed at the end of that period, probably because of an early manifestation of his chronic heart problems.[1] He nevertheless was intent on becoming a priest, and in the winter semester of 1909/10 moved into the *Collegium Borromaeum* in Freiburg to enrol at the university as a student of Catholic theology—a course reserved, at the time, for candidates for the priesthood.[2] However, in the middle of the third semester of the course, in February 1911, his career underwent a momentous change. Heidegger had to break off his studies due to a violent outbreak of his heart condition, and was forced to spend the summer semester in Meßkirch to recuperate. When he returned to university in the winter semester of 1911/12, he did not continue his theology studies, but changed to a course in mathematics and philosophy, which he completed in 1912. He continued with a doctoral dissertation in philosophy (examined in 1913) and a qualifying thesis on the doctrine of categories and signification in Duns Scotus, leading to the award of a licence to teach philosophy in 1915.[3]

---

[1] See Ott, *Martin Heidegger*, 59, and Denker, 'Denkweg', *HJB* 100–1.
[2] A list of all lectures and seminars for which Heidegger registered between 1909 and 1915, compiled by the editors, can be found in *HJB* 13–17.
[3] The author of *De modis significandi*, the primary source for Heidegger's account of Scotus' doctrine of signification, has since been determined to be Thomas of Erfurt, like Scotus a 'speculative grammarian'; see Jack Zupko, 'Thomas of Erfurt', in Edward N. Zalta (ed.), *The Stanford Encyclopedia of Philosophy* (Autumn 2008 edn.), URL = <http://plato.stanford.edu/archives/fall2008/entries/erfurt/>.

The change of academic tracks was a crucial decision, whose unsettling nature is reflected in the wide divergence of Heidegger's own retrospective interpretations of it.[4] A 1915 curriculum vitae submitted to the Catholic Philosophy Department in Freiburg presents the change as a forced decision, brought about by Heidegger's heart condition, which, he was informed at the time, rendered a clerical career 'extremely doubtful', and thus practically barred him from continuing a vocational course in theology.[5] A 1922 curriculum vitae submitted to the Protestant philosopher Georg Misch (formerly at Marburg and, at the time of Heidegger's letter, at Göttingen), by contrast, ascribes to the decision an unequivocally religious motivation:

> The direction in which my theological-philosophical studies led me during my first semesters was such that I left the [*Collegium Borromaeum*] in Spring 1911 and gave up my theological studies, because I could not take upon myself the 'Modernist oath' which had then been made mandatory.[6]

EXCURSUS: EVALUATION OF SOURCES

Accounts of this aspect and period of Heidegger's life even by conscientious scholars of the 'young Heidegger' have suffered from an uncritical reliance upon one or the other of the curricula vitae.[7] One of the results

---

[4] The most important texts are 'Lebenslauf' (1915) and 'Vita' (1922), rpt. in GA 16, 37–9 and 41–5, respectively, and discussed here. Additional sources are Heidegger's inaugural speech upon election to the Heidelberg *Akademie der Wissenschaften* (1957), first published in *Jahreshefte der Heidelberger Akademie der Wissenschaften 1957/58* (1959), 20–1; rpt. in GA 1, 55–7; and 'Mein Weg in die Phänomenologie', in *Hermann Niemeyer zum achtzigsten Geburtstag am 16. April 1963* (private printing); rpt. in *Zur Sache des Denkens*, ed. Friedrich-Wilhelm von Herrmann (Frankfurt: Klostermann, 1985), 81–90. [Hereafter cited as GA 14.]

[5] GA 16, 38.

[6] GA 16, 41. Submitted upon request to Professor Georg Misch together with Heidegger's 1919 essay 'Anmerkungen zu Karl Jaspers, *Psychologie der Weltanschauungen*' (first published in Hans Saner (ed.), *Karl Jaspers in der Diskussion* (Munich: Piper, 1973), 70–100; rpt. in *Wegmarken*, ed. Friedrich-Wilhelm von Herrmann (Frankfurt: Klostermann, 2nd edn., 1996), 1–44. [This volume is hereafter cited as GA 9.]).

[7] The term 'young Heidegger' was coined for Heidegger scholarship by John van Buren; see 'The Young Heidegger: Rumor of a Hidden King (1919–1926)', *Philosophy Today* 33 (1989), 99–109, and subsequent publications. Adherents to the 1915 curriculum vitae include Hugo Ott (see *Martin Heidegger*, 67–105), Thomas Sheehan (see 'Reading a Life: Heidegger and Hard Times', in Charles Guignon (ed.),

of this is a marked discrepancy in dating and interpreting Heidegger's break with the Catholic 'system': Alfred Denker (and those who follow him) situates his estrangement in the context of the events of 1911, while Hugo Ott, Thomas Sheehan, and John van Buren (and those who rely on them) date it to 1916/17, when Heidegger gave a first public lecture on Schleiermacher. A critical evaluation of the reliability of the sources is indispensable to a more accurate understanding of Heidegger's religious development during the years of his academic formation.

Both curricula vitae are somewhat problematic sources, in that (like all Heidegger's autobiographical writings) they tend to reflect the context of their composition more carefully than their subject. The 1915 curriculum—emphasizing that in spite of his recent engagement with post-Kantian thought and, particularly, Husserlian phenomenology, Heidegger's 'fundamental philosophical convictions remained those of Aristotelian-Scholastic philosophy'[8]—was written in keen consciousness that since 1913, Professor Finke (who held the Catholic chair in History, and examined Heidegger in medieval history for his doctoral degree) had intended him for the newly vacant professorship in Catholic Philosophy, an appointment that would require some experience in, and commitment to, Scholastic thought.[9] (In the event, Heidegger was passed over when the post came up for election in June 1916—no doubt a cause for his greater outspokenness about his growing Protestant sympathies after that year.[10])

The Cambridge Companion to Heidegger (Cambridge: Cambridge University Press, 1993), 70–96), and John van Buren (see esp. his *The Young Heidegger: Rumor of the Hidden King* (Bloomington, Ind.: University of Indiana Press, 1994), 51–5); adherents to the 1922 text include Alfred Denker (see 'Denkweg', *HJB* 97–122).

[8] GA 16, 38.

[9] Similar circumstances surround the statement of progress and intention associated with Heidegger's qualifying thesis, addressed to the cathedral chapter in Freiburg, which had funded the thesis. The award of scholarships at the time was guided by Pope Pius X's *motu proprio* of 1914, which declared the teaching of Thomas Aquinas the sole authoritative philosophy of the Catholic Church, and so intensified the neo-Scholastic revival instigated by Leo XIII's encyclical *Aeterni Patris* (1879), which had declared Thomas the 'chief and master' of medieval philosophy, and an enduring guide for the Catholic Church.

[10] See Ott, *Martin Heidegger*, 91. A partial critique of Ott's charge that Heidegger's repeated profession of neo-Scholastic sympathies up to 1916 was merely a strategic move to secure the post, that his disgruntlement with the Roman Catholic Church can be explained from his disappointment in this regard, and that a similar opportunism marks his entire career, is offered by Robert Vigliotti, 'The Young Heidegger's Ambitions for the Chair of Catholic Philosophy and Hugo Ott's Charge of Opportunism', *Studia Phænomenologica* 1, nos. 3–4 (2001), 323–50.

A recently published letter from Heidegger's friend Ernst Laslowski, written in the spring of 1911 (when Heidegger was convalescing in Meßkirch), shows that Heidegger's decision to give up his priestly training was not in fact a foreclosed one.[11] Heidegger had written Laslowski—whom he later called 'the only friend of [his] youth'[12]—a (no longer extant) letter around Easter, asking for advice whether to continue his theology course or switch to either mathematics or philosophy. Why the question arose at all remains unclear. In his reply, dated 20 April, Laslowski commends the completion of the theology course as probably the most prudent as well as the most congenial choice, both for financial reasons (the scholarship Heidegger received was subject-bound) and because Heidegger's dominant 'apologetic tendency' (fuelled by a 'let us say, "impractical honesty"') would 'cause offence' in the 'controlling' philosophical 'circles', but would be a 'tremendous propulsive force' in a projected apologetic career.[13] However, Laslowski also gives advice for a possible switch to philosophy, commending Heidegger's talent and suggesting several Catholic funding bodies which could provide financial support for post- (though not pre-)doctoral research.[14]

Heidegger's hesitation, evinced by this correspondence, relativizes both his 1915 account and his 1922 presentation of the interruption of his course as a premeditated step responding to the imposition of the Anti-Modernist Oath by Pius X in September 1910.

---

[11] Ernst Laslowski (1889–1961), Heidegger's closest friend during this period, studied history and was later employed, among other posts, as manager of the Catholic polytechnic 'Heimgarten' in Silesia (1923–3) and as archivist of Caritasverband e.V., the German branch of the Catholic Agency for Overseas Development (1951–61).

[12] Letter to Hannah Arendt dated 9 July 1925; in Ursula Ludz (ed.), *Hannah Arendt/ Martin Heidegger: Briefe 1925 bis 1975* (Frankfurt: Klostermann, 2nd edn., 1999), 40.

[13] Laslowski to Heidegger, 20 April 1911; rpt. in *HJB* 28–30; p. 29.

[14] In the event, Heidegger was awarded a scholarship by the Senate of Freiburg University (a Grieshaber-Pino Grant of 400 marks per year) in April 1912, with (retroactive) effect from February 1912 to May 1916; see Sheehan, 'Lehrjahre', in Sallis, *Collegium Phaenomenologicum*, 99 and 136 n. 175. In addition, he received post-doctoral funding (the von Schaezler Grant of 1,000 marks per year) from the cathedral chapter in Freiburg from September 1913 to spring 1916, and a private lecturer stipend from the Görres-Gesellschaft zur Pflege der Wissenschaften (a private foundation established during the *Kulturkampf* to promote Catholic scholarship) for the academic year 1916/7; see Hugo Ott, 'Der Habilitand Martin Heidegger und das von Schaezler'sche Stipendium: Ein Beitrag zur Wissenschaftsförderung der katholischen Kirche', *Freiburger Diözesan-Archiv* 106 (1986), 142–4, and Ott, 'Martin Heidegger und seine Beziehungen zur Görres-Gesellschaft zur Pflege der Wissenschaft im katholischen Deutschland', *HJB* 197–200.

This latter rendering, too, is no doubt strategic. The text is associated with Heidegger's move to the University of Marburg, the second-oldest Protestant university in the German Reich. Paul Natorp, who acted as part of the appointing committee, had communicated to Husserl, Heidegger's sponsor, in advance that there existed reservations regarding the young philosopher's arguable 'confessional narrowness'. Husserl responded decisively:

> Allow me to inform you that [by 1917], Heidegger had...freed himself...from dogmatic Catholicism. Soon after that he drew all the conclusions and cut himself off—unequivocally, energetically, and yet tactfully—from the sure and easy career of a 'philosopher of the Catholic world-view'.[15]

Heidegger no doubt wished to confirm this impression.[16]

Heidegger's explanation of the catalyst of his decision, too, seems only partly to reflect the situation of 1909 to 1911. Immediately preceding the assertion that he gave up his theological studies because he could not accept the recently imposed Anti-Modernist Oath, he writes:

> The endeavour to see beyond what was offered [by my theology course] led me to the critical investigations of Franz Overbeck and acquainted me with Protestant history of doctrine research more generally. What was decisive for me was that the modern history of religion research of Gunkel, Bousset, Wendland and Reitzenstein, and the critical work of Albert Schweitzer entered my field of vision.[17]

The immediate motivation for this narrative seems to arise from the context of its composition. Two factors indicate this. First, the Theology Faculty of Marburg University (which, although not directly responsible for Heidegger's appointment, maintained close ties with the Philosophy Faculty) was dominated by exponents of the 'history of religion' school, to which Gunkel, Bousset, Wendland, and Reitzenstein

---

[15] R I Natorp 11.II.20, Husserl Archive, Leuven; quoted in Theodore Kisiel, *The Genesis of Heidegger's Being and Time* (Berkeley and Los Angeles: University of California Press, 1995), 75.

[16] Indeed, Heidegger strove to augment the force of his impression by claiming that his relinquishment of the theology course 'caused [him] to become destitute', but that he 'pressed on' nevertheless. Though by no means unfounded, this claim is certainly exaggerated for effect. As Laslowski's letters indicate, Heidegger was already aware of possible funding bodies when he made his decision, and in fact was awarded a new scholarship (the Grieshaber-Pino Grant) within one term of his return to university.

[17] GA 16, 41.

also belonged. Before Bultmann's appointment in 1921, the chair of New Testament Studies had been held by Johannes Weiß and Wilhelm Heitmüller, two of the most prominent members of that school. At the time of Heidegger's appointment, both the Old Testament and the Patristics chair were held by proponents of the historical-critical method, Gustav Hölscher and Hans von Soden. Heidegger's account would no doubt have been welcomed by this Faculty.

Secondly, Heidegger himself seems to have developed an increasing interest in Franz Overbeck in the early 1920s. Hans-Georg Gadamer, his student in Marburg, recalls that in the discussion following a guest lecture by Eduard Thurneysen in 1923, Heidegger energetically invoked Franz Overbeck, whose 'radical self-doubt' he related to the 'true task of theology', namely to 'search for the word which was capable of calling to faith and sustaining in faith'.[18] Although it is probable that Heidegger had in fact encountered Overbeck before 1911, it is also clear that he did not, at that time, have the intellectual resources for such an interpretation of the Basle theologian. Furthermore, the 1922 curriculum vitae is the only mention of Overbeck before Heidegger's more sustained engagement with him around 1923: It is likely that Heidegger's newly revived interest both amplified and inflected the memory of Overbeck's importance during his student days.

That Heidegger probably did encounter Overbeck before 1911 is confirmed inadvertently by a slip in his memory later in the 1922 text. He recounts that after 1911, he began to attend lectures at the Philosophy Faculty by the Neo-Kantian Heinrich Rickert and the Protestant classicists Richard August Reitzenstein and Eduard Schwartz ('Gospel of John'), which 'had been forbidden him until that time'. The prohibition had been pronounced in the 1907 encyclical *Pascendi*, which ruled that candidates for the priesthood must not attend courses at state institutions which they could also attend at confessional institutions.[19] While Heidegger's recollection appears innocuous, the specific reference to Schwartz's course on the Gospel of John betrays (as Johannes Schaber's research has uncovered) that he must in fact have attended at least this course earlier than WS 1911/12: Schwartz, who was in Freiburg from WS 1909/10 to WS 1913/14, only lectured on John in

---

[18] Gadamer, 'Marburger Theologie' (1964), in Gadamer, *Heideggers Wege: Studien zum Spätwerk* (Tübingen: Mohr Siebeck, 1983), 29–40; p. 29. Overbeck's influence on Heidegger in the 1920s is discussed in greater depth in Chapter 3.

[19] Reported in Schaber, 'Herkunft', *HJB* 174–75.

WS 1910/11.[20] Overbeck's areas of research shortly before his death in 1904 overlapped substantially with Schwartz's, and it is probable that Schwartz introduced his students to the work of the senior scholar, as well as to that of the contemporary 'history of religion' school.

Qualified by these critical remarks, the curricula vitae and related texts offer a multi-faceted account of Heidegger's theological development in what he later recalled as 'the exciting years between 1910 and 1914'.[21] In the public life of the university, this period was inaugurated by a heated controversy between the Catholic-Theological Faculty and the Academic Senate over the question of scholarly objectivity, incited by the publication, on 1 September 1910, of Pope Pius X's *motu proprio Sacrorum antistitum*, imposing the Anti-Modernist Oath on 'all clergy, pastors, confessors, preachers, religious superiors, and professors in philosophical-theological seminaries'.[22] The quarrel centred on the question whether or not theologians who took the oath thereby *mutatis mutandis* compromised their scholarly credibility. It steadily intensified from November 1910 to March 1911, and was finally resolved in July 1911, when the local government in Karlsruhe enforced a compromise, allowing the continued appointment to academic posts of priests who had professed the oath. Even after this resolution, however, an ill-concealed animosity between the Senate and the Catholic-Theological Faculty prevailed.[23]

The Anti-Modernist Oath represented a formal commitment to the precepts laid down in *Lamentabili sane exitu* and *Pascendi dominici gregis*, and a rejection of the following 'errors' of Modernism: a denial that God can be known 'with certainty' as the origin and end of all things by natural reason; a denial of the validity of miracles and prophecies as 'external proofs' of the divine origin of Christian revelation; a

---

[20] In the same term, Heidegger officially attended the lecture course on the Gospel of John given by the Catholic New Testament scholar Simon Weber at the Theology Faculty; see Schaber, 'Herkunft', *HJB* 175. This slip lends a cheeky tone to Heidegger's statement that it was his 'effort to see beyond what was offered' by his theology course which led him to Overbeck and the 'history of religion' school.

[21] 'Die erregenden Jahre zwischen 1910 und 1914'; 'Antrittsrede' upon election to the Heidelberg *Akademie der Wissenschaften* (1957), rpt. in GA 1, 55–7; p. 56.

[22] *Sacrorum antistitum*; rpt. in *Acta Apostolicae Sedis* 2 (1910), 655–80.

[23] See Schaber, 'Herkunft', *HJB* 164. Relevant contemporary discussions of the Anti-Modernist Oath in its relation to scientific freedom in Germany are Hermann Mulert, *Antimodernismuseid, freie Forschung und theologische Fakultäten* (Halle: Verlag des Evangelischen Bundes, 1911), and Simon Weber, *Theologie als freie Wissenschaft und die wahren Feinde wissenschaftlicher Freiheit. Ein Wort zum Streit um den Antimodernisteneid* (Freiburg: Herder, 1912).

denial of the institution of the Church upon Peter and his successors by the 'real and historical Christ'; the representation of church dogma as a human construct subject to continuous development; and an account of faith as a 'blind sentiment of religion' rather than a 'genuine assent of the intellect' to externally revealed truth.

With respect to Catholic scholars in particular, the oath also condemned various practices, including: the assertion of the mutual independence of faith and historical scholarship, which allegedly made it possible for these spheres, though irreconcilable, to be practised in parallel; an exclusive commitment to 'textual criticism' (that is, the historical-critical method) in biblical exegesis; and a denial of the divine import of sacred tradition (in any other than a pantheistic sense). Finally, it made the demand that when expounding on a 'historico-theological subject', a Catholic scholar should proceed by purely historical-scientific principles, putting 'aside any preconceived opinion about the supernatural origin of Catholic tradition or ... the divine promise of help to preserve all revealed truth forever'. Against these 'errors', the oath affirmed the Church's divinely bestowed 'charism of truth', handed down 'absolute and immutable' from the apostles and therefore an incontestable criterion for all (Christian) scholarship.

Although Heidegger did not openly protest against the oath (the 1922 curriculum vitae is the first indication of the possible magnitude of its impact on him at the time), the tone of his publications changes after its issue. His engagement with F. W. Foerster (as well as Carl Braig and Herman Schell) had given him the means of constructing an account of scholarly objectivity on which objectivity is not in conflict with, but rather facilitated by, Catholic commitment. Nevertheless, after 1911, Heidegger's attitude to this account was no longer the pre-critical triumphalism displayed *vis-à-vis* the 'Moderns' in the 1910 Foerster review. Rather than as an asset provided by the Church, the possibility of (objective) knowledge began to appear as a *question*. In a 1911 article in the *Heuberger Volksblatt*, Heidegger called upon Catholic scholars to confront this question:

> By freedom of research we understand freedom from all preconceived opinions and unproven assumptions in the examination of scholarly (specifically, philosophical-historical) questions. This problem, philosophical-theological epistemology has to solve.[24]

---

[24] 'Dem Grenzbot-Philosophen zur Antwort', *Heuberger Volksblatt* 13, no. 42 (7 April 1911); quoted in Schaber, 'Herkunft', *HJB* 167.

Heidegger's formulation of the problem reveals his distance—if not as regards substance, yet nevertheless as regards methodology—from the papal position: by affirming the validity and urgency of 'philosophical-historical' questions, as well as the need for a 'philosophical-theological epistemology', Heidegger implicitly challenges Pius' repudiation of the relevance of these subjects as progeny of 'Kantian philosophy', 'German Idealism', or 'Protestant theology'—terms used interchangeably by Pius as antagonists of orthodox 'Scholasticism'.[25]

In Pius' writings and the general discourse of the time, 'Scholasticism' came to refer as much to a methodology as to a philosophical system. It was Scholasticism in this methodological sense which Heidegger primarily opposed. Thus, while he asserts in his 1915 curriculum vitae that his 'fundamental philosophical convictions [have] remained those of Aristotelian-Scholastic philosophy', Ernst Laslowski also warns him in a letter from December of the same year to be '*careful* in judgments about Scholasticism' (here in a methodological sense) so as not to endanger his future career.[26] The same distinction is made in a 1913 letter to Heinrich Rickert, who was to supervise Heidegger's qualifying dissertation. In response to Rickert's suggestion to take as his thesis topic an interpretation of Duns Scotus by means of modern (that is, for Rickert, primarily his own Neo-Kantian) logic, he writes:

> I must say that my own fundamental philosophical convictions are different ones; nevertheless, I want to be the last to go along with the familiar pathetic method of seeing in modern philosophy nothing but a string of 'errors', a progeny of 'godlessness' and so forth.[27]

Pius X's *motu proprio Doctoris Angelici* of 1914, declaring the teaching of Thomas Aquinas the sole authoritative philosophy of the Catholic Church, exacerbated this frustration with the perceived Catholic failure to engage with modern philosophy. In a letter to Engelbert Krebs in July of the same year, Heidegger acerbically comments:

> The *motu proprio* about philosophy was really the cherry on the cake. Perhaps you as an 'academic' could apply for an even better procedure to

[25] Cf. Otto Weiß, 'Der katholische Modernismus: Begriff—Selbstverständnis—Ausprägungen—Weiterwirkungen', in Wolf (ed.), *Antimodernismus und Modernismus in der katholischen Kirche*, 107–39; my thanks to Johannes Schaber for drawing my attention to this publication.
[26] Letter dated 6 December 1915, rpt. in *HJB* 52–3; p. 53.
[27] Letter dated 12 October 1913; in Alfred Denker (ed.), *Martin Heidegger/Heinrich Rickert: Briefe 1912–1933* (Frankfurt: Klostermann, 2002), 12.

gut the brain of anyone who dares to have an independent thought, and replace it with 'Italian salad'.[28]

Heidegger's curriculum vitae of 1922 suggests that his progressive disappointment with modern Scholasticism was wakened and nourished by his developing interests in three areas: philosophical logic, the Protestant 'history or religion' school, and hermeneutics and the study of history.

LOGIC

The inadequacy of (neo-)Scholasticism as a philosophical method was due, in Heidegger's view, primarily to its inability or unwillingness to 'encounter philosophical problems as problems', a tendency of which he became increasingly wary after the interruption of his theology course, particularly through the seminars of the Neo-Kantian Heinrich Rickert.[29] In Heidegger's view, the imperative to acknowledge philosophical thought as irreducibly problematic—which, for him, also included the refusal to reduce its questions to psychological puzzles—could be observed only through the prioritization of (a particular understanding of) philosophical logic, which he developed through an engagement with Husserl's *Logical Investigations* (first studied on Braig's advice between 1909 and 1911), as well as *vis-à-vis* the logical interpretation of Kant associated with the South-western or Baden School of Rickert, Wilhelm Windelband, and, perhaps most importantly, Emil Lask, a one-time student of Rickert also influenced by Husserl.[30]

[28] Letter to Engelbert Krebs, 19 July [?] 1914; rpt. *HJB* 61–2; p. 62.
[29] In his 1915 curriculum vitae, he comments: 'In der neuen Schule [Philosophie] lernte ich allererst die philosophischen Probleme als Probleme kennen und bekam den Einblick in das Wesen der Logik, der mich bis heute vor allem mich [*sic*] interessierenden philosophischen Disziplin. Zugleich bekam ich ein richtiges Verständnis der neueren Philosophie seit Kant, die ich in der scholastischen Literatur allzuwenig und ungenügend berücksichtigt fand'; GA 16, 38. For a list of Rickert's seminars attended by Heidegger, see *HJB* 15–17.
[30] Heidegger mentions his early reading of Husserl in both the c.v. of 1915 (see GA 16, 37) and that of 1922 (see GA 16, 41). On Heidegger's debt to Lask, see Theodore Kisiel's oft-reprinted essay 'Why Students of Heidegger Will Have to Read Emil Lask', e.g. in Theodore Kisiel, *Heidegger's Way of Thought: Critical and Interpretative Signposts*, ed. Alfred Denker and Marion Heinz (London: Continuum, 2nd edn., 2002), 101–36. On Heidegger's work on logic in the years 1912 to 1916 more generally, see esp. Steven

Between 1912 and 1916, Heidegger wrote a number of texts concerned with contemporary developments in logic, most importantly 'Das Realitätsproblem in der modernen Philosophie' (1912), 'Neuere Forschungen über die Logik' (1912), 'Charles Sentroul, *Kant und Aristoteles*' (review, 1914), *Die Lehre vom Urteil im Psychologismus* (doctoral dissertation, 1914), and *Die Kategorien- und Bedeutungslehre des Duns Scotus* (qualifying dissertation, 1915; published with an added conclusion in 1916). His leading philosophical question at the time was 'the relation between perception and thinking, and between object and perception', as requisite for a theory of objects (*Gegenstandslehre*[31]) and of judgement.[32] At least until 1916, he was hopeful that his developing response could draw from and even strengthen Scholasticism as a philosophical system, whose fundamentally realist, anti-psychologistic perspective he regarded as vital and (in early 1912) as consonant with the 'critical realism' pioneered by Eduard von Hartmann and advanced by Oswald Külpe, Husserl, and others.[33]

The importance of a realist attitude, for Heidegger, lay in its assertion that thinking is determined by the object, not vice versa. This direction of influence, he claimed until early 1912, was compromised by Kant, whose 'phenomenalism' he then still regarded as irreducibly subjectivist: 'According to [Kant], the transcendental conditions of sensual and intellectual knowledge have a genetically a priori, subjective character'.[34]

However, in 1912–13, his attitude to Kant shifted dramatically. As a consequence of his engagement with the implications of the Anti-Modernist Oath and his switch to philosophical studies, Heidegger became increasingly frustrated with the Catholic lack of an adequate epistemology, and consequent stultifying dogmatism about both the constitution of objects of perception and the nature of judgements.[35] Precisely this is what he now, discovering the Baden School's interpretation of Kant's system through his studies with Rickert, began to find

Galt Crowell, 'Making Logic Philosophical Again (1912–1916)', in Theodore Kisiel and John van Buren (eds.), *Reading Heidegger from the Start: Essays in his Earliest Thought* (Albany, NY: State University of New York Press, 1994), 55–72.

[31] Heidegger adopts this Meinongian term in his 1922 description of the aim of his qualifying thesis. See GA 1, 42; cf. Alexius Meinong, *Untersuchungen zur Gegenstandstheorie und Psychologie* (Leipzig: Barth, 1904).

[32] See Heidegger, 'Das Realitätsproblem in der modernen Philosophie', *Philosophisches Jahrbuch der Görresgesellschaft* 25 (1912), 353–63; rpt. GA 1, 1–15.

[33] See 'Das Realitätsproblem', GA 1, 15.

[34] 'Das Realitätsproblem', GA 1, 9.   [35] See 'Lebenslauf' (1915), GA 16, 38.

in Kant's transcendental-logical discoveries.[36] In late 1912, Heidegger explained that Kant's critique, as interpreted (correctly) by the Marburg and Baden Schools, 'did not enquire after the psychological origin of knowledge but after the logical value of its validity'.[37] In 1914, engaging with a recent Catholic work on Aristotle and Kant, he challenged the uncritical neo-Scholastic reliance on Aristotle and called for a proper '*wissenschaftstheoretische Einstellung*' (namely, a perspective appropriate to a philosophy of science) among 'Aristotelian-Scholastic' philosophers.[38] Aristotle's (seemingly presupposition-free) acceptance of objects of perception as 'given' or 'complete', Heidegger now argued, in fact relies on his theory of movement and the first mover, and is thus 'heavily metaphysically loaded from the start'; consequently, his epistemology is 'much more encumbered by presuppositions' than Kant's. Kant's supposedly dogmatic presupposition of the '*Sinnbestand*' (inventory of significance) of mathematics and the natural sciences, by contrast, is in fact a step towards transcendentally questioning the logical conditions of their possibility, and so, 'with radical acuity, making the object of knowledge itself (not as really existing, but according to its significance), and so the knowledge of the object, the problem'.[39] 'Kant's way of posing the problem', Heidegger concluded, 'is (even if one-sidedly oriented by mathematics and natural science) proper to a philosophy of science', while the Aristotelian remains 'anthropological, proper to a psychology of the individual'.[40]

This reframing of logic and epistemology in the widest sense would become vitally important to Heidegger's search for an adequate theological position in the following years. His own provisional answer to the puzzle of how the primacy of the object could be preserved without epistemological naivety, guided by Husserl's *Logical Investigations*[41] but

---

[36] See 'Lebenslauf' (1915), GA 16, 38. The work by Külpe to which Heidegger is referring is *Die Philosophie der Gegenwart in Deutschland* (Leipzig: B. G. Teubner, 1911).

[37] 'Neuere Forschungen über die Logik', *Literarische Rundschau für das katholische Deutschland* 38, no. 10 (1912), cols. 465–72; no. 11 (1912), cols. 517–24; no. 12 (1912), cols. 565–70; rpt. GA 1, 17–43; p. 19.

[38] See Heidegger, '*Kant und Aristoteles* von Charles Sentroul' (review), *Literarische Rundschau für das katholische Deutschland* 40, no. 7 (1914), cols. 330–2; rpt. GA 1, 49–53; p. 53. (This is a review of Charles Sentroul, *Kant und Aristoteles*, trans. L. Heinrichs (Munich: Kösel, 1911)). Heidegger here explicitly criticizes Sentroul's psychologistic interpretation of Kant, following that of Schopenhauer; see p. 51.

[39] '*Kant und Aristoteles*', GA 1, 50 (emphasis dropped).

[40] '*Kant und Aristoteles*', GA 1, 50 (emphasis dropped).

[41] Husserl is first mentioned in 'Neuere Forschungen über Logik' (1912) as having 'got the clarification of the principles of logic moving' (GA 1, 19).

motivated by theological concerns, was given in his 1915 qualifying thesis, which is discussed in the final section of this chapter.

THE 'HISTORY OF RELIGION' SCHOOL

Side by side with his philosophical criticism of its epistemological 'encumberedness', Heidegger, in the early 1910s, developed an increasingly critical historical-theological perspective on Scholasticism as a metaphysical system, at least as this was interpreted by the neo-Scholastics. This criticism was incited primarily by the Protestant 'history of religion' school, which Heidegger encountered in the winter semester of 1910/11. According to the curriculum vitae of 1922, the importance of this encounter cannot be overestimated: 'My engagement with primitive Christianity as approached by the history of religion school had rendered the [Roman Catholic position of faith] untenable'.[42] Among this school, Heidegger singles out Wilhelm Bousset, Hermann Gunkel, J. T. P. Wendland, and the Freiburg professor R. A. Reitzenstein; alongside them, he mentions Franz Overbeck and Albert Schweitzer as decisive influences of a similar kind.

The 'history of religion' school was a circle of Protestant theologians who had attained their *veniae legendi* in Göttingen in or after 1886, and who engaged in comparative studies of the history of religions, seeking to identify the common religious impulses underlying all religious texts, and the specific debts of early Christianity to Jewish and/ or Hellenistic cultic and theological trends.[43] Gunkel and Bousset were particularly interested in a historical interpretation of early Christian apocalyptic material, which they regarded as defining for the shape and direction of early Christian belief.[44] In this emphasis, they agreed

---

[42] GA 16, 43.

[43] See W. G. Kümmel, *Das Neue Testament: Geschichte der Erforschung seiner Probleme* (Freiburg: Karl Alber Verlag, 1958), chapter 5; see also Schaber, 'Herkunft', *HJB* 180–1.

[44] See esp. Hermann Gunkel, *Schöpfung und Chaos in Urzeit und Endzeit: Eine religionsgeschichtliche Untersuchung über Gen 1 und Apk Joh 21* (Göttingen: Vandenhoeck & Ruprecht, 1895); Wilhelm Bousset, *Der Antichrist in der Überlieferung des Judentums, des Neuen Testaments und der alten Kirche* (Göttingen: Vandenhoeck & Ruprecht, 1895), *Die jüdische Apokalyptik: Ihre religionsgeschichtliche Herkunft und ihre Bedeutung für das neue Testament* (Berlin, 1903), and *Die Offenbarung Johannis: Kritisch-exegetischer Kommentar über das Neue Testament* (Göttingen: Vandenhoeck & Ruprecht, 3rd edn., 1906).

with Albert Schweitzer, the most prominent member of the parallel 'consequent eschatology' school, which regarded an imminent eschatological expectation as the decisive mark of Jesus' preaching and/or of earliest Christianity.[45] Schweitzer drew a sharp distinction between early Christian eschatological fervour and the subsequent development of institutionalized liturgical forms, ethical teaching, and theology. In his view, these religious sensibilities were not merely different, but fundamentally incompatible: the second could only arise out of the failure of the first.

In this respect, Schweitzer agreed with Franz Overbeck, a New Testament and Patristics scholar of the previous generation (1837–1905), who also gained his *venia legendi* in Göttingen, but taught for most of his working life in Basle. His most influential work, *How Christian is our Present-Day Theology?* [*Über die Christlichkeit unserer heutigen Theologie*] (1873, 2nd edn. 1903), particularly impressed Heidegger; as late as 1970, he described it as 'establish[ing] the world-denying expectation of the end as the primary feature of the primordially Christian' ('das Urchristliche').[46] In this work, Overbeck posits an absolute contrast between the ascetic apocalypticism of the earliest Christians, which represents a radical rejection of any hope of salvation within world and time, and the subsequent secularization (*Verweltlichung*) and historicization (*Vergeschichtlichung*) of Christianity, effected by the development of a Christian theology and (political) establishment. Any such development, on Overbeck's view, is fundamentally misguided, because it assumes the possibility of explaining or grounding faith intellectually, and of achieving within history what can only be attained by its End.[47]

---

[45] See especially his *Leben-Jesu-Forschung: Von Reimarum zu Wrede* (Tübingen: J. C. B. Mohr, 1906).

[46] 1970 'Preface' to the 1927 lecture 'Phenomenology and Theology'; GA 9, 45–6 (followed by the lecture, 47–78). In the lecture itself, 'Christlichkeit' is distinguished from 'Christentum' as the proper subject of theology—'das, was Christentum allererst zu einem ursprünglichen geschichtlichen Ereignis werden läßt' (p. 52). Together with Overbeck's *How Christian is our Present-Day Theology?*, Heidegger mentions his friend Nietzsche's *Untimely Meditations* as a further text 'still out of season', 'für die wenigen Denkenden unter den zahllosen Rechnern bedeutend, weisend in das sagend, fragend, bildende Verharren vor dem Unsagbaren'; GA 9, 46.

[47] Overbeck's summary term for these errors is 'Jesuitism', a term Heidegger uses in a 1932 letter to Elisabeth Blochmann, where he writes that communism is 'grauenhaft', but Jesuitism 'teuflisch'; letter of 22 June 1932, in Joachim W. Storck (ed.), *Martin Heidegger/Elisabeth Blochmann: Briefwechsel 1918–1969* (Marbach: Deutsches Literaturarchiv, 2nd edn., 1990), 52.

For Heidegger, the significance of these enquiries was both methodological and substantial. Methodologically, the Protestant theologians
had, by integrating early Christianity into a wider historical picture of
human religions, emphasized the abiding nature of human religiosity
and the importance of historical development, and de-emphasized (or
even subverted) the claim of a radically new, because revealed, element in early Christianity. This both tacitly and explicitly implied a
conception of religion as an essentially human (rather than a (purely)
supernatural) phenomenon, and highlighted the irreducible historical dimension of any manifestation of religious beliefs and practices.
As regards content, Overbeck, Schweitzer, and others emphasized
the eschatological character of early Christian spirituality as a kind
of immediate, intuitive religious experience inherently resistant to
('metaphysical') systematization. While to Schweitzer or Johannes
Weiss, this spirituality did not imply an imperative for contemporary Christianity (but was rather an aberration to be left behind), to
Overbeck and Heidegger, it constituted the paradigm of 'authentic'
Christian experience, and as such formed the basis of a radical critique
of 'metaphysicizing' neo-Scholasticism.[48]

The task emerging from these enquiries, for Heidegger, was both
a religiosity marked by such aboriginal experience, and a theology
capable of giving this experience expression from within, rather than
imposing upon it a system from without. He found significant early
impulses for these in the writings of the young Luther (which he read as
early as 1909–11), Kierkegaard (whose translation he regarded as one
of the highlights of 1910–14), and the medieval mystics (particularly
Meister Eckhart).[49] Heidegger's own development of these thinkers,
within his maturing phenomenological method, in the years following
his qualifying dissertation of 1915, will be discussed in Chapter 3.

This task included a necessary sensitivity to the inherent historicity
of religious belief—its determination by the historical situation and

[48] Cf. Kisiel, *Genesis*, 218.
[49] Heidegger's surprisingly early encounter with Luther was recently established by
Otto Pöggeler; see his 'Heideggers Luther-Lektüre im Freiburger Theologenkonvikt',
HJB 185–96. Heidegger's mention of the translation of the works of Kierkegaard (and
Dostoevsky) can be found in his 1957 'Antrittsrede'; GA 1, 56. Meister Eckhart is first
mentioned in Heidegger's qualifying thesis of 1915. The Jena edition of Kierkegaard's
Gesammelte Werke in German was published in 12 volumes between 1909 and 1922:
Sören Kierkegaard, *Gesammelte Werke*, 12 vols., trans. H. Gottsched and C. Schrempf
(Jena: Eugen Diederichs, 1909–22). This is also the edition which Heidegger cites in
Being and Time (§ 40, n.1).

development of its practitioners—and an ability to give expression to this dimension from within, rather than (similarly to religious belief) stultifying it by an imposed 'objectivity' which would, by its very nature, be untrue to the phenomenon it sought to describe. Heidegger self-confessedly developed this sensitivity primarily through the Freiburg seminars of Heinrich Finke, his own study of the works of Dilthey, and his 'awakening interest' in Fichte, Schelling, and Hegel.[50]

HERMENEUTICS AND THE STUDY OF HISTORY

H. W. Dilthey's *Gesammelte Schriften* began to appear in 1914, with publications, in that year, of *Einleitung in die Geisteswissenschaften* (originally published in 1883) and *Weltanschauung und Analyse des Menschen seit Renaissance und Reformation* (not previously published).[51] Heidegger mentions these publications as a highlight of the period 1910–14 not because they marked his first encounter with Dilthey, but rather because they made work he already prized significantly more accessible. Heidegger's own study of Dilthey's (then scattered) works dates from five years earlier: Responding to a request by Karl Löwith for the temporary loan of some volumes, he writes on 3 September 1920, 'I don't have Dilthey's works, only detailed excerpts, in part hand-copied by me as a theologian in 1909–10, which are useful only if you know the context.'[52]

Dilthey's importance for Heidegger lay in his strict differentiation between the significance and methods of human and natural sciences. As Heidegger explains in 1925:

> [Dilthey's] final interest is the question after the concept of life. The history of the historical sciences has a different meaning from that of the natural sciences. Where the history of the historical sciences is pursued,

---

[50] See 'Lebenslauf' (1915), GA 16, 39; 'Vita' (1922), GA 16, 42; 'Antrittsrede' (1957), GA 1, 56.

[51] *Einleitung in die Geisteswissenschaften*, being vol. i of *Gesammelte Schriften*, ed. Bernhard Groethuysen (Stuttgart: B. G. Teubner, 1914); *Weltanschauung und Analyse des Menschen seit Renaissance und Reformation*, being vol. ii of *Gesammelte Schriften*, ed. Georg Misch (Stuttgart: B. G. Teubner, 1914). Heidegger mentions the publication of Dilthey's *Collected Works* as one of the events particularly noteworthy in the period 1910–14.

[52] Quoted in Kisiel, *Genesis*, 524 n. 43.

life is pursued under the aspect of its understanding [*Erkenntnis*]. Life as understanding pursues itself in its history. The one who understands is also the thing understood. That is the meaning of a history of the sciences of humanity and its structure.[53]

This view is expressed in Dilthey's valorization of autobiography as an indispensable tool for the historian.[54] An important goal of historiography, Dilthey contends, is to grasp the individual, who is 'an intrinsic value in the world of human spirit', rather than to reduce the individual to a part in some larger system.[55] This is the case because history is not brute facts, but both constituted and grasped in and by 'moods' (*Lebensstimmung*), 'colorations' (*Färbung*), or 'hermeneutics' (*Auslegung*) unique to each individual.[56] Consequently, we should first of all 'observe without prejudice the reality of our inner life and, proceeding from there... establish the meaning of nature and history for this inner life'.[57]

This historical consciousness, according to Dilthey, finds its roots in early Christianity. Indeed, the irreducibility of 'personal experience' just *is*, for Dilthey, 'moral-religious truth'.[58] This personal element of faith (so well conceptualized by Schleiermacher[59]) is the distinguishing mark of primitive Christianity, medieval mysticism, and Luther, and presents an enduring 'protest' against metaphysics.[60]

By the time Heidegger discusses Dilthey publicly (which happens most sustainedly between 1920 and 1925), his interpretation of the

[53] 'Wilhelm Diltheys Forschungsarbeit und der gegenwärtige Kampf um eine historische Weltanschauung (Kasseler Vorträge)', ed. Walter Bröcker and Frithjof Rodi, *Dilthey-Jahrbuch* 8 (1992–3), 143–80; 153. This and the following two paragraphs are heavily indebted to Crowe, *Heidegger's Religious Origins*, chapter 5, which represents the (so far) most detailed analysis of Heidegger's appropriation of Dilthey in English. See also Rudolf A. Makkreel, 'Dilthey, Heidegger und der Vollzugssinn der Geschichte', *HJB* 307–21.

[54] Dilthey, *Der Aufbau der geschichtlichen Welt in den Geisteswissenschaften* (1910), Gesammelte Schriften 7, ed. Bernhard Groethuysen (Stuttgart: B. G. Teubner, 8th edn., 1992), 200.

[55] Dilthey, *Aufbau der geschichtlichen Welt*, 212. All translations in this and the next paragraph are taken from Crowe, *Heidegger's Religious Origins*, 146–7.

[56] Dilthey, *Weltanschauungslehre: Abhandlungen zur Philosophie der Philosophie* (1931), *Gesammelte Schriften* 8, ed. Bernhard Groethuysen (Stuttgart: B. G. Teubner, 6th edn., 1991), 81.

[57] Dilthey, *Einleitung in die Geisteswissenschaften* (1883), *Gesammelte Schriften* i, ed. Bernhard Groethuysen (Stuttgart: B. G. Teubner, 10th edn., 2008), 408.

[58] Dilthey, *Einleitung in die Geisteswissenschaften*, 384–5.

[59] See Dilthey, *Leben Schleiermachers* (1870), 2 vols., *Gesammelte Schriften* 13–14, ed. Martin Redeker (Stuttgart: B. G. Teubner, 1966 and 1985).

[60] Dilthey, *Einleitung in die Geisteswissenschaften*, 385.

historian-philosopher is well defined. In a series of semi-popular lectures held in Kassel in 1925, 'Wilhelm Dilthey's Research and the Present Struggle for a Historical World-view' ('Wilhelm Diltheys Forschungsarbeit und der gegenwärtige Kampf um eine historische Weltanschauung'), Heidegger valorizes Dilthey's 'living question after the meaning of history and of human existence'.[61] Although it is impossible to determine how much of this interpretation was already in place in the first half of the 1910s, the relevance of Dilthey's approach to Heidegger's developing concerns in 1912 to 1916 is clear.

Dilthey's valorization of the historical individual found its counterpart, in Heidegger's developing perspective, in an idealist understanding of God as intrinsically historical. The most formidable thinker in this regard was Hegel. That Heidegger began to appreciate Hegel at around the same time as Kant is clear from the stark contrast between his disparaging remarks about the idealist philosopher in 'Das Realitätsproblem in der modernen Philosophie' (1912),[62] and the conclusion of Heidegger's qualifying thesis (1916), which culminates in the declaration that the great and immediate task of any 'philosophy of living spirit, active love, and reverential ardency for God', such as Heidegger envisions, is a 'fundamental critical engagement with that system of historical world-view which, exceeding all others in breadth and depth, wealth of experience and concept-formation, has sublated all previous fundamental philosophical problem-motifs into itself—that of Hegel'.[63]

The student absorbed Hegel both directly and through his teachers. Both Heidegger's Freiburg dogmatics professor Carl Braig and Hermann Schell, a Würzburg apologist whose work Heidegger greatly valued until at least 1915,[64] were strongly influenced by the speculative Catholic Tübingen School of J. A. Möhler and Johann Evangelist

---

[61] Heidegger, 'Diltheys Forschungsarbeit', 152.   [62] See GA 1, 3.

[63] 'Die Philosophie des lebendigen Geistes, der tatvollen Liebe, der verehrenden Gottinnigkeit, deren allgemeinste Richtpunkte nur angedeutet werden konnten ... steht vor der großen Aufgabe einer prinzipiellen Auseinandersetzung mit dem an Fülle wie Tiefe, Erlebnisreichtum und Begriffsbildung gewaltigsten System einer historischen Weltanschauung, als welches es alle vorausgegangenen fundamentalen philosophischen Problemmotive in sich aufgehoben hat, mit Hegel'; GA 1, 411. For an emphasis on Hegel's *theological* context, see also *Phänomenologische Interpretationen zu Aristoteles: Einführung in die phänomenologische Forschung* (WS 1921/22), ed. Walter Bröcker and Käte Bröcker-Oltmanns (Frankfurt: Klostermann, 2nd edn., 1994), 7. [Hereafter cited as GA 61.]

[64] See 'Lebenslauf' (1915), GA 16, 37.

Kuhn, which sought an in-depth engagement of Catholic theology with contemporary philosophy, particularly German idealism and romanticism, in the service of a renewed appreciation of Catholic doctrine.[65] In Braig's dogmatics lectures, which Heidegger attended from the winter semester of 1910/11 until the summer semester of 1912,[66] Braig covered (in an annual cycle) an introduction to Catholic dogmatics and the doctrine of God, theological anthropology, theological cosmology, and the doctrines of sin and grace.[67] Strongly influenced by Möhler's *Symbolik* and Kuhn's *Katholische Dogmatik* (the former of which Heidegger also owned[68]), Braig's lectures deeply impressed Heidegger by their speculative approach and penetrating intelligence.[69] In 1963, the erstwhile student recalled: 'On the few walks that I was allowed to take with [Braig] I heard for the first time about the significance of Schelling and Hegel for speculative theology as contrasted with the doctrinal system of Scholasticism.'[70] And in 1957, he praised the Tübingen School (as whose last exponent he regarded Braig) for giving 'rank and breadth to Catholic theology through engagement with Hegel and Schelling'.[71]

Hermann Schell (1850–1906) was, from 1884, Professor of Apologetics at the University of Würzburg, where he developed a speculative approach to apologetics which, in 1898, led to the temporary inclusion of several of his books in the Roman Index. Heidegger read his work privately before or during his theology course, and according to his 1915 curriculum vitae found in it a philosophical approach more satisfactory than those offered either in his prescribed philosophy lectures or in his private reading of 'Scholastic textbooks'.[72]

Schell adhered to what he called a 'dynamic Thomism', which identified 'the true nature' of Thomism as 'trust in the power of reason,

---

[65] The Catholic Tübingen School (contemporaneous with the better-known Protestant school of the same name) was a mid-nineteenth-century school of speculative theology represented in the first generation by Johann Adam Möhler (1796–1838) and in the second by Johann Evangelist Kuhn (1806–87), Franz Linsenmann (1835–98), and Franz Funk (1840–1907), with whom Braig studied in Tübingen.

[66] See GA 14, 82.

[67] From 'Vorlesungsverzeichnis der Katholisch-Theologischen Fakultät', reproduced in Johannes Schaber, 'Der Theologiestudent Martin Heidegger und sein Dogmatikprofessor Carl Braig', *Freiburger Diözesanarchiv* 125 (2005), 332–47; 337.

[68] Heidegger acquired *Symbolik* second-hand around 1911 and later passed it on to his still-Catholic nephew. See Schaber, 'Der Theologiestudent Martin Heidegger', 338; 'Herkunft', *HJB* 183.

[69] GA 14, 82.   [70] GA 14, 82.   [71] 'Antrittsrede' (1957), GA 1, 57.

[72] GA 16, 37.

the absolute validity of the law of causality, [and] the strictly empirical foundation of all our scientific knowledge'[73]—in short, as rationalist realism. On this methodological understanding of *'philosophia perennis'*, the *perennitas* of Catholic truth manifests itself precisely in its ability to be applied to 'everything new and vigorous'.[74] The role of apologetics in relation to this truth is that of a 'philosophical critical-speculative *Begründungswissenschaft'* which can and must remain accountable to *'all the ideals and demands* of the scientifically and historically matured spirit'.[75] The theological correlate of this understanding, which at the same time served as its theological justification, was Schell's Hegelian re-conceptualization of the aseity of God in terms not of a static *ratio sui* but of a dynamic *causa sui*: for Schell, God is pure Being, positing itself and actuating itself in thought and act.[76] This dynamic conception of God (which was partly responsible for Schell's temporary inclusion in the Index) also facilitated a conception of Christian truth as inherently open to development.[77]

TRANSITION: THE QUALIFYING THESIS OF 1915

In his 1915 qualifying thesis *Duns Scotus' Theory of the Categories and of Meaning*, Heidegger follows and extends Schell and Braig's attempts to bring the neo-Scholastic practice of reading medieval texts with a direct view to contemporary concerns into alignment with the pneumatological and historiographical theories of Hegel, and the logical investigations of Kant and Husserl.[78] Braig's philosophical

---

[73] *Apologie des Christentums*, i: *Religion und Offenbarung* (Paderborn: Schöningh, 1902), xiii; quoted in Schaber, 'Herkunft', *HJB* 168.

[74] *Religion und Offenbarung*, xxiv; quoted in Hans-Joachim Sander, 'Herman Schells Apologetik der pluralen Wahrheit des Glaubens', in Otmar Meuffels and Rainer Dvorak (eds.), *Wahrheit Gottes—Freiheit des Denkens: Herman Schell als Impulsgeber für Theologie und Kirche* (Würzburg: Schöningh, 2001), 95–108; p. 102.

[75] *Religion und Offenbarung*, xi; quoted in Meuffels and Dvorak, *Wahrheit Gottes*, 101.

[76] See Raimund Lachner, 'Schell, Herman', *Biographisch-Bibliographisches Kirchenlexikon*, vol. ix, cols. 88–99; Thomas Sheehan, 'Lehrjahre', in Sallis, *Collegium Phaenomenologicum*, 92.

[77] *Religion und Offenbarung*, xiii–xiv; cited in Schaber, 'Herkunft', *HJB* 168.

[78] In a 1959 speech, reproduced as the foreword to his earliest writings, Heidegger declared that from his dogmatics professor Carl Braig he had received the 'entscheidende und darum in Worten nicht faßbare Bestimmung für die eigene akademische Lehrtätigkeit'; GA 1, x–xi.

corpus—*Vom Sein: Abriß der Ontologie* (1896), *Vom Denken: Abriß der Logik* (1896), and *Vom Erkennen: Abriß der Noetik* (1897)—had already begun to integrate these two concerns by answering Kant's transcendental question after the condition of the possibility of knowledge with ultimate reference not to the laws of logic but to those of being: 'The laws of logic guarantee the substantial truth of their results, beyond the mere formal correctness of the procedure, only because the basic laws of thought coincide with the laws of Being of the thinking entity.'[79]

Simply put, it is the self-communication (*communicabilitas sui*) of Being—which Braig, like the Scholastics, identifies with God as the source of all beings—which enables man's passive and active intellect, that is, the self-manifestation (*manifestativa sui*) of beings on one hand and their perception/knowledge by man on the other. As Braig quotes Bonaventure:

> Just as the eye, when it turns towards the manifold differences of the colours, does not see the light . . . , so the eye of the mind, when it turns towards beings in particular and in general, does not notice being itself, . . . even though it is only through being that it encounters everything.[80]

Heidegger follows this strategy directly in his qualifying thesis. Taking up Husserl's challenge to create an 'indubitable foundation' for a 'general and, especially, an a priori grammar' through 'proof of a priori laws determining the possible forms of meaning',[81] he argues that such laws must transcend the sphere of logic: 'One cannot even begin to view logic and its problems in the right light if one does not recognise the context from within which they become visible as a trans-logical one.'[82] Ways of meaning correspond to ways of being. It is in this Bonaventurian sense that, as he continues, 'in the long run, philosophy cannot do without its essential optics, i.e. metaphysics'.[83] Logic requires an ontological, indeed a spiritual, grounding:

> If one frames the concept of the object *transcendentally-ontologically*, . . . the problem of the 'application' of the categories loses its meaning;

---

[79] Schaeffler, *Frömmigkeit des Denkens?*, 8; quoting Carl Braig, *Vom Denken: Abriß der Logik* (Freiburg: Herder, 1896), 9.

[80] Carl Braig, *Vom Sein: Abriß der Ontologie* (Freiburg: Herder, 1896), v–vi (original reference not provided).

[81] Edmund Husserl, *Logische Untersuchungen* ii/1 (Halle: Max Niemeyer, 1907), 287; quoted in GA 1, 270.

[82] GA 1, 405.   [83] GA 1, 406.

the more firmly the more courageously one affirms the in-principle
significance of the—not 'individualistically' interpreted—*proposition of
immanence*, whose ultimate grounding, which is in my opinion both
necessary and ultimately achievable only metaphysically, can be man-
aged through the already suggested concept of living spirit. If the partial-
ness of a *solely* objective-logical treatment of the problem of categories
is recognizable anywhere, then [it is] in the problem of the *application*
of the categories.[84]

This living spirit, Heidegger continues, is 'by nature historical spirit
in the widest sense of the word'.[85] Thus, a proper world-view is 'far
removed from the merely punctual existence of a theory detached from
life'. Rather, 'Spirit can only be grasped[86] if the whole abundance of his
achievements, i.e. *his history*, is sublated into him; and this ever-growing
abundance, philosophically grasped, offers an ever-increasing means
of a living grasp of the absolute spirit of God.'[87]

God here is intrinsically a historical God, to be grasped in and
through historical existence. In the years following his qualifying thesis, Heidegger will specify the disposition appropriate to such a temporal experience of God: affliction.

---

[84] GA 1, 407.   [85] GA 1, 407.
[86] The German *begriffen/begreifen*, used twice more in the sentence, plays with the
tension between the philosophical use of the term ('to conceptualize') and its visceral
roots ('to grasp', 'to finger').
[87] GA 1, 407–8.

3

Eschatological Affliction as the Centre of a Phenomenology of Religion, 1916–21

Doch uns ist gegeben,
Auf keiner Stätte zu ruhn,
Es schwinden, es fallen
Die leidenden Menschen
Blindlings von einer
Stunde zur andern,
Wie Wasser von Klippe
Zu Klippe geworfen,
Jahr lang ins Ungewisse hinab.[1]

—Friedrich Hölderlin,
'Hyperions Schicksalslied'

In the years 1916 to 1919, Heidegger's estrangement from the Catholic Church became definite and public. Heidegger navigated this move carefully, maintaining a semblance of Catholic ties while preparing the way for a professional existence within Protestant scholarship, before openly declaring his break with Catholicism in 1919. The difficulty, professionally speaking, lay in his Catholic training. After the failure of his ambition for the vacant chair in Catholic Philosophy at Freiburg in 1916, Heidegger attempted the jump to a Protestant department. Heinrich Rickert, the (nominal) supervisor of his qualifying thesis,[2] had just moved to the Protestant Heidelberg as successor of Wilhelm Windelband, and Heidegger wrote to him in early 1917, expressing a

---

[1] 'But our fate is | To find no resting place; | Suffering humanity | Faints, falls, | Blindly from one hour | To the next | Like water flung | From cliff to cliff | Year after year into the unknown.'

[2] In practice, Rickert delegated the assessment to Krebs; see Ott, *Martin Heidegger*, 82.

wish to join the Neo-Kantian there. Rickert replied that Heidelberg was 'out of the question' for Heidegger, who, being 'a committed Catholic also in his capacity as a philosopher' could only serve at a Catholic theological faculty.[3] Heidegger replied defensively: 'I never have, and never would, maintain the *narrow* Catholic standpoint that the understanding and solution of problems should take their bearings from extra-scientific considerations, traditional or whatever. Rather, according to my free personal convictions, I will seek and teach the truth.'[4]

But the move did not happen. Instead, Heidegger tried to forge a closer association with Rickert's Freiburg successor Edmund Husserl, whose work had engaged him since his student days. Husserl initially responded only partially. In 1916, he met Heidegger's request to discuss the copy of the (still unpublished) qualifying thesis he had sent to Husserl with cordial reserve.[5] In October 1917, asked for an assessment of his young colleague by the (Protestant) Marburg philosopher Paul Natorp, who was seeking to appoint an extraordinary professor in Philosophy, but wondered about Heidegger's teaching experience and, in particular, the potential danger of 'confessional narrowness',[6] Husserl replied evasively and with oblique dismissiveness. Heidegger's 'beginner's effort [*Erstlingswerk*]' on Duns Scotus was certainly 'a promising beginning for a historian of medieval philosophy', but Heidegger seemed too young and immature for 'our post', and had only mixed teaching success. In particular, however, he was clearly 'confessionally bound', standing, 'so to speak, under the protection of my colleague Finke, our "Catholic historian"'. Husserl goes on to report condescendingly that

> accordingly, last year in committee meetings to fill the chair in Catholic philosophy here in our Philosophy Department—a chair that we would like to make a professional position in the history of medieval

[3] Rickert to Heidegger, 3 February 1917; in Alfred Denker (ed.), *Martin Heidegger/ Heinrich Rickert: Briefe 1912–1933* (Frankfurt: Klostermann, 2002), 40.

[4] Heidegger to Rickert, 27 February 1917; in Denker (ed.), *Heidegger/Rickert*, 42.

[5] See Husserl's related letter to Heidegger, dated 21 July 1916; in Edmund Husserl, *Briefwechsel*, 10 vols., ed. Karl Schuhmann (The Hague: Kluwer Academic Publishers, 1994), iv. 127. On Heidegger's early relationship to Husserl, see particularly Thomas Sheehan, 'Husserl and Heidegger: The Making and Unmaking of a Relationship', in *Edmund Husserl: Psychological and Transcendental Phenomenology and the Confrontation with Heidegger (1927–1931)*, ed. and trans. Thomas Sheehan and R. E. Palmer (The Hague: Kluwer Academic Publishers, 1997), 1–40; esp. 1–22.

[6] Letter from Natorp to Husserl, October 1917, quoted in Ott, *Martin Heidegger*, 97.

philosophy—[Heidegger] was also brought up for consideration, at which point Finke discussed him as a confessionally suitable candidate.[7]

The only counter-consideration, Husserl noted, was Heidegger's recent marriage to a Protestant woman, who had 'not yet' converted to the Catholic faith.[8]

Heidegger had indeed, hurriedly and in a quiet military church ceremony on 21 March 1917, married the Protestant Elfride Petri—a move regarded with concern by his Catholic family and friends, and accepted only because of her alleged intention to convert to Roman Catholicism (which was never actualized).[9] It was she who first voiced the couple's estrangement from the Roman Church to their Catholic friends. In a conversation with Engelbert Krebs on 23 December 1918, recorded in reported speech in Krebs's diary, she explained to the theologian priest why she and her husband could not in good conscience have their expected first child baptized within the Catholic Church:

> My husband no longer has his church faith, and I have not found it. Already when we got married, his faith was undercut with doubts. But I myself urged a Catholic wedding and hoped, with his help, to find faith. We have read, talked, thought and prayed a lot together, and the result is that we now both think in a Protestant way, that is, believe in a personal God and pray to him in the spirit of Christ, but without fixed dogmatic commitment, or Protestant or Catholic orthodoxy.[10]

Husserl later confirmed this representation. A few months after his dismissive letter to Natorp, the phenomenologist learned from Heidegger's close friend Heinrich Ochsner (who was, religiously, in a similar position to his friend) that Heidegger had in fact loosened his commitment to Catholic dogma already. Accordingly, in 1920, when he was once more queried by Natorp about Heidegger's suitability for a Marburg post, Husserl proudly and pointedly declared that by 1917,

---

[7] Husserl, *Briefwechsel*, v. 131 (translation by T. Sheehan).

[8] Husserl, *Briefwechsel*, v. 131 (translation by T. Sheehan).

[9] A concerned letter from Heidegger's friend Ernst Laslowski dated 28 January 1917, as well as a series of diary entries by Heidegger's Catholic priest friend Engelbert Krebs concerning the difficulties of the marriage, are recorded in Ott, *Martin Heidegger*, 99–101 and 109.

[10] Quoted in Ott, *Martin Heidegger*, 108. Gerda Walther, a fellow student of Husserl, mentions Elfride's influence on her husband's turn from Catholicism in *Zum anderen Ufer: Vom Marxismus und Atheismus zum Christentum* (Remagen: Der Leuchter/Otto Reichl Verlag, 1960), 207; noted in Sheehan, 'Husserl and Heidegger', 12 n. 33.

'Heidegger had…and cut himself off from the sure and easy career of a "philosopher of the Catholic world-view".'[11] In a letter to Rudolf Otto around the same time, Husserl associated this conversion with Heidegger's increasing closeness to Husserl himself:

> Not without strong inner struggles did the two of them [Heidegger and Ochsner] gradually open themselves to my suggestions and also draw closer to me personally. In that same period they both underwent radical changes in their fundamental religious convictions.

He hurries to avow that

> [i]n arch-Catholic Freiburg I do not want to stand out as a corrupter of the youth, as a proselytizer, as an enemy of the Catholic Church. That I am not. I have not exercised the least influence on Heidegger's and Oxner's [*sic*] migration over to the ground of Protestantism, even though it can only be very pleasing to me as a 'non-dogmatic Protestant' and a free Christian.[12]

The same year, Heidegger became Husserl's assistant, a post he held until his belated appointment to an associate (*ausserordentlich*) professorship in Philosophy at Marburg in 1922. By that move, Heidegger was, as Rudolf Bultmann, the local New Testament professor, reported in a 1923 letter to Hans von Soden, 'thoroughly Protestant'.[13]

It is at the point of Heidegger's more or less completed turn to Protestantism—coinciding professionally with having moved from being a 'protégé' of the Catholic historian Finke to being assistant to the Jewish/Lutheran phenomenologist Edmund Husserl—that scholarly engagement with his theological roots, at least in English-language scholarship, usually begins. One of the most consequential results of this foreshortening of Heidegger's religious-intellectual path is the

[11] Husserl to Natorp, dated 11 February 1920; in Husserl, *Briefwechsel*, v. 139 (translation by T. Sheehan).
[12] Husserl to Rudolf Otto, dated 5 March 1919; in Husserl, *Briefwechsel*, v. 205–8; pp. 205 and 207 (translation by T. Sheehan). See also Sheehan, 'Husserl and Heidegger', 12.
[13] 'Das Seminar ist diesmal besonders lehrreich, weil unser neuer Philosoph Heidegger, ein Schüler Husserls, daran teilnimmt. Er kommt aus dem Katholizismus, ist aber ganz Protestant…'; Bultmann to Hans Freiherr von Soden, 23 December 1923; published in Antje Bultmann Lemke, 'Der unveröffentlichte Nachlaß von Rudolf Bultmann—Ausschnitte aus dem biographischen Quellenmaterial', in Bernd Jaspert (ed.), *Rudolf Bultmanns Werk und Wirkung* (Darmstadt: Wissenschaftliche Buchgesellschaft, 1984), 194–210; p. 202.

assumption that his interest in religion was secondary from the beginning: that Heidegger never regarded religion as more than one among many fields of phenomenological enquiry. The sources suggest, on the contrary, that Heidegger discovered the phenomenological method, together with Protestantism, in large part as a means to adequately describing religious experience.

Husserlian phenomenology adopted the motto, 'To the things themselves!' ('*Zu den Sachen selbst!*'). In other words, it called for a bottom-up approach to the description of objects, bracketing any preconceived notions or classifications in favour of concentrated attention to the experience of the 'constitution' of these objects for the observer. Heidegger felt this method to be internally akin to religious experience as described by Schleiermacher and others, and so to be uniquely capable of illuminating that experience from within. Not only that: in 1919/20, he argued that it was in fact 'one of the inmost tendencies of phenomenology' to strive away from the metaphysization of Christianity that had occurred through its forced assimilation to Greek philosophy—a metaphysization only overcome partially and periodically by the medieval mystics, the young Luther, Schleiermacher, and Kierkegaard.[14]

Personal testimony to the religious origins of Heidegger's characteristic form of the phenomenological method, his 'hermeneutics of facticity', is easily forthcoming. In a letter to Heidegger on 10 September 1918, Husserl calls his younger colleague 'my phenomenologist of religion'.[15] And as late as 1921, Heidegger himself corrects his student Karl Löwith by insisting that he is not a philosopher but a 'Christian theo*logian*'.[16] When he first presents his 'hermeneutics of facticity' publicly in 1923, Heidegger (sardonically) prefaces it with a partial genealogy: 'The companion of my search was the young Luther and its model Aristotle, whom the former hated. Kierkegaard provided

---

[14] Heidegger, *Grundprobleme der Phänomenologie* (WS 1919/20), ed. Hans-Helmuth Gander (Frankfurt: Klostermann, 1992), 61. [Hereafter cited as GA 58.]

[15] Kisiel, *Genesis*, 75. In a conversation on 13 August 1931, Husserl told Dorion Lairns that he had long realized how far Heidegger was from him, and laid this to Heidegger never having freed himself completely from his theological prejudices (as well as to the weight of the war on him); see Dorion Lairns, *Conversations with Husserl and Fink*, ed. Richard M. Zaner (The Hague: Martinus Nijhoff, 1976).

[16] Letter dated 19 August 1921; in Hartmut Tietjen (ed.), 'Drei Briefe Martin Heideggers an Karl Löwith', in *Zur philosophischen Aktualität Heideggers*, vol. ii, ed. Dietrich Papenfuss and Otto Pöggeler (Frankfurt: Klostermann, 1990), 27–38; pp. 28–9.

impulses, and Husserl gave me my eyes.'[17] On other occasions, he mentions a number of other important Christian influences: the apostle Paul, Augustine, the medieval mystics (particularly Bernard of Clairvaux, Meister Eckhart, and Tauler), Kierkegaard, Dostoevsky, and Franz Overbeck.[18]

Recently published letters, notes, and lecture transcripts from the period between 1915 and 1924 make it possible, for the first time, to determine and evaluate the substance of this strand of influence. This chapter presents the provisional outcome of Heidegger's early reading of Schleiermacher and the young Luther, strongly inflected by his prevailing interest in Romantic and post-Romantic poetry. Specifically, it argues that Heidegger revises Schleiermacher's basic religious experience of absolute dependency in line with Luther's and St Paul's emphases on crucicentrism and eschatological anxiety, presenting the basic religious experience (which is determinative of the phenomenological examination of religion) as *affliction* rather than dependency or (as his colleague Adolf Reinach suggests) 'shelteredness'.

But Heidegger's assimilation of Paul and Luther is not purely theological, but inflected by his intense engagement, during the same years, with Rainer Maria Rilke and, particularly, Friedrich Hölderlin. Through Hölderlin and his tradition, Heidegger arrives at an interpretation of (Christian) affliction neither as a result of sin nor as a participation in the suffering of Christ, but as the constitutive experience of irreducible human finitude—an experience which highlights the radical otherness of the human *vis-à-vis* the divine, but which alone also enables authentic existence.

This experience of human finitude, for the Heidegger of the late 1910s and early 1920s, has its horizon and paradigmatic expression in eschatological expectation—an idea he works out in *Introduction to the Phenomenology of Religion* (his lecture series for the winter semester of 1920/1), and refines in *Augustine and Neo-Platonism* (his lecture series the following semester). This chapter will follow Heidegger's development in both its theological-philosophical and its literary forms from his first interest in Schleiermacher to his 1920/1 lecture series on Pauline eschatology.

---

[17] GA 63, 5.
[18] On Paul, Augustine, and the medieval mystics, see Heidegger, *Phänomenologie des religiösen Lebens* (1918/19, WS 1920/21 and SS 1921), ed. Matthias Jung, Thomas Regehly, and Claudius Strube (Frankfurt: Klostermann, 1995), *passim* [hereafter cited as GA 60]; on Dostoevsky, see GA 1, 57; see also GA 16, 42.

RELIGION AS A DISPOSITION OF TEMPORALITY

As already discussed, Heidegger remained, until the achievement of his *venia legendi* in 1915, broadly committed to 'Aristotelian-Scholastic philosophy', but increasingly reinterpreted this thought system in the light of contemporary philosophy, particularly Husserlian phenomenology, which he had encountered via his training in Neo-Kantianism.[19] In the conclusion of his qualifying thesis, *Duns Scotus' Theory of the Categories and of Meaning*, he calls for an integration of medieval scholasticism and medieval mysticism, which latter he associates with a proper appreciation of the significance of the irreducibly temporal, individual experience of the believer for any understanding of God. This significance arises because temporal experience is the natural human counterpart of God's Spirit, which as 'living Spirit is… essentially historical Spirit'.[20] Consequently, theological philosophy 'as rationalistic construct detached from life is powerless'.[21] What is required is a 'philosophy of living Spirit, of active love, of reverential ardency for God'.[22]

Drawing on his developing phenomenological method, Heidegger devoted much of the years 1915 to 1921 to the attempt to formulate a more authentic Christian theology, moving as an *exitus/reditus* from and to 'factic life experience'.[23] In this effort, Heidegger turned, among others, to the Protestant sensibilities of Schleiermacher and Luther.[24] At the same time, his abiding interest in Romantic literature sensitized him to a decisive dimension of factic life experience: suffering or, more precisely, affliction.

---

[19] GA 16, 38–9.   [20] GA 1, 407.   [21] GA 1, 409.   [22] GA 1, 410.

[23] See esp. 'Introduction to the Phenomenology of Religion', GA 60, 9–14; and compare his 19 August 1921 letter to Karl Löwith, in which he affirms his commitment to his own 'facticity', which involves being 'a Christian theo*logian*' ('Drei Briefe', in Papenfuss and Pöggeler (eds.), *Zur philosophischen Aktualität Heideggers*, 29).

[24] Cf. Heidegger's reminiscence in his 1923 lecture series *Ontologie: Hermeneutik der Faktizität*: 'Begleiter im Suchen war der junge Luther und Vorbild Aristoteles, den jener haßte. Stöße gab Kierkegaard, und die Augen hat mir Husserl eingesetzt'; published under the same title as GA 63; here p. 5. Heidegger began reading Kierkegaard between 1910 and 1914; see his 'Antrittsrede' upon election to the Heidelberg *Akademie der Wissenschaften* (1957); rpt. in GA 1, 55–57; p. 56. He read Luther (it now appears) as early as 1908 (see Pöggeler, 'Heideggers Luther-Lektüre im Freiburger Theologenkonvikt', *HJB* 185–96). He first engaged with Schleiermacher in depth in 1917, when he held a private lecture entitled 'Das Problem des Religiösen bei Schleiermacher' on the occasion of Elfride Heidegger's birthday, 1 August 1917. The lecture is remembered in two letters by Heinrich Ochsner, dated 2 and 5 August 1917; noted in 'Schriftenverzeichnis (1909–2004)', compiled by Chris Bremmers, *HJB* 419–598; p. 469.

FRIEDRICH SCHLEIERMACHER

On 1 August 1917, shortly after being passed over for the vacant chair in Catholic Philosophy at Freiburg, Heidegger gave a private lecture on Schleiermacher's Second Speech on Religion, entitled 'The Problem of the Religious in Schleiermacher'.[25] This was a radical gesture for a Catholic scholar, and the first public indication of his announcement, two years later, that the 'system of Catholicism' had become 'unacceptable' to him. No lecture notes or summaries are preserved; however, Heidegger's approach to Schleiermacher's Second Speech is attested in notes which he took during the same year towards a lecture series on the philosophical foundations of medieval mysticism, announced for the winter semester of 1919/20, but never delivered.[26] (At the end of August 1919, Heidegger requested a cancellation of the course, explaining that he had insufficient time for an adequately rigorous development of the material.[27])

In Schleiermacher, Heidegger found a proto-phenomenological conception of religion as a 'disposition' or 'form of experience' (*Erlebnisform*), which overcame the traditional conflation of religion with 'metaphysics'.[28] In his 1917 notes, he defined religion (after Schleiermacher's Second Speech, 'On the Essence of Religion') as 'the specific religiously intentional, emotional [*gefühlsartige*] relation of every experiential content to an infinite whole as [its] originary sense [*Grundsinn*]'.[29] This 'infinite whole', for Schleiermacher as read by Heidegger, is not the God of traditional theism, who is prior to and independent of the world, but that world itself in its infinite variety (for which 'God' is one appropriate 'auxiliary means of representation').[30]

[25] 'Das Problem des Religiösen bei Schleiermacher'; attested in two letters by Heinrich Ochsner dated 2 and 5 August 1917; see Curd Ochwadt and Erwin Tecklenborg (eds.), *Das Maß des Verborgenen: Heinrich Ochsner zum Gedächtnis* (Hannover: Charis-Verlag, 1981), 92 and 266; cited in *HJB* 469 n. 24.

[26] 'Zu Schleiermachers zweiter Rede "Über das Wesen der Religion"' (1917), in 'Die philosophischen Grundlagen der mittelalterlichen Mystik', GA 60, 301–37; pp. 319–22.

[27] 'Bei der Aufstellung des Planes rechnete der Unterzeichnete mit längeren Herbstferien. Unter den jetzigen Umständen wird aber eine strengen Anforderungen genügende Durcharbeitung des Materials für die angekündigte Vorlesung...unmöglich'; letter to the Faculty of Philosophy dated 30 August 1919; cited in GA 60, 348.

[28] GA 60, 321.

[29] GA 60, 322. (The term *Dasein*, so significant ten years later, is already used in this note for '[human] existence'.)

[30] Friedrich Schleiermacher, *Über die Religion: an die Gebildeten unter ihren Verächtern*, ed. Günter Meckenstock (Berlin: Walter de Gruyter, 2001 [1799]), 82–3.

'Religion', in the Second Speech, is the recognition of every finite being as a 'part', a 'cut-out', an 'imprint', or a 'representation' of that whole, and the consequent liberation of the 'believer' to 'love the World Spirit and joyfully observe its work'.[31] It is in this sense that, as Heidegger excerpts the Second Speech, '*history*, in its most proper sense, is the highest object of religion; with [history] it begins and ends'.[32]

For Heidegger, one of the most important implications of this conception of religion is the dependence of the object of religious experience on the act of intuition. In the Second Speech, Schleiermacher notes: 'Intuition without feeling is nothing and can have neither the proper origin nor the proper force; feeling without intuition is also nothing: both are therefore something only when and because they are originally one and unseparated'.[33] Heidegger formalizes this thought as a phenomenological description of the way in which the content of religious experience is constituted: '*Mysterious* moment of unstructured unity between intuition [*Anschauung*] and feeling', he notes. '[T]he former is nothing without the latter. The noetic moment is itself constitutive of the noematic content [*Gesamtgehalt*] of the experience'.[34] This experienced co-originality of *noesis* and *noema* sharply distinguishes authentic religious feeling and its object (which are not transferable or delegable) from conventional religiosity, which, by merely appropriating the experiences, thoughts, and precepts of others, inherently falls short of what is 'living' and 'holy'.[35]

The crucial question that arises for and within such an approach to faith is the identification of the specific feeling that is (claimed to be) constitutive of religious experience. In order to form an adequate epistemological basis for religious faith, this feeling must be self-evident (or, in Cartesian terms, properly basic). For Schleiermacher, this basic feeling is (as an unargued matter of course) one of 'absolute dependence'.[36] But Heidegger will develop a different account of the basic feeling of religious experience, in conversation with his First World War

---

[31] Schleiermacher, *Über die Religion*, 80–2, 92.

[32] GA 60, 322, citing Schleiermacher, *Über die Religion*, 100 (emphasis added by Heidegger).

[33] Schleiermacher, *Über die Religion*, 89.

[34] GA 60, 322, referring to Schleiermacher, *Über die Religion*, 89–90 (emphasis added by Heidegger).

[35] GA 60, 307, 336. Cf. Schleiermacher, *Über die Religion*, 90.

[36] Schleiermacher, *Der christliche Glaube nach den Grundsätzen der evangelischen Kirche im Zusammenhang dargestellt*, ed. Rolf Schäfer (Berlin: Walter de Gruyter, 2008 [1830/1]), § 4.

contemporaries, (post-)Romantic poetry, and voices of the late Middle Ages and the Reformation.[37] This is affliction (or later, care).

SHELTER AND ASCENT: ADOLF REINACH
AND BERNARD OF CLAIRVAUX

In the years 1915 to 1919 and beyond, several of Husserl's students attempted to formulate phenomenological accounts of religious experience, often—as in the prominent cases of Adolf Reinach and Edith Stein—in response to personal conversion experiences. These young philosophers regarded as the primary task of such an account a description of the experiential constitution of 'God' as an object for the believer. Adolf Reinach, one of Husserl's most brilliant students, converted to Christianity in the trenches shortly before his death in 1916; Edith Stein reports discussing his fragmentary work with 'little Heidegger' in 1919.[38] Reinach postulated that the constitutive experience of faith was that of a super-natural *Geborgensein*. The acknowledgement of the experience of 'being sheltered', and of one's own existential implication in that experience, became for him the epistemological condition for the recognition of God's existence: 'We have to distinguish two things: first the recognition of being sheltered, and secondly the recognition of the presence of God.'[39]

In a long note on Reinach's fragment, dated June 1918, Heidegger emphasizes the temporal (or 'historical') dimension of this statement, and sketches its implications:

> Our experiential conduct *vis-à-vis* God—which is primary, because it wells up inside us by grace—determines the direction of the specifically *religious* constitution of 'God' as a 'phenomenological object'.... Therefore, determinations of the meaning of this, i.e. of the 'Absolute', are only to be discovered in the specific structures of the constitutive experience.... The 'Absolute'... receives its full concretization within each sphere only by manifesting itself in a form of *historicity*; and accordingly, the analysis

---

[37] For an alternative account of Heidegger's 'basic experience', see Benjamin Crowe, *Heidegger's Religious Origins* (Indianapolis: Indiana University Press, 2006), 29–37.

[38] Letter from Edith Stein to Roman Ingarden, dated 8 June 1918; in Stein, *Selbstbildnis in Briefen III: Briefe an Roman Ingarden*, ed. Maria Amata Neyer (Freiburg: Herder, 2nd edn., 2005), 85–6; p. 85. [Hereafter cited as ESGA (=Edith Stein Gesamtausgabe) 4.]

[39] Adolf Reinach, 'Das Absolute', in *Sämtliche Werke*, 2 vols., ed. Karl Schuhmann and Barry Smith (Munich: Philosophia Verlag, 1989), i. 610; quoted GA 60, 327.

must manifest the '*historical*' as an element of living consciousness as such, bestowing basic sense and structure.[40]

In a contemporaneous note on Bernard of Clairvaux's third Sermon on the Song of Songs, Heidegger expounds the significance of such 'historicity' in the relevant (religious) context. He glosses Bernard's opening sentence, '*Hodie legimus in libro experientiae*': "Today we want to move with understanding (description) in the field of personal experience', noting as a 'basic tendency' of human experience the ability or wish to 'live more'.[41] This experience is central to the 'process of the constitution of God's presence', which is itself 'originary'.[42] In other words, God cannot be understood in the manner of a 'rationalist metaphysics' as an 'absolute', a 'highest measure' or 'measure *per se*';[43] rather, the sense of the term 'God' is determined by the inherently temporal experience of perpetual ascent, which is nothing other than a recognition of one's interminable tendency to '*Mehr-Leben*' ('living more' or 'more life') in a specifically religious mood.

From 1918 onward, Heidegger develops this sense of ascent or progress, in other words, of the *specifically religious experience of one's own temporality*, as defining for the Christian life and life in general. In a letter written to his friend and colleague Elisabeth Blochmann on 15 June 1918, he insists that an authentic life can only be lived in awareness of one's essential, dynamic God-directedness:

> Where belief in the proper value of one's own destiny is truly alive, everything unworthy in one's chance circumstances is overcome from within and forever. Every accomplishment achieves the character of finality in accordance with its authenticity, i.e. its inner belonging to the central 'I' and its God-directed determination.[44]

However, Heidegger's sense of this '*gottgerichtete Zielstrebigkeit*' diverges from those of St Bernard and Adolf Reinach in the increasing displacement of the object or goal of this teleological process by the process itself. For both St Bernard and Reinach, the believer's ascent is directed both by and towards a God who is present and active beyond and independently of human comprehension. Thus, in his fourth sermon on the Song of Songs, which immediately follows the sermon discussed by Heidegger, St Bernard emphasizes that the gradual human approach to God just described is inferior to that of the 'dwellers in

[40] GA 60, 324–5.   [41] GA 60, 334 and 336.   [42] GA 60, 336.
[43] GA 60, 325.   [44] In Storck (ed.), *Martin Heidegger/Elisabeth Blochmann*, 7.

the heavens', who can 'read in the Book of Life without contradiction, and understand it without difficulty'.[45] Similarly, further on in the fragment discussed by Heidegger, Reinach argues that the believer's experiential relation to God is determined by his or her actual position *vis-à-vis* him.[46] For Heidegger, by contrast, there is no meaningful viewpoint outside the human: 'What does "position *vis-à-vis* God" mean? Meaningfully and constitutedly this can be formulated only as a disposition of consciousness, rather than, ontically, as being next to or "under" an (absolute) Being'.[47]

The fact that the Christian is always in movement towards God means that he or she can make no authentic assertions about God that do not arise from *within* this movement. In a letter to his former teacher Engelbert Krebs on 9 January 1919, Heidegger presents this insight as the reason for his declared break with Catholicism:

> Epistemological insights, extending to the theory of historical cognition, have made the system of Catholicism problematic and unacceptable to me—but not Christianity and metaphysics, these however in a new sense.... I believe that I have the inner calling to philosophy, and that by realizing this calling through research and teaching I will achieve what is in my power for the eternal destiny of the inner man—*and only for this*. Thus, I hope to justify my existence and work even before God.[48]

Similarly, in a letter to his wife Elfride of 12 May 1918, Heidegger projects the development of a 'wholly original religious life' as the well-spring of his entire future work: 'The creation of a wholly original [alt.: originary] religious life of our own will succeed, and all our work will grow from it.'[49]

THE CROSS OF CHRIST AND THE CROSS OF MAN: MARTIN LUTHER AND HERMAN SCHELL

Heidegger's declared companion in the endeavour of a 'wholly original/originary religious life' was the 'young Luther'.[50] Since his

---

[45] Bernard of Clairvaux, Sermon IV, *Sermones super Cantica Canticorum*.
[46] Reinach, 'Das Absolute', 10, quoted in GA 60, 324.
[47] GA 60, 324.   [48] Letter rpt. in *HJB* 67.
[49] In Gertrud Heidegger (ed.), *'Mein liebes Seelchen!' Briefe Martin Heideggers an seine Frau Elfride, 1915–1970* (Munich: Deutsche Verlags-Anstalt, 2005), 66.
[50] GA 63, 5.

first encounter with the Reformation theologian ten years earlier in
Johannes Ficker's 1908 Weimar edition of the Lectures on Romans,
Heidegger had come to regard Luther's path, as described in Ficker's
preface, as reflective of his own.[51]

It was specifically Luther's early, radical *theologia crucis* which influenced Heidegger. In his 1921 lecture series on Augustine, he specified:
'In his first works, Luther opened up a new understanding of primitive
Christianity. Later, he himself fell prey to the burden of tradition; this
was the beginning of Protestant Scholasticism.'[52] This theology of the
cross—formulated in response to the Scholastic *theologi gloriae*—is
expressed most clearly in the proof of Theological Thesis XX of the
1518 Heidelberg Disputation:

> The nature of God which is turned towards us and visible to us—i.e. his
> humanity, weakness, foolishness—is opposed to the invisible nature of
> God, as 1 Corinthians 1.25 states of divine weakness and foolishness. You
> see, because men abused the knowledge of God from his works, God
> wished now to be known through suffering. He wished to condemn such
> 'wisdom of the invisible' through a 'wisdom of the visible', so that those
> who did not revere God as he is revealed in his works would revere him as
> the One Who is hidden in suffering [*absconditum in passionibus*].[53]

Ironically, Heidegger had been prepared for an experiential interpretation of this theological claim of the Reformer by his reading of a
dissident Catholic theologian, Herman Schell (1850–1906). Schell,
whom Heidegger read with enthusiasm between 1909 and 1911,[54]
had, like Hölderlin, been a one-time student of the Tübingen *Stift*,
and was strongly influenced by the Catholic Tübingen School. In
1898, his works were temporarily placed on the Roman Index, partly
(as he was informed the following year) for their 'over-emphasis of the
quasi-sacramental efficacy of death and suffering, and concomitant

[51] Thus Otto Pöggeler, 'Heideggers Luther-Lektüre', *HJB* 194. Cf. Heidegger's 1922
essay 'Phänomenologische Interpretationen zu Aristoteles (Anzeige der herme-
neutischen Situation)', also known as the 'Natorp Report', where he describes Luther's
'new basic religious position' as arising from his 'original appropriation of Paul and
Augustine, and simultaneous engagement with late scholastic theology (Duns Scotus,
Occam, Gabriel Biel, Gregor von Rimini)'; in Frithjof Rodi (ed.), *Dilthey-Jahrbuch
für Philosophie und Geschichte der Geisteswissenschaften* 6 (1989), 237–69; p. 250;
rpt. in Heidegger, *Phänomenologische Interpretationen ausgewählter Abhandlungen
des Aristoteles zu Ontologie und Logik* (1922 and SS 1922), ed. Günther Neumann
(Frankfurt: Klostermann, 2005). [Hereafter cited as GA 62.] The close resemblance to
Heidegger's own path is obvious.
[52] GA 60, 281–2.   [53] WA 1, 362.   [54] See the curriculum vitae of 1915; GA
16, 37.

endangerment of the necessity of [the sacraments of] baptism and extreme unction'.[55] In *Katholische Dogmatik* (1889–93), his *magnum opus*, Schell explicitly defines the essence of martyrdom or *martyrium* ('witness') as suffering, and describes this suffering as sacramental, that is, as a channel of man's participation in the life of God:

> The essential quality of the baptism of blood [martyrdom] is the *suffer-ing* that is borne.... Therefore the Holy Scriptures call *every suffering* a baptism; the baptism of blood is only the highest degree of the baptism of suffering and sorrow. Through Christ's weakness and suffering, all *evils* that man is subject to until the dissolution of death have been trans-figured into a *means of salvation*..., a bond that unites the sorrowful, the oppressed, [and] the weak... in a special way with the crucified.[56]

Fittingly, Heidegger came, increasingly, to regard the mood of the ascensive character of human experience of the divine as one of *afflic-tion* or *suffering*. Referring to Luther's interpretation of Romans 1, he wrote to his wife on 9 September 1919:

> Since I have read Luther's Commentary on Romans, much that was pre-viously painful and dark to me has become luminous and liberating— I understand the Middle Ages and the development of Christian religiosity in an entirely new way, and wholly new perspectives on the problems posed by the philosophy of religion have opened up to me.[57]

SUFFERING FROM OUR DIFFERENCE FROM THE DIVINE: HEIDEGGER AND ROMANTICISM

Although it depended on Luther, Heidegger's interpretation of his *the-ologia crucis* also diverged significantly from its source. He inflected Luther by relocating the centre of the revelatory significance of suffer-ing from the passion of Christ to the passion of *man* in and from his own finitude—a finitude revealed particularly in the ascensive character

---

[55] Raimund Lachner, 'Herman Schell', in *Biographisch-Bibliographisches Kirchen-lexikon*, vol. ix (1995), cols. 88–99. See especially Schell, *Menschwerdung und Erlösung. Heiligung und Vollendung*, ed. Heinrich Petri and Paul-Werner Scheele (Munich: Schöningh, 1994), 407 (being vol. iii of *Katholische Dogmatik in sechs Büchern*, 3 vols., ed. Josef Hasenfuss and Paul-Werner Scheele (Munich: Schöningh, 1968–94)).
[56] Schell, *Menschwerdung und Erlösung*, 407 (author's emphases).
[57] Heidegger (ed.), *Mein liebes Seelchen!*, 100.

of religious experience. His main source for this reinterpretation was Romantic literature, and in particular, Hölderlin.

Heidegger first encountered Hölderlin in 1908 in a Reclam edition of his poems when Heidegger was still in grammar school.[58] His headmaster, in Heidegger's graduation report, remarks that Martin 'read a little too much German literature, in which he was very well versed, at the expense of other subjects.'[59] Shortly thereafter, the publication of several volumes of Rilke's (post- or neo-Romantic) poems became one of the highlights of Heidegger's university years.[60]

Heidegger's earliest writings, dating from 1909 (the year of his graduation from high school), display little of this literature's influence on him. As we have seen, these essays are polemical pieces in the service of the Catholic anti-Modernist cause, and exemplify a muscular, Darwinist Christianity. Thus, for example, Heidegger argues in a 1910 review that just as all 'higher life is predicated on the demise of the lower forms', so the higher, 'spiritual life' requires the 'killing' of 'what is low' in oneself. Rather than being a cause of suffering, such self-mortification or 'carrying [the] cross' naturally brings joy. The truth must *naturaliter* lead to happiness, the lie to downfall.'[61]

But during the physical and vocational difficulties of 1911, and again during another period of personal crisis, in 1915, when his engagement to the Catholic Gretl Weninger was dissolved, Heidegger wrote a number of poems that are strongly indebted to Romantic ideas and styles. The 1911 poems are recognizable pastiches of Romantic poetry, both thematically and stylistically; they also give first expression to Heidegger's frequent return to Rilke's 'angel' motif, as initially developed in *Mir zur Feier* (1899) and *Neue Gedichte* (1907).[62]

[58] GA 1, 56.

[59] Rpt. in Sheehan, 'Lehrjahre', in Sallis, *Collegium Phaenomenologicum*, 127 n. 49.

[60] See GA 1, 57–9.

[61] '*Per mortem ad vitam*: Gedanken über Jörgensens "Lebenslüge und Lebenswahrheit"', *Der Akademiker* 2, no. 5 (March 1910), 72–3; rpt. in GA 16, 3–6; 5.

[62] Heidegger mentions his reading of Rilke's poetry as one of the most significant intellectual experiences of the 'tumultuous' years 1910–14 (GA 1, 56). The then recent *Neue Gedichte* (Leipzig: Insel-Verlag, 1907) contains both 'L'Ange du Méridien' and 'Der Ölbaum-Garten', by which Heidegger's 1911 poem 'Ölbergstunden' is clearly influenced. A return to Rilke in the mid-1920s may well have been occasioned by the publication, in 1923, of Rilke's *Duineser Elegien* (Leipzig: Insel-Verlag), to which Heidegger makes frequent reference in his later work.

The lasting impression of these early Rilke poems can be gauged from Heidegger's later correspondence. In a letter to Elisabeth Blochman dated 12 September 1929, Heidegger describes the Compline service that the friends had attended a few months earlier at Beuron Abbey as 'a symbol of the fact that existence is always a being-immersed [*Hineingehaltensein*] in the night'.[63] In his inaugural lecture 'What is Metaphysics?', delivered the same autumn, the idea appears in an alternative formulation: 'Existence means: immersion [*Hineingehaltenheit*] in Nothingness.'[64] The phrase is lifted from the last line of Rilke's 'L'Ange du Méridien' (*Neue Gedichte*), a meditation on the statue of an angel with a sundial, now housed in the crypt of Chartres Cathedral, but originally part of a trumeau that supported a tympanum depicting the Last Judgement. In his poem, Rilke addresses the angel, who—in his eschatological serenity—is imagined as providing a refuge from the intellectual and natural 'storm' besieging the cathedral. This refuge, however, may not, after all, be suitable for humans: the still and smiling angel is oblivious that 'our hours' 'slide off' his sundial, whose simultaneous representation of all the hours of the day—'as if [they] were all ripe and rich'—is, by implication, an inadequate representation of lived time. The poem ends in questions: 'What do you, stony figure, know of our being? | Do you, perhaps, with even more blessed countenance | hold the tablet into the night?'

Vis-à-vis the anti-Modernist texts of 1909 and 1910, Heidegger's 'Romantic' poems show an abrupt change of perspective on pain and suffering. In contrast to the prose texts, the poems present pain not merely as a temporary or secondary effect of the emancipation from the 'lower drives', but as a permanent condition or companion of joy and solace. In 'Ölbergstunden' ('Hours on the Mount of Olives', published April 1911), the experience of spiritual solace, which constitutes an assurance of authentic faith, is wrested—and can arguably arise only—from intense emotional conflict. In 'Julinacht' ('July Night', written summer 1911), joy is not so much born of sorrow as permanently wedded to it: 'joy, is thy bride's name "mourning"?'.

Gethsemane Hours

Gethsemane hours of my life:
in the dusky glow
of despondent apprehension
you have often seen me.

---

[63] In Storck (ed.), *Heidegger/Blochmann*, 32.   [64] GA 9, 35.

Weeping I cried: never in vain.
My young being,
tired of lamenting,
put all its trust in the angel 'Grace'.[65]

July Night

Once again, you sing to me
Songs of eternity
You spirit away my soul
To wood-quiet expanses,
You dip me into God-close
Infinities.
July night
Enchantress,
Homesickness-releasing
Artist.
That the sun died early
In the field today,
That what I earned by day
Has sunk into dusk,
That the finch falls silent,
Tired of singing,
And cantankerously and cold
The night wind growls,
That the lime trees listen
To the song of death,
That the leaves rustle
As if I was parting from you—
All this shapes itself into the harsh
Shuddering question: Happiness,
Do you call your bride 'Mourning'?[66]

A similar sense of the abiding importance of suffering pervades
Heidegger's correspondence of the time. In 1915, amid the physical and
emotional breakdown that has followed the breaking-off of Heidegger's
engagement, Ernst Laslowski writes his friend a long letter pitying the
'inhuman difficulty [*Schwere*] of this sacrifice', but also acknowledging
that the intensity of Heidegger's philosophical 'vocation', which raises
him 'above the sphere in which "love" and "happiness" can flourish',

---

[65] First published in *Allgemeine Rundschau* 8, no. 14 (8 April 1911), 246; rpt. GA 13, 6.
[66] Written in July 1911; first published in Ott, *Martin Heidegger*, 72; rpt. GA 16, 17.
Compare, among many other examples, Keats's 'Ode on Melancholy' for a similar sensibility in English Romantic Poetry.

demands it. 'This suffering', Ernst assures him, 'will be a source of strength to you and make you wise for many things'. And not only Heidegger himself: 'How peculiar it is; this sacrifice, like all real, great renunciation, does not embitter ... but enlivens and enriches, me also; I too feel the purifying power of your decision.'[67]

Heidegger's 1916 poem 'Einsamkeit' ('Loneliness') goes so far as presenting this experience of anguish as potentially conflicting with—and as ultimately stronger than—even the offer of God's love to dispel it. In his qualifying thesis, Heidegger calls the individual 'ein *unzurückführbares Letztes*', something ultimate and underivable.[68] A growing awareness of the irreducible significance of human existence, with its pain and finitude, for any manifestation of 'the Absolute'[69] will accompany and partly motivate Heidegger's progressive disenchantment with the Catholic 'system':

> Pale green light swims around the books,
> Outside, angels spread shrouds.
> It is snowing.
> In the oven, a buzzing, a crackling,
> Tic-tac-clock sleeps. The winds whisper.
> It is snowing.
> Haggard shapes who never find the light
> drift around me,
> my wailing sins.
> It is snowing.
> Memory dies. The world stands still.
> I feel divine love wanting to flare up—
> It is snowing.[70]

The war years which followed this breakdown brought a more systematic development of this general sense of the significance of suffering, in dialogue with both theology and poetry. Years later, Heidegger remarked: 'During the campaign [of the Great War], Hölderlin's hymns were stuffed into one's backpack right along with the cleaning gear.'[71] On 30 August 1918, he wrote to his wife Elfride from the front, 'Hölderlin

---

[67] Letter dated 21 November 1915; published in *HJB* 50–2; 51. Note the arguable parallels to Kierkegaard's dissolution, after a year, of his 1840 engagement to Regine Olsen.

[68] GA 1, 253.   [69] Cf. the note of this title (dated June 1918) in GA 60, 324–7.

[70] GA 16, 40.

[71] 'Der Ursprung des Kunstwerkes' (1935/6), in *Holzwege* (1935–46), ed. Friedrich-Wilhelm von Herrmann (Frankfurt: Klostermann, 2nd edn., 2003), 3. [This volume is hereafter cited as GA 5.]

is becoming a new experience for me at the moment—almost as if I am approaching him wholly originally (and) for the first time.'[72]

What Heidegger was discovering at the time was Hölderlin's justification of human suffering as the necessary supplement of divine perfection. Perfection, in his view, implies a complete being-at-rest in oneself, and consequently, beatitude. At the same time, however, complete self-sufficiency excludes self-awareness, because self-awareness can only arise in the 'space' of an enduring self-difference, that is, within (or for) an incomplete self.[73] Although in one sense self-sufficient in themselves, the gods thus require humans to *witness* to their perfection, and thus to supplement their lacking awareness of that perfection:

> The gods, however, are sufficient
> In their own immortality, and if
> The dwellers of heaven require one thing,
> It is heroes and humans
> And other mortals. For because
> The blessed do not of themselves feel,
> Someone else, if it is permitted
> To say so, must sympathetically feel on their behalf—
> That one they need....[74]

More often than not, this vicarious (or 'participating') 'feeling' of humans for gods takes the form of suffering, which functions as a negative witness to divine perfection, and awakens the gods to their own contrasting blessedness. Hölderlin sees his own poetry as both evoking and continuing this witness, for example in 'Hyperion's Song of Fate', sung by the protagonist towards the end of the epistolary novel *Hyperion*[75]:

> You walk in the light above,
> On soft ground, blissful spirits!
> Bright divine airs
> Touch you lightly
> As the fingers of the harpist
> her holy strings.

---

[72] Heidegger (ed.), *Mein liebes Seelchen!*, 77.

[73] See Gerhard Kurz's marginal notes to 'Der Rhein' (1801), in Friedrich Hölderlin, *Gedichte*, ed. Gerhard Kurz (Stuttgart: Reclam, 2003), 162–6; p. 164. The following discussion and selection of quotes is deeply indebted to Damian Love, 'Samuel Beckett and the Art of Madness' (unpublished D.Phil. dissertation, Oxford, 2004), 159–69.

[74] 'Der Rhein', ll. 105–14; in Hölderlin, *Sämtliche Werke und Briefe*, vol. i, ed. Jochen Schmidt (Frankfurt: Deutscher Klassiker Verlag, 1992), 328–34; p. 331.

[75] Heidegger writes to Hannah Arendt on 23 August 1925 that 'among the few books on [his] "desk" is Hölderlin's *Hyperion*'; Ludz (ed.), *Hannah Arendt/Martin Heidegger*, 46.

Fatelessly as the sleeping
Infant, the heavenly ones breathe;
Chastely preserved
In a modest bud,
Spirit blooms for them
Eternally,
And the blessed eyes
Gaze in still
Eternal clarity.
But our fate is
To find no resting place,
Suffering humanity
Faints, falls
Blindly from one hour
To the next,
Like water flung
From cliff to cliff,
Year after year into the unknown.[76]

The temporal and restless existence of humans, in its difference and distance from divine peacefulness and stasis, is the main source of our suffering. However, in its role as witness, suffering, for Hölderlin, also becomes a source of joy for humans, because it constitutes their own proper participation in, indeed their excess over the divine, recalling the gods from the 'Nothing' of oblivion:

Oh my divinity!, that you should be capable of suffering as you are blessed, I was long unable to grasp. But bliss which does not suffer is sleep, and without death, there is no life. Should you be eternal as a child and slumber, resembling Nothing? lack victory? not traverse all perfections? Yes! yes! Pain is worthy of lying at the heart of humans, and of being your intimate, oh Nature! For it alone leads from one bliss to the other, and there is no other companion than it.[77]

THE CROSS OF FINITUDE AS ESCHATOLOGICAL AFFLICTION: HEIDEGGER'S READING OF PAUL

For Heidegger, these poetic insights were consonant with the phenomenological method, and answered to his dual search, already

---

[76] Hölderlin, *Sämtliche Werke und Briefe*, ii. 157–8.
[77] Ibid. 164.

formulated in 1915, for a religiosity marked by aboriginal experience and a theology capable of giving this experience expression
from within (rather than imposing upon it a system from without).
Consequently, he derived from his readings a personal programme:
one focused on suffering not as a participation in Christ's passion, nor
as prolegomena to an experience of the divine, obliterating human
satisfaction and so opening the subject to the influx of divine grace,
but as in itself significant. Following soon after his May 1918 letter to
Elfride, in which he announces that 'the creation of a wholly original
[or primal] religious life' will become the well-spring of all his future
work, he writes to Elisabeth Blochmann on 15 June 1918:

> Where a personal life, with inner truthfulness, is on the *way* to
> perfection—and we are, after all, always *essentially on the way*—it is nec-
> essarily beset by the asperity of tornness, of relapses and new attempts,
> and by an unstaunchable suffering from the problematic and question-
> able; these are essential components of the ethos of the truly scholarly
> and spiritual man.[78]

In 1919, Heidegger announces his break with institutional Catholicism.
The language of his famous letter to Krebs echoes that of his recent correspondence: 'It is *hard* [*schwer*] to live as a philosopher—the inner
truthfulness *vis-à-vis* oneself and in relation to those one is called to
teach requires sacrifices and renunciations and struggles which remain
forever foreign to the mere scholarly craftsman.'[79] And in a 1921 letter
to his student Karl Löwith, Heidegger recommends acceptance of this
yoke as an active principle of the work of a theologian: 'We must *sacrifice*
ourselves and find our way back into *existential* limitation and facticity,
instead of deflecting these by programmes and universal problems.'[80]
    In the years following this breakthrough of 1918/19, Heidegger
crystallizes this understanding of suffering in his interpretation of
Christian eschatology.

---

[78] Storck (ed.), *Heidegger/Blochmann*, 7.

[79] Letter dated 9 January 1919; rpt. in *HJB* 67–8; p. 67.

[80] Letter dated 19 August 1921; in 'Drei Briefe', in Papenfuss and Pöggeler, *Zur philosophischen Aktualität Heideggers*, 31. Compare Heidegger's letter to Matthäus Lang
(who was from 1905 Rektor of Heidegger's grammar school in Constance) dated 30
May 1928, where he associates this attitude firmly with philosophy (rather than theology): 'Vielleicht zeigt die Philosophie am eindringlichsten und nachhaltigsten, wie
anfängerhaft der Mensch ist. Philosophieren heißt am Ende nichts anderes als Anfänger
sein. Aber wenn wir bei unserem Knirpstum zu uns selbst die innere Treue bewahren
und aus ihr heraus zu wirken suchen, dann muß auch das Wenige zum Guten sein'; in
Ott, *Martin Heidegger*, 55–6.

INTRODUCTION TO THE
PHENOMENOLOGY OF RELIGION (1920/1)

Heidegger's dual concern with a religiosity marked by aboriginal experience and a theology capable of giving this experience expression
from within culminated in the now famous lecture series of the winter semester of 1920/1, *Introduction to the Phenomenology of Religion*.
This lecture series, concerned in equal parts with the provisional and
temporal nature of philosophy and life and with an eschatological passage in Paul's First Letter to the Thessalonians, locates the meeting
point of these two concerns in early Christian eschatology.

In his winter semester 1919/20 lectures, *Basic Problems in
Phenomenology*, Heidegger has already stated that the consolidation
of a *Selbstwelt* ('world of self')—a focus on the self as the locus of the
expression and perception of 'being', which alone makes possible
'history' in a Hegelian sense—was a consequence of the emergence
of Christianity. The basic disposition of this primitive Christianity,
according to Heidegger, is *crede ut intelligas*, which he glosses: 'Live
your self animatedly—and only on this ground of experience, your
last and fullest experience of self, knowledge will grow.'[81] After the era
of the early Church, this basic disposition has been exemplified most
strikingly by Augustine, the medieval mystics (Bernard of Clairvaux,
Bonaventure, Eckhard, and Tauler), and Luther. The phenomenological method is ally and handmaid of this Christian thought world,
which alone has the inner power to deconstruct Aristotelian metaphysics. The emergence of Christianity, Heidegger writes, was

> [a] great revolution against classical science, particularly Aristotle,
> who, however, in the coming millennium, would once again triumph,
> indeed become the philosopher of official Christianity—such that
> the inner experiences and the new attitude to life [characteristic of
> Christianity] would be yoked to the forms of expression of classical
> science. [This is] a process, still showing deep and confusing repercus-
> sions, radical liberation from which is one of the innermost tendencies
> of phenomenology.[82]

In his lecture series *Introduction to the Phenomenology of Religion*,
Heidegger gives a fuller account of this convergence of Christian
experience and phenomenology. Specifically, he seeks to show how

---

[81] GA 58, 61–2.   [82] GA 58, 61.

the disposition towards temporality fostered by early Christian eschatology overlaps with—or motivates—the disposition necessary to
be a true philosopher: a disposition of uncertainty, questioning, and
Anfängertum ('beginner-dom'):

> The criticism of remaining stuck in preliminary questions can only be
> levelled against philosophy if the criteria of its evaluation are borrowed
> from the idea of the sciences, demanding the solution of concrete prob-
> lems and the construction of a world-view. I, for my part, want to keep
> awake and acuminate this affliction of philosophy...to such an extent
> that it turns into a virtue.[83]

How semantically close this is to Heidegger's subsequent description
of eschatological expectation will be apparent in a moment.

The standard of the 'sciences' (*Wissenschaften*)—a category appropriated, as so much in this field, from Dilthey—Heidegger continues,
is as inappropriate to religion as it is to philosophy.[84] He criticizes Ernst
Troeltsch for treating the philosophy of religion as a *science* of religion,
shaped by a scientific conception of philosophy as the perception/
knowledge of objects (*Objekterkenntnis*). In this false conception, religion becomes an 'object' for philosophy, and so is defined by 'contexts
[lit.: object relations] which already existed *before* religion'.[85] By contrast, 'what characterizes a religion-phenomenological understanding
is to lay the ground for an original/originary way of approach' to the
Christian religion.[86]

This can only grow out of factic life experience, and therefore
requires, first of all, an aboriginal approach to that experience: 'The
meaning of temporality is defined by a basic relation to God—such,
however, that eternity can only be understood through the practice
of temporality.'[87] This, he believes, is the characteristic disposition of
early Christian eschatological expectation.

Heidegger expounds on this by way of an exposition of Paul's
exhortation regarding the Coming of Christ in chapter 5 of the First

---

[83] GA 60, 4–5. Compare the quote from Kierkegaard, *Entweder-Oder* I (Jena:
Diederichs, 1911), 35, which Heidegger chooses as a motto for his WS 1921/2 lecture
series 'Phenomenological Interpretations of Aristotle'; see GA 61, 81. Cf. the discussion in Chapter 4.

[84] For Heidegger's debt to Dilthey in the developing opposition between the explana-
tory and the understanding sciences, as well as in his account of intellectual history,
see Kisiel, *Genesis*, 101–8.

[85] 'Sachzusammenhänge[n], die schon vor der Religion an sich bestanden'; GA 60, 67.

[86] GA 60, 67.   [87] GA 60, 117 (on 1 Thessalonians 3: 3 and 5: 9).

Epistle to the Thessalonians. The relevant passage in Paul's Epistle is as follows:

> Now concerning the times and the seasons [of Christ's return], brothers and sisters, you do not need to have anything written to you. For you yourselves know very well that the day of the Lord will come like a thief in the night. When they say, 'There is peace and security', then sudden destruction will come upon them, as labour pains come upon a pregnant woman, and there will be no escape! But you, beloved, are not in darkness, for that day to surprise you like a thief; for you are all children of light and children of the day; we are not of the night or of darkness. So then, let us not fall asleep as others do, but let us keep awake and sober.[88]

For Heidegger, the phenomenological significance of this passage lies in the fact that Paul's expectation of the *parousia* is not controlled by speculation about the exact time of Christ's return but, on the contrary, effects a complete transformation of his experience of time or temporality as such. It calls forth a subjective experience of time 'without order and fixed spots, which cannot be grasped by any objective notion of time', and thus gives rise to eschatological 'affliction' (*Bedrängnis*), characterized by an existential insecurity or uncertainty which arouses an intense and undelegable 'watchfulness'.[89] Heidegger's gloss on the passage (reconstructed from students' transcripts) is worth quoting in full:

> For the Christian life there is no security; constant insecurity [or uncertainty] is also the characteristic of the basic meaningfuls of factic life. The uncertain is not coincidental, but necessary. This necessity is not logical or merely natural. To see clearly here, we have to recollect our own life and its practice. Those 'who speak of peace and safety' ([1 Thess.] 5.3) pour themselves out into that which life brings their way, occupy themselves with any random tasks of life. They are absorbed by that which life offers; they are in the dark as far as self-knowledge is concerned. The faithful, by contrast, are sons of light and of the day. Paul's answer to the question of the 'when' of the *parousia*, then, is the exhortation to watch and be sober. This implies an attack on the enthusiasm, the compulsive speculation, of those who pursue and speculate about questions like that of the 'when' of the *parousia*. They are only concerned with the

---

[88] 1 Thessalonians 5: 1–5. All biblical citations are taken from the *New Revised Standard Version*.
[89] 'Einleitung in die Phänomenologie der Religion', GA 60, 98, and 104.

'when', the 'what', the objective determination; they have no actual [or authentic] personal interest in it. They remain stuck in the worldly.[90]

In Heidegger's Overbeckian reading, this experience soon gave way in the history of Christianity to dispersion, hustle, and dogmatism. Consequently, Christianity today presents itself most commonly as a closed system of 'answers' precluding rather than opening existential uncertainty or questioning.[91]

Heidegger is interested primarily in a *Befindlichkeit*—a '*gestimmtes Sichbefinden*' or intuitive, situated 'attunement' within and to the world.[92] Heidegger labels this disposition 'eschatological' affliction; yet his etymological understanding of *Befindlichkeit* (influenced by Schleiermacher[93]) as a function precisely of human situatedness *in* a world resists the inclusion of the traditional Christian object of this disposition, namely the anticipated irruption into the world from without of Christ's *parousia*, as a term of the analysis. Consequently, the object of eschatological 'care' or 'affliction' is no longer (as for Paul) the dark and death-filled world *inflected by* its imminent 'solicitation' by Christ, but only that world in its transience.

It is important to note that although Heidegger presents this as a phenomenologically precise representation of Paul's eschatology, which

---

[90] GA 60, 105.

[91] Thus, Heidegger, asserts in his 1935 lecture series 'Introduction to Metaphysics': 'Wem z.B. die Bibel göttliche Offenbarung und Wahrheit ist, der hat *vor allem Fragen* der Frage "Warum ist überhaupt Seiendes und nicht vielmehr Nichts?" schon die Antwort: das Seiende, soweit es nicht Gott selbst ist, ist durch diesen geschaffen' (emphasis added); *Einführung in die Metaphysik*, ed. Petra Jaeger (Frankfurt: Klostermann, 1983), 5. [Hereafter cited as GA 40.] Compare his famous remark, in a letter to Engelbert Krebs dated 9 January 1919, that certain 'epistemological realisations' have made the '*system* of Catholicism' 'unacceptable' to him (author's emphasis); cited in Ott, *Martin Heidegger*, 106.

[92] See Heidegger, *Sein und Zeit* (Tübingen: Max Niemeyer Verlag, 18th edn., 2001 [1927]), §29 [hereafter cited as *SZ*]. 'Attunement' is Stephen Mulhall's (Cavellian) translation of '*Befindlichkeit*' (see his *Heidegger and Being and Time* [London: Routledge, 2nd edn., 2005], 116). The German *Befinden* (from the verb *sich befinden*), from which *Befindlichkeit* is coined, means both 'residing' or 'being situated', and 'condition' or 'disposition'.

[93] Theodore Kisiel also cites Schleiermacher's 'felt intuition' as a precursor and model of Heidegger's *Befindlichkeit*, which enters his vocabulary in the 1919/20 lecture series *Grundprobleme der Phänomenologie*, a series which grew partly out of his engagement with Schleiermacher and medieval mysticism (compare his 1917–19 notes in GA 60, 301–37). In his 1924 lecture series *Grundbegriffe der aristotelischen Philosophie* (published under the same title as GA 18, ed. Mark Michalski (Frankfurt: Klostermann, 2002)), Heidegger identifies the term as an equivalent of Aristotle's '*diathesis*'. Cf. Kisiel, *Genesis*, 492.

he has stripped only of its heuristic appeal to a specific object of anticipation (the *parousia*), his 'phenomenological reduction' in fact causes
him to misidentify Paul's basic eschatological mood (*Befindlichkeit*),
which is not affliction but hope. Paul offers his discourse on the *parousia* to increase the hope of the faithful (1 Thessalonians 5: 13), and
closes it with an appeal, 'therefore', to persevere in faith, love, and hope
(5: 8–11).[94] Nor is this misreading accidental. On the contrary, 'hope'
(alone among the three theological virtues) is entirely absent from
Heidegger's writings on the phenomenology of religion. The reason
may be that Christian hope, as Alexander Jones puts it, 'is to be con-
fident of receiving the eschatological gifts'—in other words, is inherently directed towards that which exceeds the 'naturally' human, and
is gratuitously bestowed on *Dasein* by Another.[95] What is more, Paul
identifies precisely this hope as the 'ownmost' calling (*Beruf*) of the
faithful, thus suggesting, paradoxically, that what is most proper to a
person is also beyond his or her natural capacity—which is bounded
by death—and must be received from Christ through his Resurrection
and Return.[96] Heidegger's early phenomenology is fundamentally at
odds with such a vision.

---

[94] Parallels can be found in all Pauline Epistles. See, among many other examples,
Rom. 5: 2, 8: 18–23; 1 Cor. 15: 19f.; Gal. 5: 5; Eph. 1: 17f.; Col. 1: 5, 1: 27; Tit. 1: 2, 2: 13.

[95] In his note to Rom. 5: 2 in the *New Jerusalem Bible* (London: Darton, Longman &
Todd, 1994), 1873.

[96] See the verses listed above, especially 1 Cor. 15: 19f. For the most influential formulation of this Christian position, see Thomas Aquinas, *Summa Theologiae* 1–2.114.2
ad 1. (*Beruf* is a favourite Heideggerian term, though he does not, of course, apply it
to this context.)

4

From Theology to Philosophy I: The Problem of Sin

Humanitatis seu…carnis regno, quod in fide agitur, nos sibi
conformes facit et crucifigit, faciens ex infoelicibus et superbis
diis homines veros, idest miseros et peccatores.

—Martin Luther[1]

It has become well known in recent years that during the 1920s,
Heidegger's focus shifted from the development of a phenomenology of religion to that of a principled a-theistic method.[2] This said,
no detailed account of this shift has so far been attempted. One consequence is a persistent uncertainty in the secondary sources regarding the question of Heidegger's resulting attitude to Christianity in
general and theology in particular: especially, whether he emerged

---

[1] 'Through the regime of his humanity and his flesh, in which we live by faith,
[Christ] makes us of the same form as himself and crucifies us by making us true men
instead of unhappy and proud gods: men, that is, in their misery and their sin'; Luther,
Psalmenvorlesung (1519/21), in *D. Martin Luthers Werke: Kritische Gesammtausgabe*,
120 vols. (Weimar: Hermann Böhlaus, 1883–2009), v. 128–9. [This edition is hereafter
cited as WA followed by volume number.]

[2] 'A-theistic', as should become clear in the course of the chapter, here refers to a
philosophical methodology that brackets God from its analyses, rather than to a
more definitive world-view.Those chiefly responsible for advancing knowledge of
Heidegger's religious origins in the English-language academy are John van Buren,
Thomas Sheehan, and more recently Benjamin Crowe and Sean McGrath; see van
Buren's translations of early Heideggerian writings in *Supplements: From the Earliest
Essays to Being and Time and Beyond* (Albany, NY: SUNY Press, 2002), as well as his
own *The Young Heidegger*; Sheehan, 'Heidegger's *Lehrjahre*'; Crowe, *Heidegger's Reli-
gious Origins* and *Heidegger's Phenomenology of Religion: Realism and Cultural Criticism*
(Indianapolis: Indiana University Press, 2007); McGrath, *The Early Heidegger &
Medieval Philosophy: Phenomenology for the Godforsaken* (Washington: Catholic
University of America Press, 2006).

regarding philosophy as a *praeparatio evangeliae*, or as a competitor
for or successor to the rank of the queen of sciences.[3] This cluster of
chapters presents the development of Heidegger's religious thought
in the 1920s as a three-stage process: The first stage, whose genealogy is given in the previous two chapters, is a prioritization of the
earliest, eschatologically oriented Christian experience as capable of
disclosing the deepest structures of existence, namely eschatological affliction or anxiety—a prioritization consistently coupled with
a critique of Christianity as quickly abandoning its earliest eschatological experience for secure philosophical and political *systems* (represented in Heidegger's own time by neo-Scholasticism). The attempt
to 'deconstruct'[4] these systems leads Heidegger to look increasingly
to the 'anti-metaphysical' strands of Christian tradition—including
the early Luther, Kierkegaard, Dostoevsky, and Franz Overbeck—to
develop his sense of a constitutive and absolute *rift* between God and
man which perpetuates affliction or anxiety as the proper mood both
of human existence and of theological enquiry. But ironically, this
radical externality of God, for Heidegger, comes to imply that God's
agency must remain irretrievably beyond the purview of the phenomenological method: what originally attracted Heidegger as a method
adequate to describing Christian faith now emerges as a demarcation
of the philosopher's territory against that of the theologian. In 1921,
Heidegger still called himself, emphatically, 'a Christian theo*logian*'.[5]
In 1922, this ceases to be an option for him.

For Luther, Kierkegaard, *et al.*, the rift between God and man is
rooted and embodied in the absolute depravity of man. Committing
himself to the phenomenological method rather than a specifically
Christian standpoint, Heidegger is immediately aware that his analysis, rather than simply and uncontroversially limiting itself to the
status corruptionis, must in so doing *itself* appear, from a Christian
perspective, as sinful, since for the Christian, any attempt to describe

---

[3] Among the former are, e.g. Hans Meyer, *Martin Heidegger und Thomas von Aquin* (Munich: Schöningh, 1964), Maurice Corvez, *L'Être et la conscience morale* (Louvain: Éditions Nauwelaerts, 1968), Schaeffler, *Frömmigkeit des Denkens*, and most recently Stephen Reynolds, 'Heidegger's *Introduction to the Phenomenology of Religion*' (unpublished D.Phil. dissertation, University of Oxford, 2008). Among the latter are van Buren, *Young Heidegger*; Kisiel, *Genesis*, and most recently McGrath, *Heidegger: A (Very) Critical Introduction* (Grand Rapids, Minn.: Eerdmans, 2008).
[4] Heidegger first borrows this phrase from Luther in GA 63.
[5] Letter to Karl Löwith dated 19 August 1921; in 'Drei Briefe', Papenfuss and Pöggeler, *Zur philosophischen Aktualität Heideggers*, 28–9.

the sinful state from a standpoint outside grace (which alone brings sin into view) implicitly rejects grace. As Heidegger puts it, clear-eyed, in 1922:

> Any philosophy that understands itself in terms of what it is, that is, as the factic how of the interpretation of life, must know—and know it precisely if it also has an "intimation" of God—that this throwing of life back upon itself which gets actualized in philosophy is something that in religious terms amounts to raising one's hands against God.[6]

But this opposition destabilizes Heidegger's initial sense of a possible coexistence, in which philosophy acts as a (substantially and methodologically autonomous) *praeparatio evangeliae*. Rather, philosophy and theology now stake competing claims to the same territory, namely man's (sinful) existence and the possibility of its interpretation.

In the years 1923–5, Heidegger seeks orientation in this field of problems by explicitly confronting the problem of sin, particularly in the writings of Luther and Kierkegaard. His conclusion is the resolute rejection of grace as the horizon of an interpretation of sin, carrying with it a more radical rejection of God as the horizon of an interpretation of human existence. While in 1919, Heidegger spoke of the 'mystery and *graced* character [*Gnadencharakter*] of all life',[7] he says resolutely in 1929 that existence at its deepest means 'immersion in Nothingness'.[8]

This chapter traces Heidegger's growing opposition to an eschatology framed by beliefs in death as the consequence of sin, and in eternal life as the object of eschatological hope; he reformulates eschatology against a horizon of death as the natural (rather than imposed) boundary of human existence and consequently Nothingness (rather than God) as the Other *vis-à-vis* which human existence shapes itself. The next chapter will discuss the methodological shift concomitant with this thematic shift, namely the developing distinction between philosophy as ontological science and theology as ontic science. This shift occurred in proximity to dialectical theology, and a first appraisal of Heidegger's complex relationship to that movement is an integral part of the chapter.

---

[6] GA 61, 198.

[7] Letter to Elisabeth Blochmann dated 1 May 1919; in Storck (ed.), *Heidegger/Blochmann*, 14–16; p. 14 (emphasis added).

[8] 'Da-sein heißt: Hineingehaltenheit ins Nichts'; *Was ist Metaphysik?* (Bonn: Friedrich Cohen, 1929); rpt. in GA 9, 1–41; p. 35.

FROM ETERNAL LIFE TO DEATH AS THE HORIZON OF ESCHATOLOGY: AUGUSTINE, LUTHER, AND OVERBECK

It was, recalls Heidegger in 1925,

> seven years ago, while I was investigating the [basic] structures [of Dasein] in conjunction with my attempts to arrive at the ontological foundations of Augustinian anthropology, that I first came across the phenomenon of care. Of course, Augustine and ancient Christian anthropology did not know the phenomenon explicitly, nor even directly as a term, although *cura*, care, as is well known, already played a role in Seneca as well as in the New Testament.[9]

Augustine is a major interlocutor in the period of Heidegger's first formation as a phenomenologist. He appears in notes and lectures from as early as 1919, and a whole lecture series—*Augustine and Neoplatonism*—is devoted to him in 1921. In his winter semester 1919/20 lecture series *Basic Problems of Phenomenology*, Heidegger praises Augustine as 'elementally compassing' ('*elementar umfassend*') the insight of primitive Christianity, which, as he emphasizes (correcting Dilthey), can never be merely epistemological, but must be 'lived': 'Augustine saw in the '*inquietum cor nostrum*' the great unceasing restlessness of life. He achieved a wholly original [alt.: originary] view which was not merely theoretical, but lived and brought to expression.'[10]

In his great reading of *Confessiones* X in the 1921 lecture series *Augustine and Neoplatonism*, Heidegger frames Augustine's marvelling discovery that the memory exceeds the grasp of the conscious spirit as a proto-phenomenological insight:

> '*Penetrale amplum et infinitum.*' All this belongs to myself, and yet I do not grasp [or contain] it myself. The spirit is too narrow to possess itself.[11]

---

[9] Heidegger, *Prolegomena zur Geschichte des Zeitbegriffs*, ed. Petra Jaeger (Frankfurt: Klostermann, 2nd edn., 1988), 418. [Hereafter cited as GA 20.]

[10] GA 58, 61–2. For Heidegger's similar endorsement of Luther; see Sean McGrath, 'The Facticity of Being GodForsaken: The Young Heidegger and Luther's Theology of the Cross', *American Catholic Philosophical Quarterly* 79, no. 2 (2005), 273–90; p. 285 (re-worked as chapter 6 of McGrath, *The Early Heidegger & Medieval Philosophy*).

[11] 'Augustinus und der Neuplatonismus', first published in GA 60, 157–299; p. 182 (commenting on *Confessiones* X. xvii (26)). Cf. Philippe Capelle, '"Katholizismus", "Protestantismus", "Christentum" und "Religion" im Denken Martin Heideggers: Tragweite und Abgrenzungen', *HJB* 346–71; p. 362.

For Heidegger, it is precisely the self's non-coincidence with itself (contrasting with divine self-possession) which is at the root of Augustine's central insight into human facticity, *'inquietum est cor nostrum'*.[12] This non-coincidence enables and perpetuates *curare* or *Bekümmertsein*, the existential mood which Heidegger describes as eschatological affliction in the *Introduction to the Phenomenology of Religion* (WS 1920/1), and as *Sorge* (care) in *Being and Time*.

However, for Heidegger this 'eschatological' affliction is radically compromised by Augustine's actual eschatological vision, centring on the eternal beatific vision of the *summum bonum*. In Augustine's work, this great eschatological theme frames the baring of his 'restless heart' in the exordium, and is developed in Book X: 'You have made us for yourself, O Lord, and our hearts are restless until they rest in you.'[13] But for Heidegger, the professed desire for the joyful contemplation of God is not an integral or authentic part of Augustine's insight into the human, but a Neo-Platonic vitiation of his phenomenological analysis. In his reading, Augustine's 'beatific vision' is merely a version of the Neo-Platonic notion of *theoria* or *contemplatio*, a static contemplation of God as a metaphysical object.[14] But this passive vision of an objectified God is inherently incompatible with the living experience of the holy which Heidegger has defined as authentic religion. Specifically, unlike the inherently 'unfulfilled' character of human willing (which is always directed to something it 'does not yet have' or 'not yet is'), contemplation of God as *'das Seiende selbst'* 'no longer points beyond itself, [but] is fulfilled in itself'.[15] Thus, it betrays the existential experience of eschatological 'affliction' or 'care' to which both Paul and Augustine himself have, in Heidegger's reading, testified.

One of the sources of disagreement between Heidegger and Augustine regarding the question of what constitutes human 'facticity' (and, consequently, what falls within the purview of phenomenological analysis) is their divergent understanding of the *diastasis* or *distensio* of human existence. Like Heidegger (and Plotinus), Augustine locates the source of the ordinary concept of time in 'temporality', that is, in a

---

[12] *Confessiones* I. i (1).

[13] *Confessiones* I. i (1). See also X. xxii (32) to xxiii (33).

[14] See GA 60, 199–203.

[15] In the 1925/6 lecture series *Logik. Die Frage nach der Wahrheit*; published under the same title as GA 21, ed. Walter Biemel (Frankfurt: Klostermann, 2nd edn., 1995), 122. I owe the reference to GA 21 to John van Buren, *Young Heidegger*, 187.

'distension' of the soul.[16] For Augustine (as later for Kierkegaard), the *diastasis* of human existence is caused precisely by the fact that, while within time, we strain towards eternity. Echoing Paul's commitment to 'stretching forward' (*epekteinomenos*) towards the 'prize of the upward call of God in Christ Jesus' (Phil. 3: 13–14), he writes (conforming Plotinus to the image of Psalmist and apostle):

> 'Because your mercy is more than lives' (Ps 62.4), see how my life is a dis-tension in several directions. 'Your right hand upheld me' (Ps 17.36; 62.9) in my Lord, the Son of man who is mediator between you the One and us the many, who live in a multiplicity of distractions by many things; so 'I might apprehend him in whom also I am apprehended' (Phil 3.12–14), and leaving behind the old days I might be gathered to follow the One, 'forgetting the past' and moving not towards those future things which are transitory but to 'the things which are before' me, not stretched out in distraction but extended in reach, not by being pulled apart but by concentration. So I 'pursue the prize of the high calling' where I 'may hear the voice of praise' and 'contemplate your delight' (Ps 25.7; 26.4) which neither comes nor goes. But now 'my years pass in groans' (Ps 30.11) and you, Lord, are my consolation. You are my eternal Father, but I am scattered in times whose order I do not understand. The storms of incoherent events tear to pieces my thoughts, the inmost entrails of my soul, until that day when, purified and molten by the fire of your love, I flow together... into you [*in te confluam*].[17]

For Heidegger, by contrast, *diastasis* is conditioned by *diathesis*: like Schleiermacher's religious feeling (which reveals Dasein as part of the world as an 'infinite whole', and thus cannot extend to 'the being of God before the world and outside the world'), the 'thrown projection' characterizing (authentic) Dasein necessarily moves within the horizons of this world and this time.[18]

---

[16] See *SZ* §§ 65–71; *Confessiones* XI. xxvi (33). Cf. Plotinus, *Enneads* 3. 7. 11 (cited in Augustine, *Confessions*, trans. and ed. Henry Chadwick (Oxford: Oxford University Press, 1992), 240 n. 27).

[17] *Confessiones* XI. xxix (39); Chadwick's translation. There is no doubt about the Neo-Platonic influence on this passage; nevertheless, it is not reducible to Neo-Platonism. Cf. also Gregory of Nyssa's mystical appropriation of *epektasis*, curiously absent from Heidegger's catena of mystical sources.

[18] Cf. Schleiermacher, *Über die Religion*, 82. Heidegger does not use the terminology of '*Geworfenheit*' and '*Entwurf*' until *Being and Time*; however, he expresses a similar concept from 1919 onwards. In the 1924 lecture series *Grundbegriffe der aristotelischen Philosophie* (published under the same title as GA 18), he thematizes this issue in relation to *Befindlichkeit* (see Kisiel, *Genesis*, 498).

A fuller development of this concept of temporality is not achieved until a few years later, in Heidegger's 1924 essay on 'The Concept of Time' and subsequent work.[19] But one immediate consequence of his disagreement with Augustine is directly relevant: For Heidegger, death and not eternal life becomes the authentic object of eschatology. This shift, already anticipated in his reading of Paul, is confirmed in his contemporaneous references to Luther. In his notes towards the winter semester 1921/2 lecture series *Phenomenological Interpretations of Aristotle: Introduction to Phenomenological Research*, Heidegger notes as a motto for the series a quote from Luther's Lectures on Genesis: '*Statim enim ab utero matris mori incipimus.*'[20] The passage from which this sentence is taken is Luther's commentary on Genesis 3: 15, which prophesies the striking of the serpent's head by the 'seed of the woman'. This prophecy incites Luther to speak about the promise of eternal life:

> This...is the text that made Adam and Eve alive and brought them back from death into the life which they had lost through sin. Nevertheless, the life is hoped for rather than one already possessed. Similarly, Paul also often says (1 Cor 15.31): 'Daily we die.'[21] Although we do not wish to call the life we live here a death, nevertheless it surely is nothing else than a continuous journey toward death [*perpetuus cursus ad mortem*]. Just as a person infected with a plague has already started to die when the infection has begun, so—because of sin, and death, the punishment for sin—this life can no longer properly be called life after it has been infected by sin. Right from our mother's womb we begin to die.[22]

Heidegger's term *Vorlaufen zum Tode* (anticipation of death), in *Sein und Zeit* and other texts, is a direct German translation of Luther's *cursus ad mortem*; but its use depends on a bracketing of Luther's aetiology of that condition, namely that human life tends towards death because it is infected with sin, and that Christ's conquest of sin and death proleptically overcame this predicament, opening the way

---

[19] Published as *Der Begriff der Zeit*, ed. Friedrich-Wilhelm von Herrmann (Frankfurt: Klostermann, 2004). [Hereafter cited as GA 64.]

[20] 'Right from our mother's womb we begin to die'; in WA 42, 146; quoted as 'Motto und zugleich dankbare Anzeige der Quelle' in GA 61, 182.

[21] This proclamation comes in the centre of Paul's great discourse on eschatology (1 Cor. 15).

[22] *Luther's Works*, i: *Lectures on Genesis Chapters 1–5*, ed. Jaroslav Pelikan, trans. George V. Schick (Saint Louis, Mo.: Concordia Publishing House, 1958), 196.

to eternal life (which is man's 'ownmost' vocation).[23] In Heidegger's re-reading, mortality is no longer a curse imposed on human existence *post hoc*, but the inmost and ownmost condition of humanity. Similarly, existence is no longer inherently directed towards eternity as its eschatological end, but distended only between birth and death.

In these 'phenomenological reductions' ('reduction' not in Husserl's technical sense, but in that dictated by the *lex parsimoniae*), Heidegger follows Franz Overbeck, with whose thought he engaged intensely in the early 1920s. Heidegger particularly approved of Overbeck's 'Christian scepticism'.[24] This 'scepticism' is expressed most systematically in Overbeck's sense that at the heart of Christianity lies its 'eschatology', which he interprets as nothing other than a self-reflexive *memento mori*—in other words, an acknowledgement of the mortality of all things, which must necessarily include even the transience of Christianity itself. 'The highest wisdom' of Christianity, Overbeck writes, is found 'in [its] eschatology, that is, its *doctrine of the future* or *of death*. For Christianity is nothing other than the wisdom of death. It teaches us exactly what death teaches us, not more nor less.'[25]

MORTALITY AND THE PROBLEM OF SIN

It is not until a few years later, when he moves to Marburg and develops a close working relationship with his theological colleague Rudolf Bultmann, that Heidegger begins to work systematically through the theological context of the question of death and mortality that he has been re-posing: the problem of sin.

---

[23] The alternative term *Sein zum Tode* is, of course, modelled on Kierkegaard's 'sickness unto death' (in the German translation, *Krankheit zum Tode*), to which it bears a similar relationship as *Vorlaufen zum Tode* to *cursus ad mortem*.

[24] Gadamer, Heidegger's student in Marburg, recalls that in 1923, following a lecture by Thurneysen, Heidegger energetically invoked Overbeck, whose 'radical self-doubt' he related to the 'true task of theology', namely to 'search for the word which was capable of calling to faith and sustaining in faith'; Gadamer, 'Marburger Theologie' (1964), in Gadamer, *Heideggers Wege*, 29–40; p. 29.

[25] From the unpublished 'Kirchenlexikon' (a collection of several thousand index cards), on a series of cards entitled 'Christentum Eschatologie Allg.', 2–3; quoted in Rudolf Wehrli, *Alter und Tod des Christentums bei Franz Overbeck* (Zurich: Theologischer Verlag, 1977), 229. Cf. Franz Overbeck, *Christentum und Kultur*, ed. C. A. Bernoulli (Darmstadt: Wissenschaftliche Buchgesellschaft, 1963), 297–8.

The context of this collaborative project is the fact that any Christian account of death must include reference to sin. The causal connection between sin and death (at least 'as it meets us'[26]) in the source texts is inescapable: '[S]in came into the world through one man, and death came through sin, and so death spread to all because all have sinned' (Rom. 5: 12); 'For the wages of sin is death' (Rom. 6: 23). This New Testament correlation—consistently accepted by the Christian tradition—is a complex interpretation of Genesis 2: 16–17 and 3: 1–24 in the light of the Christ event. God had declared upon placing the newly created man in Paradise, 'You may freely eat of every tree of the garden; but of the tree of the knowledge of good and evil you shall not eat, for in the day that you eat of it you shall die' (Gen. 2: 16–17). Man, having trespassed the command, incurred the curse of mortality: 'By the sweat of your face you shall eat bread until you return to the ground, for out of it you were taken; you are dust, and to dust you shall return' (Gen. 3: 19).

Whether death here is an intrinsic or punitive consequence of sin remains a matter of theological debate, closely connected, of course, to the concurrent debate how to interpret the Atonement.[27] But the general claim, only rarely contested until recently, is that mortality is not a natural feature of human life, but a violation of that life in its original (that is, prelapsarian) integrity—and that the primary significance of Christ's Incarnation, death, and resurrection is precisely the overcoming of death: '[W]here sin increased, grace abounded all the more, so that, just as sin exercised dominion in death, so grace might also exercise dominion through justification leading to eternal life through Jesus Christ our Lord' (Rom. 5: 20–1).[28] This victory over death is conceived both in individual and in cosmic terms: as an eternal life with

---

[26] Karl Barth, *Church Dogmatics*, iii/2: *The Doctrine of Creation*, ed. G. W. Bromiley and T. F. Torrance, trans. H. Knight, G. W. Bromiley, J. K. S. Reid, and R. H. Fuller (Edinburgh: T. & T. Clark, 1960), 596.

[27] The key text for this debate in the twentieth century, though it has undergone severe and justified criticism, is still Gustaf Aulén, *Christus Victor: An Historical Study of the Three Main Types of the Idea of Atonement*, trans. A. G. Herber (London: SPCK, 1931; New York: Macmillan, 1969).

[28] Schleiermacher makes an early attempt at reframing death not as an imposition but as the natural and necessary limit of human life since its creation; see Schleiermacher, *The Christian Faith* (Edinburgh: T. & T. Clark, translated from the 2nd (1830) edn., 1928), 243–4. Karl Barth's position on the subject is somewhat ambiguous, but the passages in the *Church Dogmatics* directly relating to the subject are clear in their conception of death 'as it actually meets us' as 'the sign of divine judgement', 'standing [under which] is not something intrinsic to our human nature'; Barth, *Church Dogmatics*, iii/2. 596–7.

God after death, consequent upon the forgiveness of one's sin through faith in Christ (John 3: 16, 11: 25; etc.), and as the general resurrection of all the dead unto divine judgement and eternal life with or punished by God (1 Cor. 15: 12–28, 50–7; Rev. 20: 11–15; etc.).

The *temporality* of human existence is not directly linked with sinfulness in the Old or New Testaments; nevertheless, its inescapable association with mortality[29] means that it, too, is envisioned as being overcome by the eschatological defeat of death: 'time shall be no more' (Rev. 10: 6).[30] The question whether this anticipated timelessness is a return to prelapsarian existence or a radically new mode of human existence—in other words, whether biblical anthropology is in this respect fundamentally nostalgic or dynamic ('evolutionary')—is never raised in the source text, but becomes an important underlying concern in the Reformation era.

It is on this basis alone that Paul and Augustine can await with hope the 'coming of the Lord' (1 Thess. 5: 2) and eternal 'rest in Thee' (*Confessions* I. 1[i]). For both thinkers (speaking anachronistically with Heidegger here), a hermeneutics of facticity, or a description of what it is to be human, must involve an account of the *disruption* of human existence by sin and consequently death, and of the hoped-for restoration of authentic human existence through an outstripping of that disruption. Heidegger confronted the problem of this explicitly theological, yet nevertheless inalienable dimension of Paul's and Augustine's thought in the course of his attempt to develop his own phenomenological perspective in dialogue with their work. The key to shaping an eschatological phenomenology without hope of salvation, I will argue in the course of this section, was the adaptation of Luther's radical account of original sin.

ONTOLOGY: HERMENEUTICS OF FACTICITY (SS 1923)

In the last lecture series before his move to Marburg, *Ontology: Hermeneutics of Facticity* (SS 1923), Heidegger first explicitly engages

---

[29] See, among many other examples, Ps. 90: 10 and Ecclesiastes (*passim*).

[30] 'χρόνος οὐκ ἔσται ἔτι'. Some recent translations have rendered the verse, 'there shall be no more delay', but this is an ideologically motivated translation with no influence on the relevant Christian tradition.

with the Christian understanding of sin as the state in which postlapsarian humanity finds itself, i.e. the *status corruptionis*. In seeking to isolate 'the idea of facticity and the concept of man', Heidegger vigorously criticizes Max Scheler's 'phenomenological' claim that man's difference from the rest of the animal kingdom rests not in his rationality but in his perception of spiritual values and of God for its insufficient differentiation between theological and philosophical claims.[31] In particular, Scheler's definition of man as an '"intention and gesture of 'transcendence' itself," a "God-seeker"'[32] is ridiculed for importing theological categories without observing the fundamental theological distinction between human existence in its prelapsarian integrity, its postlapsarian corruption, its Christian state of grace, and its eschatological glory: '[W]hat gets overlooked again is that... in theology, man's various states, modes of being, must in principle be distinguished (*status integritatis, status corruptionis, status gratiae, status gloriae*) and that one cannot arbitrarily exchange one for the other.'[33]

Heidegger then draws special attention to Luther's understanding of the *status corruptionis*:

> See Luther: *Porro caro significant totum hominem, cum ratione et omnibus naturalibus donis.*[34] This flesh is in a *status corruptionis* which is from the start fully defined: to it belong *ignorantia Dei, securitas, incredulitas, odium erga Deum*, a definitely negative relation to God in which man stands against God. *This* is as such *constitutive!*'[35]

In his supplementary notes to the lecture series, Heidegger adds, in difficult shorthand:

> *homo iustus—rectus—bona voluntas—caritas dei*; that is: *homo primus in gratia conditus est*; i.e. *in beata vita constitutus.* Cf. De lib. arb., cap. 11 in fine.[36]
>
> Formal deduction: *faciamus hominem*; intention about *man!* Salvation here—the more originally and absolutely it is taken, the more weight

[31] See GA 63, 25–6.
[32] GA 63, 26, quoting Max Scheler, 'Zur Idee des Menschen', *Abhandlungen und Aufsätze* (Leipzig: Weisse Bücher, 1915), 346.
[33] GA 63, 27.
[34] 'Flesh means further the whole man with his reason and all his natural endowments'; Luther, *In Esaiam Prophetam Scholia praelectionibus collecta, multis in locis non parva accessione aucta* (1534), ch. 40; in *Exegetica opera latina*, vol. xxii, ed. H. Schmidt (Erlangen, 1860), 318.
[35] GA 63, 27. Cf. Luther's *Lectures on Genesis Chapters 1–5*, 166.
[36] Augustine, *De libero arbitrio*, I. 11.

must sin have. It has such weight only if the Fall is absolute, i.e.: first origin, ἀρχή, absolute *gratia Dei*. The τέλος: pure sinfulness.[37]

What Heidegger is isolating here is the essential difference between a Scholastic and a Lutheran understanding of the *status corruptionis*—a dispute in which he firmly sides with Luther. For Scholastic theology, the Fall into sin impaired but did not obliterate human nature as it was constituted before the Fall. There was for Scholasticism, consequently, a large degree of continuity between man's prelapsarian and postlapsarian states, which expressed itself primarily in his continued ability to discern God by natural reason (as affirmed in Rom. 1: 18–20).[38] For Luther, by contrast, the term 'flesh' (as opposed to 'Spirit') now encompasses 'the whole man with his reason and all his natural endowments': The *status corruptionis* 'is as such *constitutive*'; human nature as originally created 'in the image of God' (Gen. 1: 27) is obliterated. In the supplementary note quoted above, Heidegger explains the Christological rationale for this radical position: 'the more originally [alt.: originarily] and absolutely [salvation] is understood, the weightier sin must be. But it can have such weight only if the Fall is absolute,...its result [being] pure sinfulness.'

It was in Marburg that Heidegger followed this line of thought further.

LUTHER

After an initial immersion in the work of Luther in his early student days, Heidegger returned to the Reformation theologian around 1919.[39] Karl Jaspers recalled that, during his visit in Freiburg in April 1920, he 'sat alone with [Heidegger] in his den, watched him at his Luther studies, and saw the intensity of his work'.[40] To his wife

---

[37] GA 63, 111 (appendix X).

[38] There were significant internal disagreements whether the 'original justice' of Adam was natural (i.e. inherent to his existence) or supernatural (i.e. superadded from without), that is, whether the Fall reduced man *from* his natural state (Aquinas) or merely from the supernatural state of Adam *to* a natural state (Scotus). These disputes, however important, are not immediately relevant to the present discussion.

[39] Heidegger's early reading of Luther is documented in Otto Pöggeler, 'Heideggers Luther-Lektüre im Freiburger Theologenkonvikt', *HJB* 185–96.

[40] Quoted in van Buren, *Young Heidegger*, 149; no reference is provided. Julius Ebbinghaus similarly recounted that after the war, his friend and colleague Heidegger

Elfride, Heidegger wrote in late 1920 that his 'edition of Luther' had become 'indispensable' to him.[41] But only after his move to Marburg in 1923 did Heidegger attempt a more systematic engagement with the Reformation thinker, in dialogue with his theological colleague Rudolf Bultmann. Bultmann wrote at the time that Heidegger 'not only [had] excellent knowledge of Scholasticism, but also of Luther'—so much so that he 'rather put' the resident church historian Heinrich Hermelink 'on the spot'.[42] His student Karl Löwith recalled attending a joint seminar by Heidegger and Bultmann on the young Luther,[43] and Heidegger lectured on Luther at least twice in Bultmann's New Testament seminar: on 'The Problem of Sin in Luther' in 1924, and on Luther's commentary on Paul's Letter to the Galatians in 1927.[44]

Heidegger's engagement with Luther was definitive of his own path. Bultmann avers that Heidegger 'never made a secret of the fact that he was influenced...most notably by Luther'.[45] Hans Georg Gadamer similarly thought that Heidegger's 'inspiration came from the young

'had received the Erlangen edition of Luther's work as a prize or gift—and so we read Luther's reformatory writings for a while in the evenings we spent together', a practice from which his own essay 'Luther and Kant', as well as a joint colloquium on the influence of Luther on Kant and German Idealism more generally emerged. See Ebbinghaus, 'Julius Ebbinghaus', in Ludwig Pongratz (ed.), *Philosophie in Selbstdarstellungen*, vol. iii (Hamburg: Felix Meiner, 1977), 33. Ebbinghaus's essay on Luther and Kant is found in Ebbinghaus, *Interpretation und Kritik*, ed. Hariolf Oberer and Georg Geismann (Bonn: Bouvier, 1981). The joint colloquium was entitled 'Die theologischen Grundlagen von Kant, *Religion innerhalb der Grenzen der blossen Vernunft*', and held in SS 1923 (see 'Schriftenverzeichnis', *HJB* 476). A proposed journal article by Heidegger on 'The Ontological Foundations of Late Medieval Anthropology and the Theology of the Young Luther' never appeared; see van Buren, *Young Heidegger*, 149.

[41] Letter of 20 August 1920, in Heidegger (ed.), *Mein liebes Seelchen!*, 111–12; p. 112.
[42] Letter to Hans Freiherr von Soden, 23 December 1923; published in Bultmann Lemke, 'Der unveröffentlichte Nachlaß von Rudolf Bultmann', in Jaspert (ed.), *Rudolf Bultmanns Werk und Wirkung*, 202. Bultmann gives a similar account in a letter to Friedrich Gogarten dated 22 December 1923; see Rudolf Bultmann and Friedrich Gogarten, *Briefwechsel 1921–1967*, ed. Hermann Götz Göckeritz (Tübingen: Mohr Siebeck, 2002), 53.
[43] In Löwith, *Mein Leben in Deutschland vor und nach 1933. Ein Bericht* (Stuttgart: J. B. Metzler, 1986), 29.
[44] The first is reprinted as 'Das Problem der Sünde bei Martin Luther', in Bernd Jaspert (ed.), *Sachgemäße Exegese: Die Protokolle aus Rudolf Bultmanns Neutestamentlichen Seminaren 1921–1951* (Marburg: Elwert, 1996), 28–33. The second is reported by Heinrich Schlier, 'Denken im Nachdenken', in Günther Neske (ed.), *Erinnerungen an Martin Heidegger* (Pfullingen: Neske, 1977), 217–21; p. 219.
[45] Quoted in van Buren, *Young Heidegger*, 150; no reference provided. See also Bultmann, 'Martin Heidegger', in Hermann Gunkel and Leopold Zscharnack (eds.), *Religion in Geschichte und Gegenwart* (Tubingen: Mohr Siebeck, 2nd edn., 1927–31), vol. ii, cols. 1687–8.

Luther'. Luther scholar Edmund Schlink even claimed that 'Heidegger's existential analytic of human Dasein is a radical secularization of Luther's anthropology'.[46]

In his February 1924 seminar presentation on the problem of sin in Luther, Heidegger elaborated on the radical rift between pre- and postlapsarian existence which had already interested him in his 1923 *Ontology* lectures. In seeking to give a theological elucidation of Luther's understanding of sin, the presentation reiterates the Christological reasoning cited in the earlier lecture notes:

> The more the radicalness of sin is underestimated, the more salvation is undervalued and God's Incarnation stripped of its necessity. Thus, one finds in Luther the basic tendency: The *corruptio* of the being of man can't be understood radically enough; this in contrast to Scholasticism, which had always spoken of an attenuated *corruptio*.[47]

This position—that the '*natura hominis* is *corrupta*'—is then translated into characteristically Heideggerian language: 'The being of man as such is sin. . . . In other words, it does not attach itself to the moral make-up of man, but is his actual [alt.: authentic] core. Sin, in Luther, is an existential term'.[48] Defining this state of sin as 'nothing other than the opposite of faith',[49] Heidegger comes to the startling conclusion that 'one can only understand faith if one understands sin, and one can only understand sin if one has a correct understanding of the being of man itself'.[50]

The constitutive significance of this interpretation of Luther for *Being and Time*'s discussion of *Verfall* (which, though in a Heideggerian context usually clumsily translated into English as 'falling', is merely a German rendering of the Latin *corruptio*) is one of the concerns of Chapter 5.[51] For now, our focus should be on two specific, closely interrelated moves.

---

[46] Quoted in van Buren, *Young Heidegger*, 150; no reference provided.
[47] 'Das Problem der Sünde bei Martin Luther', 29. Cf., for example, Luther's *Lectures on Genesis 1–5*, 142.
[48] 'Das Problem der Sünde bei Luther', 31. Later, Heidegger will say, 'das eigentliche Selbstsein ist eine existenzielle Modifikation des Man als eines wesenhaften Existenzials'; *SZ* § 27, p. 130.
[49] 'Das Problem der Sünde bei Luther', 31.
[50] 'Das Problem der Sünde bei Luther', 33.
[51] *Ruinanz*, the early term for *Verfall* used in Heidegger's WS 1921/2 Introduction to Phenomenology, is probably also a Germanization of the Latin Luther: *ruina* (in the sense of death or downfall, and often in immediate juxtaposition to *resurrectio*) occurs over 300 times in Luther's Latin writings.

First, Heidegger defines sinfulness as the mode of being in which postlapsarian humanity always finds itself, and so—for a phenomenology like his that 'also has an "intimation" of God'[52]—as that existence which it is phenomenology's primary task to interpret. Secondly, he inverts Luther's epistemological hierarchy by making an understanding of faith dependent on an understanding of sin. For Luther (as for the entire Christian tradition), the depth of human corruption can only be fathomed by a consideration, in faith, of the magnitude of Christ's deed, which alone reveals the magnitude of the sin that required such an atonement.[53] For Heidegger, by contrast, sin—as the mode of being in which humanity always already finds itself—is logically prior to faith, which can be understood only by contrast to sin.

If Heidegger can regard this as a legitimate interpretation of Luther, it is because Luther so often emphasizes the (proto-phenomenological) need to argue 'from experience' rather than from debased Scholastic reason in describing the *status corruptionis*: 'Let us rather follow experience, which shows that we are born from unclean seed and that from the very nature of the seed we acquire ignorance of God, smugness, unbelief, hatred against God, disobedience, impatience, and similar grave faults.'[54] It is a vital difference between Luther and Heidegger that for Luther, this is (in principle) always the experience *of the believer*, so that the Scholastics' lack of true faith, for example, is revealed precisely in their blindness to their own corruption.[55] And yet a reading such as Heidegger's cannot be fully excised from Luther's texts. In Luther's thought, Christ's death and resurrection can only be interpreted by reference to the *status corruptionis*; indeed, the Fall into sin is the ontological condition for the deed of Christ as much as the deed of Christ is the epistemological condition for recognizing that Fall for what it is. In Heidegger, correspondingly, *Verfall* (corruption) is the ontological condition of the possibility of authenticity, even if authenticity is the epistemological condition for recognizing the state of corruption. In both cases, the analysis moves within the boundaries of corruption. If, for Luther, salvation leads away from that state of corruption, then Heidegger can, with some justification, exclude this departure from the scope of his phenomenological analysis.

---

[52] GA 61, 246.
[53] See, for example, Luther's *Lectures on Genesis 1–5*, 142, 164–6.
[54] *Lectures on Genesis 1–5*, 166.   [55] *Lectures on Genesis 1–5*, 164–6.

'PHENOMENOLOGICAL INTERPRETATIONS
OF ARISTOTLE' (1922)

These explorations come to a provisional conclusion in Heidegger's 1922 essay 'Phenomenological Interpretations of Aristotle', also known as the 'Natorp Report'. From Paul and Augustine as interpreted by Luther,[56] and in more recent thought from Kierkegaard, Dostoevsky, and Overbeck, Heidegger had acquired an image of the movement of theology as governed by a radical disruption between the natural human condition, with its arrogation of metaphysical insight into the transcendent, and the deep realization, in genuine religious experience, of one's own finitude as limitedness and burden. For Paul, Augustine, Luther, and Kierkegaard, this experience is associated with the conviction of our own depravity, and should lead the believer to a humble and trusting turn toward God in expectation of his help—a help which comes as a radical antithesis to the natural order of the world. For Heidegger, by contrast, their position seems, increasingly, to imply the need for a different route than that taken by the theological thinkers themselves. Their interpretation of the natural human state as sinful, he begins to argue in 1920/1, is a secondary and partly imposed description from the perspective of already-achieved salvation. This salvation, however, because it is granted as a gift by an external source, is not itself part of the primordial human condition which it is the task of phenomenology to investigate. While Heidegger continues to regard talk of 'sin' and 'salvation' as justified in a certain sphere (namely that of theology), he comes to regard it as a more fundamental and authentic task to describe the 'sinful' state in which humans naturally find themselves *from within*. If this implies a moral task, it is to acknowledge and work with the '*Schwere*' (heaviness/difficulty) of human existence rather than to wish to neutralize it. This, he comes to regard as the task of philosophy. To work philosophically, he writes in 1922, is to sustain the fact that 'factic life has the ontological character of being heavily burdened with itself'. Theology, by contrast, is constantly tempted to 'curry favour with our needs'.[57]

This approach, Heidegger realizes, has the paradoxical result that it is at the same time a more authentically human way of being true to the acknowledgement of God than theology itself (because it does

[56] See GA 61, 250.
[57] GA 61, 238.

not seek to exceed the limits of the human, and so implicitly acknowl-
edges the absolute transcendence of God), and a rebellion against God
(because it resists his intervention). This is the 'specific factic "ascesis"
of the scientific life'.[58] Philosophy, thus the conclusion, must be methodologically a-theistic:

> 'Atheistic' not in the sense of a theory such as materialism or the like.
> Any philosophy that understands itself in terms of what it is, that is, as
> the factic how of the interpretation of life, must know—and know it
> precisely if it also has an 'intimation' of God—that this throwing of life
> back upon itself which gets actualized in philosophy is something that
> in religious terms amounts to raising one's hands against God. But phi-
> losophy is thereby only being honest with itself and standing firm on
> this, that is, it is comporting itself in a manner that is fitting to the only
> possibility of standing before God that is available to it as such. And
> here 'atheistic' means: keeping itself free from the temptations of that
> kind of concern and apprehension that only talk glibly about religiosity.
> Could it be that the very idea of a philosophy of religion, and especially
> if it does not take into account the facticity of human being, is pure
> nonsense?[59]

This is a long way from Heidegger's enthusiastic letter to his wife in
1919 that 'entirely new perspectives' have opened up to him *within*
the philosophy of religion; yet the shift is itself made possible only
by Heidegger's engagement with the tradition of the early Luther,
predicated as that tradition is on a belief in the total depravity of the
unsaved human person.

The pressing question now is: is this phenomenological analysis
of the *status corruptionis* (as the state in which humanity always
already finds itself) a *praeparatio evangeliae*—the analysis by a
believer in his capacity as philosopher of the state from which (faith
in) God alone can save? Or is it much rather an alternative to salvation? In his famous 1966 interview with *Der Spiegel*, 'Nur noch ein
Gott kann uns retten' ('Only a god can now save us'), Heidegger has
poignantly returned to the former position, which he had held until
around 1920:

> Philosophy will not be able to bring about an immediate change in the
> current state of the world. This is true not only of philosophy, but of all

---

[58] GA 61, 198.
[59] GA 61, 246.

merely human thought and desire. Only a god can now save us. I see the only possibility of rescue in preparing, through thought and poetry, a preparedness for the appearance of this god or for the absence of this god in our downfall; so that we will not, to put it crudely, 'croak', but, if we go down, go down in the face of the absent god.[60]

But in the mid-1920s, Heidegger proposes a substitution of philosophy for theology as the means to an 'authentic' existence. Just as for Luther, the main mark of the true believer was the ability to perceive the *status corruptionis* and to resist its dispersion in the present in favour of an 'expectant awaiting' of God,[61] so for Heidegger, the main mark of the philosopher is the recognition of Dasein's ordinary dispersion in worldliness (later termed *das Man*) and resolute self-projection onto the future. Because Dasein is ineluctably temporal (and thus also finite), this future includes the ineluctable possibility of his non-being, his death.[62] Consequently, *Angst* (anxiety, affliction) and not hope is the dominant mood of eschatological expectation and the mood most revelatory of Dasein's own being. As Overbeck had said, eschatology (that 'highest wisdom' of Christianity) 'teaches us exactly what death teaches us, not more nor less.'[63] 'The bright night of the Nothing of Angst', Heidegger will say a few years later, is what first gives rise to 'the original openness of that which is as... something that *is*—i.e. is not nothing.'[64] 'Only in the Nothing of Dasein does that-which-is come to itself according to its ownmost possibility, i.e. in a finite way.'[65] Nothingness (and its manifestation in death) has here replaced God as the horizon of man's self-recognition.

---

[60] '"Nur noch ein Gott kann uns retten": *Spiegel*-Gespräch mit Martin Heidegger am 23. September 1966', *Der Spiegel* 30, no. 23 (31 May 1976): 193–219; rpt. in Günther Neske and Emil Kettering (eds.), *Antwort: Martin Heidegger im Gespräch* (Pfullingen: Neske, 1988), 81–114; p. 100.

[61] '*Expectatio Creature*'; Luther, *Diui Pauli apostoli ad Romanos epistola* (1515–16); WA 56, 371.

[62] The masculine pronoun here is not accidental; Heidegger repeatedly suggests at this time that only a man can be a philosopher. In his first letter to Hannah Arendt (10 February 1925), for example, he writes of the 'terrible solitude of scholarly work [furchtbare Einsamkeit wissenschaftlichen Forschens] which only a man can bear'; Ludz (ed.), *Hannah Arendt/Martin Heidegger*, 11. An incisive critique of Heidegger's association of philosophy with masculinity can be found in Ben Morgan, 'Heidegger and the Mysticism of Everyday Life', *Heidegger and Religion 1: Heidegger and the Theology of Crisis* (Oxford Research Archive, 2008), 10–24.

[63] 'Christentum Eschatologie Allg.', 2–3.   [64] GA 9, 34.   [65] GA 9, 40.

FROM 'GOD' TO 'NOTHING': HEIDEGGER ON KIERKEGAARD

Begrebet Angest (1844)

In his developing understanding of this 'eschatology without eschaton', Heidegger was formatively influenced by Kierkegaard's analysis of sin and anxiety in *Begrebet Angest* (*The Concept of Anxiety*, 1844). In *Being and Time*, he commends the book in no fewer than three of his notoriously sparse footnotes: 'The one who has penetrated the phenomenon of anxiety [*Angst*] furthest is S. Kierkegaard', though his 'existential interpretation [*existenziale Interpretation*]' of the phenomenon remains deficient.[66]

Begrebet Angest brings together our concerns with original sin and eschatology. Here, Kierkegaard's pseudonym Vigilius Haufniensis— conscious that he is speaking psychologically of a matter that cannot adequately be discussed other than dogmatically[67]—posits anxiety (Heidegger's *Angst*) in the face of future possibility as the psychological condition (or environment) of sin.

Essential to Vigilius' claim is his understanding of temporality. Sin happens in a 'moment' (*øjeblik*) of decision; it is a 'leap' not conditioned by anything but itself.[68] But the term '*øjeblik*' so innocuously deployed here is by no means simple; on the contrary, it is the linchpin of Vigilius' whole concept of temporality. As for Heidegger, Augustine, and (Heidegger's) Paul, temporality, for Vigilius, is the specifically *human* existence in time, which is characterized by awareness of its own transience, or of itself as temporal; and as for Augustine and Paul (but contrasting with Heidegger[69]), that awareness—and with it the whole human phenomenon of temporality—can only arise on the background of the eternal, in which man also participates:

---

[66] *SZ* § 40, n. 4; § 45, n. 6; § 68, n. 2.

[67] Søren Kierkegaard, *Begrebet Angest: En simpel psychologisk-paapegende Overveielse i Retning af det dogmatiske*, attr. to Vigilius Haufniensis (Copenhagen, 1844), introduction.

[68] *Begrebet Angest*, ch. 1, § 2 [475]. I take it that this is a definitional rather than an empirical statement: If the relevant act were thus conditioned, it could not be called 'sin', and its relevant discourse would no longer be dogmatics, but psychology, sociology, or medicine. The impossibility of Vigilius' project rests precisely in the attempt to speak psychologically of *sin*, which by definition can only be discussed ethically or dogmatically.

[69] Cf. *SZ* § 68, n. 2.

The moment is that ambiguity in which time and eternity touch each other, and with this the concept of *temporality* is posited, whereby time constantly intersects eternity and eternity constantly pervades time. As a result, the above-mentioned division acquires its significance: the present time, the past time, the future time.[70]

Vigilius finds the biblical source for this idea in Paul's eschatological vision of the Resurrection, which is to happen 'in a flash, *in the twinkling of an eye* [Gk: ἐν ῥιπῇ ὀφθαλμοῦ; Dn: *i et Øjeblik*], at the last trumpet' (1 Cor. 15: 52): 'With this', he claims, Paul 'also expresses the fact that the moment [*øjeblik*] is commensurate with eternity, since the moment of destruction at that same moment expresses eternity'.[71]

Psychologically, the *øjeblik* as a moment of decision requires a particular relation to the future. The reason is that to the human subject, eternity appears, for the time being, primarily as the not-yet: 'The eternal means first of all the futural'; or, expressed differently, 'the futural [is] the incognito... under which the eternal, being incommensurable with time, nevertheless keeps company with time'.[72] Vigilius is ambiguous here: for on one hand, he talks ('objectively') of that 'fullness of time' which, for human beings, still lies in the future,[73] and on the other hand, he talks ('subjectively') of the future as *possibility*, which is infinite in two senses: the uncountable number of possible events and choices, and the 'limitlessness' (i.e. lack of delimitation) of 'possibility' as a term whose criteria include lack of realization (and so, to a certain extent, concretization).

It is the second, subjective sense—in which 'infinity' is quietly substituted for 'eternity'—which gains precedence in the following discussion. For the *øjieblik* turns out to be simultaneous with the awakening of the human spirit (in Adam and in each person) as the synthesis of body and soul, or of time and eternity.[74] The human spirit awakens in its realization of the infinity of its own potential (*mulighedens selviske uendelighed*).[75] But this self-revelation is always, already, psychologically speaking, anxiety: Anxiety 'is freedom's actuality as the

---

[70] *Begrebet Angest*, ch. 3. ET: *The Concept of Anxiety*, trans. and ed. Reidar Thomte (Princeton: Princeton University Press, 1980), 89.

[71] *Begrebet Angest*, ch. 3, n. 30 (ET 88).

[72] *Begrebet Angest*, ch. 3 (ET 89; my translation).

[73] *Begrebet Angest*, ch. 3 (ET 89).   [74] *Begrebet Angest*, ch. 3 (ET 88).

[75] *Begrebet Angest*, ch. 2, § 2 (ET 61).

possibility of possibility';[76] it 'is defined as freedom's disclosure to itself in possibility'.[77] To enter a conscious relation to one's own future is here inherently self-reflexive,[78] and to come to oneself in this way is anxiety-ful because it is to confront Nothing in a double sense: as the 'nothing' of events and choices that are not yet and may never be, and *vis-à-vis* which the human spirit experiences its own immense (creative) infinity;[79] and as the 'nothing' of possibility which the human spirit itself *is*. 'The actuality of the spirit constantly shows itself as a form that tempts its possibility but disappears as soon as it seeks to grasp for it, and it is a nothing that can only bring anxiety.'[80]

It is in the 'vertigo' induced by finding oneself thus between infinity and Nothing that one makes the leap of sin,[81] which is the attempt to stave off these enormities by declaring something merely finite absolute. But this sin produces more anxiety, epitomized in the anxiety of death as punishment.[82] 'The moment sin is posited', Vigilius puts it radically, 'temporality is sinfulness.'[83] For Luther, the *status corruptionis* was 'as such constitutive'; for Vigilius, that sinfulness is inextricable from temporal existence itself. 'Authentic selfhood', as Heidegger will say, 'is an existentiell modification of the "they" as an essential existentiale.'[84]

Although anxiety is the psychological condition of sin, it is also potentially redemptive precisely because it 'consumes all finities, uncovers all their deceptions',[85] and reveals the human subject to herself not only in her actual but also her possible existence. 'Whoever is educated by [anxiety] is educated by possibility, and only [she] who is educated by possibility is educated according to [her] infinitude.'[86]

The potential benefit is twofold. First, anxiety teaches the true power of faith:

> However, in order that an individual may thus be educated absolutely and infinitely by the possibility, he must be honest toward possibility and have faith. By faith I understand here what Hegel somewhere in his

---

[76] *Begrebet Angest*, ch. 1, § 5 (ET 42).   [77] *Begrebet Angest*, ch. 4 (ET 111).

[78] In Adam's innocence, by contrast, his spirit was 'dreaming'; *Begrebet Angest*, ch. 1, § 5 (ET 41).

[79] *Begrebet Angest*, ch. 2, § 2 (ET 61).   [80] *Begrebet Angest*, ch. 1, §5 (ET 42).

[81] *Begrebet Angest*, ch. 2, § 2 (ET 61).

[82] *Begrebet Angest*, ch. 2 (ET 53); ch. 3, n. 32 (ET 92).

[83] *Begrebet Angest*, ch. 3 (ET 92).

[84] *SZ* § 27, p. 130 (emphasis removed).

[85] *Begrebet Angest*, ch. 5 (ET 155; my translation).

[86] *Begrebet Angest*, ch. 5 (ET 156).

way correctly calls the inner certainty that anticipates infinity. When the discoveries of possibility are honestly administered, possibility will discover all the finitudes, but it will idealize them in the form of infinity and in anxiety overwhelm the individual until he again overcomes them in the anticipation of faith.[87]

Secondly, anxiety allows the human person to gather up her entire self and surrender herself to God in faith *in her entirety*:

> In that very moment, he is absolutely identified with the unfortunate man; he knows no finite evasion by which he may escape. Now the anxiety of possibility holds him as its prey until, saved, it must hand him over to faith.[88]

HEIDEGGER AFTER KIERKEGAARD

An in-depth discussion of Heidegger's immediate response to Kierkegaard—§§ 39–40 and §§ 46–53 of *Being and Time*—will be given in Chapter 6. But a few aspects must be highlighted immediately. In Heidegger's development of an eschatology without eschaton, Kierkegaard's analysis of anxiety was formative but not definitive— the latter because it lacked, to Heidegger, an ontological perspective, and remained on an ontic level insufficient to Heidegger's own existential analytic.[89] This, according to Heidegger, was particularly true of Kierkegaard's understanding of eternity: 'Kierkegaard probably penetrated the *existentiell* phenomenon of the moment most deeply— which doesn't mean that his existential interpretation was equally successful. He remains stuck in the vulgar concept of time, and defines the moment by way of the now and eternity.'[90] For Heidegger, this definition of time *vis-à-vis* a postulated eternity was a structural correlate of Kierkegaard's definition of man *vis-à-vis* a postulated Absolute or

---

[87] *Begrebet Angest*, ch. 5 (ET 157).   [88] *Begrebet Angest*, ch. 5 (ET 158).

[89] Cf. Heidegger's 1923 comment about his own hermeneutics of facticity: 'Starke Anstöße für die hier vorgelegte Explikation kommen von der Arbeit Kierkegaards. Aber Voraussetzungen, Ansatz, Art der Durchführung und das Ziel sind grundsätzlich verschieden, weil er es sich zu leicht macht. Im Grunde war für ihn nichts fraglich als die eigene Reflexion, die er betrieb. Er war Theologe und stand innerhalb des Glaubens, grundsätzlich außerhalb der Philosophie. Die heutige Lage ist eine andere'; GA 63, 30. Cf. also *SZ* § 40, n. 4; § 45, n. 6; § 68, n. 2.

[90] *SZ* § 68, n. 2.

God. Both are ontologically unnecessary: the *Christian* sense of anxiety as related to sin is merely one ontic manifestation of—indeed, one religious attempt to answer the question posed by—that anxiety which is an *ontological* moment of man. Heidegger, consequently, attempts a more radically ontological/phenomenological account of anxiety which does not appeal to extraneous postulates such as eternity or God, but reveals the structural 'self-sufficiency' of factic life.[91]

The central move of this reworking is the replacement of the Absolute (God) with Nothing. Heidegger shares Kierkegaard's correlation of authenticity and wholeness: as for Kierkegaard, it is, for Heidegger, a vital concern for the human subject to 'take the measure of herself', even if this leads only to the realization that she cannot complete that action. However, Heidegger argues, this does not require the final term of Kierkegaard's analysis. For Vigilius, anxiety (once sin is posited) is and remains part of the sinful state; salvation is through the faith that overcomes anxiety by consuming what anxiety has gathered up-the infinite possibility of human existence. For Heidegger, anxiety is enough. We will follow up this thought in the next section.

What interests me now is that although this is clearly a reinterpretation of Kierkegaard, it is made possible as an interpretation of the Christian thinker by the structure of that thinker's own work. In Vigilius' analysis, although anxiety is penultimate, it comes first, that is, before faith. The human subject is alone with it until—once anxiety has searched out and burnt away all mere 'finities' of her being—she can hand over the whole she has thus gathered up to God in faith and hope of salvation. The criteria of 'salvation', here, are wholly external to the terms of the psychological analysis: they are imported from traditional Christian belief and 'take over' once the psychological analysis is complete. *Within* that analysis, there is an implicit, competing conception of 'salvation', namely 'wholeness', achieved by a grasping of one's own infinity. Vigilius' protestations that this is merely a penultimate term are unlikely to stick with the phenomenologist Heidegger.

But there is a deeper level of analysis, for Kierkegaard is perfectly aware of this importation. What justifies it, in his view, is that the very concept to which he attempts a psychological approach is a concept only given by Christian belief. He could not attempt an analysis of sin

---

[91] Cf. GA 58, 42. An insightful discussion of Heidegger's (very partial) emancipation from the Christian Kierkegaard is found in Stephen Mulhall, *Philosophical Myths of the Fall* (Princeton: Princeton University Press, 2005), 46–66. The following paragraphs are indirectly indebted to that discussion.

without the concept of 'sin'—as a moment of decision within the free will of the human subject, not fully conditioned by anything outside itself—having been revealed by Christian doctrine. The handing over of his subject to dogmatics after the completion of the psychological analysis thus merely completes the circle. There is an obvious parallel between this practice and the Lutheran account of consciousness of sin discussed above: for Luther, the significance of sin could only be revealed (in history and in each individual's consciousness) through faithful contemplation of Christ, the magnitude of whose deed revealed, by implication, the corresponding magnitude of man's corruption. Both thinkers' appeal to 'phenomenology' (or 'psychology') in recognizing sin is firmly rooted within the phenomenon of faith.

Although Heidegger wishes to draw a firm line between the 'ontic' level of faith—which postulates entities such as God to resolve the questions posed by factic life—and the 'ontological' level of his own analysis, the distinction between corruption (*Verfall*) and authenticity which is so central to that analysis is dependent, at least genealogically, on Christian belief, and hovers uncomfortably between it and his professed a-theism.

5

From Theology to Philosophy II: Heidegger and Dialectical Theology

Die Marburger Zeit brachte dazu noch die nähere Erfahrung eines protestantischen Christentums—alles aber schon als Jenes, was von Grund aus überwunden, nicht aber zerstört werden muß.

—Martin Heidegger (1937/8)[1]

As already apparent in Chapter 4, Heidegger's ontological concerns regarding Pauline and Augustinian eschatology were inseparable from his methodological concerns, in the early to late 1920s, regarding the scope and limits of philosophy—concerns worked out from the starting point of a phenomenology of religion. In this work, Heidegger's theological exemplars were (besides the ever-present Luther) Søren Kierkegaard, Fyodor Dostoevsky, and Franz Overbeck. But Heidegger was not the only young theological thinker rediscovering these writers. During the years 1920 to 1922, Karl Barth revised his revolutionary commentary on Paul's Letter to the Romans under the acknowledged influence (beside those of Plato and Kant) of Overbeck, Kierkegaard, and Dostoevsky.[2] The simultaneous interest is not surprising; after all, Gadamer later wrote of the sense of excitement pervading the war years: 'the red Piper copies of Dostoevsky's novels burned on every desk.'[3] But Barth and Thurneysen on one

---

[1] 'My Marburg period also brought a more intimate experience of a Protestant Christianity—but always already as that which must be fundamentally overcome, though not destroyed'; GA 66, 415.

[2] Karl Barth, *Der Römerbrief* (Munich: Christian Kaiser, 2nd fully revised edn., 1922), xiii–xiv.

[3] Hans-Georg Gadamer, 'Selbstdarstellung 1975', in *Gadamer Lesebuch*, ed. Jean Grondin (Tübingen: Mohr Siebeck, 1997), 1–30; p. 4.

hand, and Heidegger on the other, were not merely independent readers of the great nineteenth-century writers, but pioneered competing interpretations of their work and its implications. What is more, both internal evidence and the newly available correspondences of Rudolf Bultmann with Karl Barth, Emil Brunner, and Friedrich Gogarten suggest that Heidegger reached his conviction of the need for a strictly a-theistic method in philosophy in express opposition to Barth and Thurneysen's resolutely Christian reading of Kierkegaard, Dostoevsky, and Overbeck. This opposition is reflected in competing eschatologies: Barth's 'consistent eschatology'[4] and Heidegger's 'eschatology without an eschaton'.

What Barth and Heidegger share in their competing appropriations of Kierkegaard, Dostoevsky, and Overbeck is the conviction of a methodological gulf between theology and philosophy: theology must proceed from faith to faith, whereas philosophy 'cannot' even 'say sin'[5]. In the years leading up to his 1927 lecture 'Phenomenology and Theology', Heidegger formalizes his assessment of this difference in the distinction between ontic sciences and ontological science, which governs his work from the late 1920s onwards. The critical distinction, here, is between those sciences— including theology—which deal with 'what is' (*Seiendes*), and the one science—philosophy—which deals with Being itself (*Sein*). More fully expressed, 'the ontic [or positive] sciences take as their theme a present something [*Seiendes*], which has always already in some way been revealed *before* its scientific revelation.... The science of being, ontology, on the other hand, requires a fundamental reorientation of the gaze directed towards what *is*...towards being.'[6] In 1927, Heidegger's guiding thesis, accordingly, is that 'theology is a positive science and consequently as such absolutely different from philosophy'.[7]

---

[4] The definitive discussion of Barth's shift, between the first and second editions of his *Römerbrief* (i.e. between 1918 and 1922), from a process eschatology to a consistent eschatology, is Bruce L. McCormack, *Karl Barth's Critically Realistic Dialectical Theology: Its Genesis and Development, 1909–1936* (Oxford: Oxford University Press, 1997), ch. 5.

[5] SZ § 62, 306n.

[6] Delivered on 9 March 1927 in Tübingen and on 14 February 1928 in Marburg. First published (with a French translation) in *Archives de philosophie* 32 (1969), 355–95; rpt. in GA 9, 45–67; p. 48.

[7] GA 9, 49 (italics removed).

THE DEVELOPING DISTINCTION BETWEEN
THE ONTIC AND THE ONTOLOGICAL

The classification of theology as an ontic or positive science was one of the significant steps in Heidegger's development from a 'Christian theo*logian*' (as he identified himself in 1921[8]) to the pioneer of a methodologically a-theistic philosophy of being.[9] Until his two lecture series on the phenomenology of religion, *Introduction to a Phenomenology of Religion* (WS 1920/1) and *Augustine and Neoplatonism* (SS 1921), Heidegger still regarded any description of human existence as necessarily including reference to God. Thus, in mid-1918, he could write to Elisabeth Blochmann that '[e]very accomplishment achieves the character of finality in accordance with its authenticity, i.e. its inner belonging to the central "I" and its God-directed determination'.[10] A year later, he assured Blochmann of the 'mystery and grace-character of all life',[11] calling her to 'trust…in [her] inner calling'[12] and 'quiet humility before the Spirit':[13] 'I have firm faith in the Spirit and his power—whoever lives in him and for him will never fight a losing battle.'[14]

However, in his winter semester 1919/20 lecture series *Basic Problems in Phenomenology*, Heidegger began to develop a view of the 'structure(s) of life' that would eventually ground the independence of phenomenology from religiosity. This view was supported by increased attention to the historical and geographical differences between different forms of religion:

> 'Self-sufficiency' does not refer to the question which particular religiosity and form of religion…fulfils, in this or that (arbitrarily) historically motivated shape, this particular historically morphologically motivated meaning, but rather to the fact that this fulfilment happens at all, and is something that happens *out of life's own forms*—that life always speaks itself and answers itself in its own language, that life, structurally

---

[8] Letter to Karl Löwith dated 19 August 1921; in 'Drei Briefe', Papenfuss and Pöggeler, *Zur philosophischen Aktualität Heideggers*, 28–9.

[9] See e.g. GA 61, 197.

[10] Letter dated 15 June 1918; in Storck (ed.), *Heidegger/Blochmann*, 7.

[11] Letter dated 1 May 1919; Storck (ed.), *Heidegger/Blochmann*, 14.

[12] Ibid.

[13] Letter dated 2 October 1918; Storck (ed.), *Heidegger/Blochmann*, 9.

[14] Letter dated 6 November 1918; Storck (ed.), *Heidegger/Blochmann*, 10. For earlier comments in this vein, see particularly the epilogue of Heidegger's qualifying thesis (GA 1) and his 1917 note 'Phänomenologie des religiösen Erlebnisses und der Religion', in GA 60, 322–4.

speaking, does not need to unscrew itself from itself to maintain its meaning, that its structure suffices unto itself, in all its possible shapes and coincidences and conditionalities, even in order somehow, time and again, to overcome its imperfections, its insufficiencies. The term ['self-sufficiency'] refers to a structural character of life, ... [namely] that it is an 'in itself'. It carries in its own structure (which most deeply determines all substantial how and what) the availabilities it requires as possibilities of the fulfilment of its own tendencies.[15]

Phenomenology as a 'science of the origin of life' or 'original/originary science of life' [*Ursprungswissenschaft vom Leben*], then, does not explore 'factic life itself and the boundless plethora of worlds lived in it', but 'life *as originating*, as emerging from an origin'.[16] This is the beginning of Heidegger's distinction between the ontic and the ontological.

Religion, on this model, is authentic when it is the case that 'in religion ... the ultimate questions [alt.: questionables] are alive and in some way answered'.[17] But religion is only one field among others in which these 'ultimate questions' can arise, and theology (and other expressions of religious life) are an attempt to *answer* them, not, like phenomenology, an attempt to sustain them *as questions*.

It is precisely because of this that Heidegger writes in preparation for his summer semester 1922 lecture series *Phenomenological Interpretations of Aristotle*:

> Questionability is not religious, but is rather what leads to a situation of religious decision in the first place. I do not act religiously in philosophizing, even if I, as a philosopher, can be a religious person. But the art lies in philosophizing and in this being truly religious, which means factically taking philosophizing as one's worldly, historical task, in doing and a concrete world of doing, not in religious ideology and fantasy.[18]

From this, Heidegger concludes:

> Philosophy must, in its radical, self-reliant questionability, be in principle *a-theistic*. It must, precisely in light of its basic tendency, not falsely claim to have God or to determine God. The more radical it is, the more determinedly it is an 'away' from him, and precisely in the radical execution of the 'away' a difficult 'with' him.[19]

---

[15] GA 58, 42.
[16] GA 58, 81.
[17] GA 58, 42.
[18] GA 61, 197 (loose leaf entitled 'Zur Einleitung').
[19] Ibid.

By 1927, Heidegger's conviction of the priority of philosophy is firm. After his delivery of 'Phenomenology and Theology' to the Lutheran Theological Faculty in Tübingen, he writes to Elisabeth Blochmann that the very remit of the lecture, namely to make philosophy fruitful for theology, puts himself 'as a philosopher in a terribly skewed light... and makes the whole thing into an apology for Christian theology rather than', as it should be, 'a confrontation'.[20] Later in the letter, he feels compelled to return to the subject: the lecture, a 'document of my *Marburg* time', was merely meant to show '*how, given* that someone stands in the Christian Protestant faith and busies himself with theology, he ought to take philosophy, assuming that he wants it to be a help and not', as it really is, 'a fundamental agitation'.[21]

Heidegger's rejection of God as the horizon of an interpretation of human existence, then, is more than a declaration of allegiance to one field rather than another: It implies a revaluation of theology as at best an ontic science, one that already takes for granted the being of its object. But in tending to *claim* the place of the ontological science, it can be pernicious—indeed, can be the very embodiment of evil, claiming a grasp of that which must be acknowledged as ungraspable.[22] Consequently, in a 1928 letter to Julius Stenzel, one of the reviewers of *Being and Time*, Heidegger writes that 'in the *philosophical* problem of existence there is necessarily... an absolute opposition to all Christianity'.[23]

This attitude encourages and is reinforced by an increasingly exclusive focus, in the late 1920s and 1930s, on the 'degenerate' form of Christianity which Heidegger has criticized from the beginning. His developing understanding of the history of Being confirms to Heidegger Overbeck's conviction that Christianity's earliest experience is no longer an option for it, and consequently no viable model for the present.[24] Accordingly, the philosopher's dominant perspective on Christian faith and theology is increasingly less historical and

[20] Letter dated 8 August 1928; Storck (ed.), *Heidegger/Blochmann*, 24–6; p. 24.

[21] Ibid., 26.

[22] For an analysis of this Heideggerian concept of evil (though without reference to theology as a possible instantiation of it), see Bernd Irlenborn, *Der Ingrimm des Aufruhrs: Heidegger und das Problem des Bösen* (Vienna: Passagen Verlag, 2000), ch. 1.

[23] Letter dated 14 April 1928; quoted from MS by permission of Prof. Karl Schuhmann, University of Utrecht, in Ott, *Martin Heidegger*, 159.

[24] See Franz Overbeck, *Über die Christlichkeit unserer heutigen Theologie* (Leipzig: C. G. Naumann, 1873), *passim*, and *Christentum und Kultur*, 7. Heidegger writes to Blochmann in the same 1928 letter: 'Die Vergangenheit des menschlichen Daseins im Großen ist nicht nichts, sondern das, wohin wir immer wieder zurückkehren, wenn wir in die Tiefe gewachsen sind. Aber diese Rückkehr ist kein Übernehmen

more systematic: 'Faith' and 'theology', in the late 1920s and early 1930s, become co-terminous with systematic theology in its urge for *answers*. As Heidegger puts it in his summer semester 1935 lecture series, *Introduction to Metaphysics*:

> Anyone for whom e.g. the Bible is divine revelation and truth has the answer to the question 'Why are there beings rather than nothing?' even before it is asked: all beings that are not God himself have been created by Him. God himself 'is' as the uncreated creator. Anyone who stands on the ground of such faith can in some way trace and participate in the asking of our question, but he cannot really ask it without giving himself up as a believer, with all the consequences of such a step. He can only act 'as if'...[...] From the standpoint of faith our question is 'foolishness'. Precisely this foolishness constitutes philosophy. 'Christian philosophy' is a round square and a misunderstanding.[25]

TOWARDS AN A-THEISTIC METHOD: CONTESTING BARTH'S READING OF OVERBECK, DOSTOEVSKY, AND KIERKEGAARD

As already indicated, Heidegger's theological exemplars in the attempt to define the scope and limits of phenomenology were (besides the ever-present Luther) Søren Kierkegaard, Fyodor Dostoevsky, and Franz Overbeck. He mentions all three as important parts of his student years—the publications of the Collected Works of both Kierkegaard and Dostoevsky in German during the early 1910s are later cited as two of the highlights of these 'exciting years',[26] and Overbeck's work claimed as a decisive influence in his separation from the Roman magisterium.[27] Evidence of a more sustained engagement with Overbeck,

---

des Gewesenen sondern die Verwandlung. So muß uns der heutige Katholizismus u. all dergleichen, der Protestantismus nicht minder, ein Greuel bleiben'; Storck (ed.), *Heidegger/Blochmann*, 32.

[25] GA 40, 9.

[26] See GA 1, 59. The Jena edition of Kierkegaard's *Gesammelte Werke* in German was published in twelve volumes between 1909 and 1922: Sören Kierkegaard, *Gesammelte Werke*, 12 vols., trans. H. Gottsched and C. Schrempf (Jena: Eugen Diederichs, 1909–22). The Piper edition of Dostoevsky's *Sämtliche Werke* in German appeared in 22 volumes between 1908 and 1914: Fjodor Dostojewski, *Sämtliche Werke*, 22 vols., trans. Dmitri Mereschkowski (Munich: Piper, 1908–14).

[27] GA 16, 41.

Kierkegaard, and Dostoevsky, however, dates from the period 1919 to 1923. In August 1918, on his way to the front in Lorraine during the Hundred Days Offensive, Heidegger writes to his wife Elfride to ask her to find him a copy of Dostoevsky's *Brothers Karamazov*.[28] Otto Pöggeler also recalls Heidegger telling him how important Dostoevsky was for him in the years surrounding 1919.[29] Hans-Georg Gadamer remembers a heated argument between Heidegger and Eduard Thurneysen about Overbeck in 1923.[30] And Karl Jaspers recalls in rela-tion to his visits to Heidegger from 1920 onward that they 'shared a passion for Kierkegaard'.[31] What follows is a brief assessment of their significance for his methodological project, which partially emerged in conscious opposition to their contemporaneous reception by Karl Barth and Eduard Thurneysen.

SØREN KIERKEGAARD

When Heidegger worked on his 'hermeneutics of facticity' in the late 1910s and early 1920s, he rediscovered Kierkegaard's Christian writ-ings as corroborating his sense of the *Schwere* (the difficulty or, literally, heaviness) of engaging with the Absolute as an inherently finite, tem-poral being, and of the moral obligation implied in this sense. Evidence of a first serious engagement with the Danish philosopher dates from 1919–21, when Heidegger worked on a review of Karl Jaspers's monumental *Psychology of World Views*, which included a section on Kierkegaard. Heidegger was interested in Jaspers's attempt to distil a pre- or non-theological meaning from Kierkegaard's religious concept of the Absolute: Jaspers's own key concept of the Absolute, he noted in passing, was clearly a synthesis of 'the Kantian doctrine of antinomies with its guiding concept of infinity, and of a Kierkegaardian concept of the "Absolute" "purified" of its specifically Lutheran-religious or

---

[28] Letter dated 28 August 1918 from Nouillon-Pont, in Heidegger (ed.), *Mein liebes Seelchen!*, 74–5; p. 75.
[29] In private conversation; recalled in Pöggler, 'Heideggers Luther-Lektüre im Freiburger Theologenkonvikt', *HJB* 185–96; p. 192.
[30] Hans-Georg Gadamer, *Philosophische Lehrjahre: Eine Rückschau* (Frankfurt: Klostermann, 1977), 37; and Gadamer, 'Marburger Theologie' (1964), in *Heideggers Wege*, 29–40; p. 29.
[31] Quoted in John van Buren, *Young Heidegger*, 150; no reference provided.

theological character'.[31] However, in Heidegger's reading, Jaspers falls short of Kierkegaard in short-circuiting the methodological awareness of the latter, whose rigour, rarely surpassed in philosophy or theology, Heidegger regards as the real essence of Kierkegaard's work.[33]

> [Consciousness of self] can only be authentically roused by in some sense driving the other ruthlessly into reflexion, so that he may see that the acquisition of the objects of philosophy is tied to a rigour of methodic execution which leaves all [mere] sciences behind. For what is decisive in the sciences is merely the demand for objectivity, while in philosophy, the philosopher himself in his notoriously pathetic being is part of the subject matter. One can only drive [another] to reflexion, make [another] alert, by leading the way along a stretch of the path.[34]

Among Heidegger's 'mottos' for his WS 1921/2 lecture course *Phenomenological Interpretations of Aristotle: Introduction to Phenomenological Research* are two passages from Kierkegaard, which emphasize the methodological implications of our constitutive 'paltriness' or 'puniness'. 'But what philosophy and the philosopher find difficult', writes Kierkegaard, 'is to stop'.[35] Rather than retaining a proper dread in the face of inescapable doubt, modern philosophy tends to 'float, as abstract, in the indeterminacy of the metaphysical'.

> But instead of admitting this of itself, and so to point men (the single man) to the ethical, the religious, the existential, philosophy has created the illusion that men can, prosaically put, speculate themselves out of their skin into mere appearance.[36]

FYODOR DOSTOEVSKY AND FRANZ OVERBECK

Dostoevsky became for Heidegger a paradigm of the consistent practice, within the literary medium, of this form of self-sacrifice through conscious acceptance of one's 'existential limitation and facticity'. As with Overbeck, he developed this attitude to Dostoevsky within, but

---

[32] Heidegger, 'Anmerkungen zu Karl Jaspers' *Psychologie der Weltanschauungen*' (1919/21), in GA 9, 1–44; p. 27.

[33] GA 9, 41.   [34] GA 9, 42.

[35] Quoted in GA 61, 182 from Kierkegaard, *Entweder-Oder* I, trans. H. Gottsched and C. Schrempf (Jena: Diederichs, 1911), 35.

[36] Kierkegaard, *Einübung im Christentum* (Diederichs IX, 1912), 70; quoted in GA 61, 182.

also in opposition to, the contemporary theological reception of the Russian writer.[37]

The 1906–19 edition by Piper Verlag of Dostoevsky's Collected Works in German caused a furore among young theological and philosophical thinkers. Hans-Georg Gadamer later remembered:

> It was about the kind of truth that would be manifested not so much in general statements and insights, as in the immediacy of one's own experience and in one's own existence, which could not be lived vicariously. Dostoevsky above all seemed to us to know of this truth. The red Piper copies of Dostoevsky's novels burned on every desk.[38]

The theological reception of Dostoevsky in Germany was decisively shaped by Karl Barth's close collaborator Eduard Thurneysen, whose 1921 book *Dostojewski*, among other things, strongly influenced Barth's own revision of his 1919 *Römerbrief* for re-publication in 1922. Heidegger (as Rudolf Bultmann later recalls) followed Barth and Thurneysen's work with interest, but he was very critical of their appropriation of Dostoevsky (as of Kierkegaard and Franz Overbeck) for a confessional Christian agenda.[39]

Thurneysen interpreted Dostoevsky as apophatically witnessing to the true transcendence of God, which cannot be appropriated by human discourse and thus also cannot be portrayed directly in literature. Instead, it can only be indirectly suggested by portraying the persistent doubts and questions of his protagonists, and their continual moral failures, within an overall gesture towards the hope of redemption and resurrection.

> The works of Dostoevsky are full of annunciation, full of the suggestion of that final turn towards the transformation of all things on earth, towards truly eternal lives lifted above all problems. But they remain suggestion and annunciation! To want more would here mean to want less. Dostoevsky is no Romantic. Precisely for the sake of the purity,

---

[37] One of the earliest appreciations of Heidegger's pursuit of 'the path of Dostoevsky' is by the French-Romanian poet, critic and philosopher Benjamin Fondane: 'Sur la route de Dostoyewski: Martin Heidegger', *Cahiers du sud* 19 (1932), 378–92.

[38] Gadamer, 'Selbstdarstellung', *Gadamer Lesebuch*, 4. For more information on the publication of the Piper edition of Dostoevsky's works, see Christoph Garstka, *Arthur Moeller van den Bruck und die erste deutsche Gesamtausgabe der Werke Dostojewskijs im Piper-Verlag 1906–1919* (Frankfurt: Peter Lang, 1998).

[39] Note Bultmann's recollection that Heidegger was 'familiar with modern theology' and knew Barth's writings; in Bultmann Lemke, 'Der unveröffentlichte Nachlaß von Rudolf Bultmann', in Jaspert (ed.), *Rudolf Bultmanns Werk und Wirkung*, 202.

the meaning and power of this *last* turn, he did not oppose anything more violently than all attempts to turn this last, eternal moment into a merely penultimate one, to turn that which is only *divinely* possible into something, after all, *humanly* possible and representable. To attempt this means to tempt God. But Dostoevsky knew that this attempt constitutes man's one, strongest temptation, which threatens his entire humanity and his entire transcendence.[40]

This interpretation, merging with a rediscovery, in the same vein, of Franz Overbeck, became an important impetus for Barth's revised edition of *Der Römerbrief.*

In January 1920, Karl Barth wrote to his friend Eduard Thurneysen, 'Our Melchizedek is probably—Overbeck. Perhaps I will write something about him in the *Neue Werke.*'[41] Half a year later, he published a review essay of Overbeck's posthumously edited *Christentum und Kultur,* entitled 'Unerledigte Anfragen an die heutige Theologie' ('Unsettled Questions for Theology Today'), in a small volume also containing a sermon by Thurneysen.[42] Upon publication, Barth notified his colleague in Leutwil: 'Our Overbeck has appeared. What course will this rocket take? At any rate it will not win us many friends or doctoral degrees!'[43]

Franz Overbeck, a nineteenth-century New Testament and Patristics scholar teaching in Basle, had presented a radical critique of the possibility of institutional theology in his controversial *Über die Christlichkeit unserer heutigen Theologie* (*How Christian is our Present-Day Theology?*; 1873, 2nd edn. 1903). In this 'Streit- und Friedensschrift', published as a 'twin' volume to the first *Untimely Meditations* of his friend Friedrich Nietzsche, Overbeck posits an absolute contrast between the ascetic apocalypticism of the earliest Church, which constitutes a radical rejection of any hope of salvation within world and time, and the subsequent secularization and

---

[40] Eduard Thurneysen, *Dostojewski* (Zurich: Zwingli Verlag, 1963), 53.

[41] Barth to Thurneysen, 5 January 1920; in Karl Barth and Eduard Thurneysen, *Briefwechsel,* i: *1913–1921* (Zurich: Theologischer Verlag, 1973), 364; quoted in Ryan Glomsrud, 'The Cat-Eyed Theologians: Franz Overbeck and Karl Barth', *Journal for the History of Modern Theology/Zeitschrift für neuere Theologiegeschichte* 16 (2009), 37–57; p. 1.

[42] Karl Barth, 'Unerledigte Anfragen an die heutige Theologie', in Karl Barth and Eduard Thurneysen, *Zur inneren Lage des Christentums* (Munich: Christian Kaiser, 1920), 1–24. See also Franz Overbeck, *Christentum und Kultur. Gedanken und Anmerkungen zur modernen Theologie von Franz Overbeck,* ed. Carl Albrecht Bernoulli (Basle: Benno Schwabe & Co. Verlag, 1919).

[43] Barth to Thurneysen, 16 June 1920; in Barth and Thurneysen, *Briefwechsel,* i. 399.

historicization of Christianity, brought about by the emergence of a Christian theology and (political) establishment. Any such development, in Overbeck's view, is fundamentally misguided, because it assumes the possibility of explaining or grounding faith intellectually, and of achieving within history what can only be attained by its End. For Overbeck, these dichotomies constitute an insurmountable dilemma for Christianity. Whether it remains world-denying apocalypticism or develops a theology, faith has lost itself by making itself, at the very least, superfluous: 'In this world, no truly existing faith can extricate itself from knowledge unless it really wants to; but knowledge, as soon as it is called, stands beside faith and remains in all eternity something other than it.'[44] It is for this reason that Christianity is a self-reflexive *memento mori*—an acknowledgement of the mortality of all things, even itself.[45]

In his 1920 review essay 'Unerledigte Anfragen an die heutige Theologie', Barth calls for a rediscovery of Overbeck (who had been his father's teacher in Basle[46]), interpreting his sharp critique of theology as a rhetorical move similar to that of Dostoevsky (and, in a different register, Kierkegaard). He reads Overbeck's work as a 'call into the desert': a necessary stripping-away of the theologian's temptation to believe that he is able to comprehend and appropriate the Word of God, which teaches him to discover and accept his own poverty, his need to receive that Word in all its 'otherness' and even its repudiation of the natural human condition.[47] If Overbeck had called Christianity a *memento mori*, Barth gives this a transcendent interpretation:

> If the concept of death marks the limit of human understanding, then it must also mark its transcendental origin. If it can be 'useful as an iron broom that sweeps away all lies and deceptions weighing down on our earthly life', if a rightly understood *memento mori* is beneficial to life (p. 297), then it must also have a positive, creative, fertile significance without compare.[48]

[44] Overbeck, *Über die Christlichkeit unserer heutigen Theologie*.
[45] See 'Christentum Eschatologie Allg', 2–3; quoted in Wehrli, *Alter und Tod*, 229.
[46] See Klauspeter Blaser, 'Fritz Barth', *Historisches Lexikon der Schweiz*, ed. Marco Jorio (Basle: Schwabe, 2002), i. 697.
[47] Barth, 'Unerledigte Anfragen', 5.
[48] Barth, 'Unerledigte Anfragen', 8. Barth's page reference is to the first edition of Overbeck, *Christentum und Kultur* (Basle: Schwabe, 1919).On 7 May 1920, Thurneysen reports to Barth: '[Hermann Kutter] begleitet unsere Gänge auf seine Weise. Es schien mir nur, er befürchte, unsere "Todesweisheit" könnte zu einem selbstständigen Prinzip werden. Ich beruhigte ihn darüber'; in Barth and Thurneysen, *Briefwechsel*, i. 389.

Barth gallantly concludes the section:

> We, for our part, choose to understand Overbeck's fundamental, critical
> doctrine of primal history and of death, with the deep understanding
> expressed in it of the dialectic of creation and salvation,... as an over-
> coming of all 'ideology', and count its author, along with the Socrates
> of the *Phaedo*, among those 'pagan enunciators of the Resurrection' of
> whom it is said: 'Not even in Israel have I found such faith.'[49]

The revisions of Barth's second, thoroughly reworked edition of his
Römerbrief (published four years after the first edition, in 1922) were
motivated to a large degree by his and Thurneysen's work on Overbeck as well as, subsidiarily, Dostoevsky and Kierkegaard.[50] Bruce L.
McCormack, in the authoritative account of Barth's theological development, summarizes these revisions as a shift to a particular eschatology: "'*Ein Denken von Gott aus*" became—in the phase of *Romans
II*—"*ein Denken von Eschatologie aus*."[51] Specifically, Barth adopted a
radically future-oriented, 'consistent' (*konsequente*) eschatology which
expected the Kingdom of God to bring about 'the dissolution of all
things, the cessation of all becoming, the passing away of this world's
time.'[52] Only in such a radical contrast to human forms of being and
communicating could God truly reveal himself; and it was precisely
because of this radical difference that humans must not attempt to
speak of God directly or in human form.

This interpretation incited a storm of controversy. The beginning of
the movement known as dialectical theology and the occasion of an
honorary doctorate from the University of Münster, it also incurred
strong criticism.[53] Paul Wernle, Professor of New Testament Studies in

---

[49] Barth, 'Unerledigte Anfragen', 9.

[50] See Karl Barth, *Der Römerbrief*, xiii–xiv ('Vorwort zur zweiten Auflage').

[51] 'Thinking from the standpoint of God became, in *Romans* II, thinking from the standpoint of eschatology'; McCormack, *Karl Barth's Critically Realistic Dialectical Theology*,
208. Hans Schindler, in his 1936 book-length critique *Barth und Overbeck*, criticized
Barth's Overbeck-interpretation precisely for making eschatology 'zur Denkmethode...,
zu einem erkenntnistheoretischen Prinzip [das sie] ins rein Intellektualistische ver-
flüchtigt'; *Barth und Overbeck* (Gotha: Leopold Klotz Verlag, 1936), 125.

[52] See Barth's 1920 address to the Aarau Student Conference, 'Biblische Fragen,
Einblicke und Aussichten', in Barth, *Das Wort Gottes und die Theologie*, 88; cited in
McCormack, *Karl Barth's Critically Realistic Dialectical Theology*, 208.

[53] The 1920 edition periodical *Der Kirchenfreund* carried an urgent call for a review of
Zur inneren Lage des Christentums: 'Barth und Overbeck stellen unsere ganze bisherige
Theologie nach Form und Inhalt in Frage. Wir dürfen diese Erscheinung nicht länger
ignorieren'; *Der Kirchenfreund: Blätter für evangelische Wahrheit und kirchliches Leben*
54 (1920), 415. (There was, however, no immediate take-up of the challenge.)

Basle, wrote scathingly in 1921 of 'Karl Barth's Overbeck-falsification', which 'looks pretty good to readers who never knew Overbeck & can be made to believe anything about him'[54]—a criticism echoed in 1936 in Hans Schindler's book-length critique *Barth und Overbeck*, and as late as 1982 in Eberhard Jüngel's *Barth-Studien*, in which he dismisses Barth's Overbeck-interpretation as resting on a 'grotesque misunderstanding'.[55] Heidegger seems to have been ambiguous. On one hand, he almost certainly had Barth's dialectical theology in mind when he wrote approvingly in 1927 that theology 'is slowly beginning once more to understand Luther's insight that its dogmatic system rests on a "foundation" that is not rooted in ... faithful [i.e. believing] question-ing, and whose concepts therefore are not merely inadequate to theol-ogy's field of problems, but obscure and distort it'.[56] On the other hand, he too was critical towards Barth and Thurneysen's 'misappropriation'. In 1923, shortly after his move to Marburg, Heidegger attended a guest lecture by Thurneysen. According to the recollections of his student Hans-Georg Gadamer, he offered a vigorous response to Thurneysen in which he appealed to the 'radical self-doubt' of Franz Overbeck.[57] Although viable for *theology*, Barth and Thurneysen's attempt to for-mulate a framework within which this radical self-doubt served as nothing but a first step to affirmation denied the *phenomenological* practice in which Overbeck was engaged, which necessarily includes acknowledgement and acceptance of (rather than an attempt to over-come) the inherent finitude or limitation of the human condition.

HEIDEGGER AND DIALECTICAL THEOLOGY

Heidegger's relations with the dialectical movement were, however, far from ended after his intervention in Thurneysen's interpretation of

---

[54] Letter to Martin Rade dated 13 February 1921, published in Jaspert (ed.), *Bultmanns Werk und Wirkung*, 33–5; p. 35.

[55] Eberhard Jüngel, *Barth-Studien* (Gütersloh: Mohn, 1982), 63. The possibility of such criticism seems to have troubled Barth from the beginnnig. In June 1920, he wrote to Thurneysen: 'Jüngst erschien mir im Traum—Overbeck. Ich hatte ein langes Gespräch mit ihm, bei dem ich Frage an Frage reihte und vernahm, wir hätten ihn dur-chaus richtig verstanden'; Barth to Thurneysen, 7 June 1920; in Barth and Thurneysen, *Briefwechsel*, i. 395.

[56] *SZ* § 3, p. 10 (italics removed).

[57] Hans-Georg Gadamer, *Philosophische Lehrjahre*, 37.

Overbeck and, by extension, Dostoevsky. The extent and the fraught nature of these relations has become at least partially biographically assessable with the publication of Bultmann's correspondences with Barth, Gogarten, and Heidegger, and Barth's correspondences with Brunner and Thurneysen.[57] What follows is an initial appraisal of the information made available by these volumes and surrounding material.

As is commonly known, Heidegger and Bultmann met upon Heidegger's 1923 appointment to an extraordinary professorship in philosophy at Marburg, and struck up a close friendship that lasted until their deaths in 1976.[58] They also developed a productive working relationship immediately expressed in private joint readings of the Gospel of John, Heidegger's participation in Bultmann's New Testament seminars,[59] and Bultmann's attendance at Heidegger's lectures on time and on logic.[60] Bultmann—then in the *Aufbruchstimmung* of the new turn against liberal theology which he spearheaded with Barth, Thurneysen, Gogarten, and Brunner in the movement soon called dialectical theology—tried for many years to integrate Heidegger into his circle. But his association with Heidegger, rather than a boost to the movement, became instead a catalyst for the differences that led Barth, Brunner, Gogarten, and Bultmann, in the aftermath of the publication of *Being and Time*, to disperse.

The ambivalence reflected in this rocky association—Bultmann's persistent conviction that Heidegger and dialectical theology had common ground on the one hand, and the cold distance between Heidegger and Bultmann's associates on the other—arose from the subject matter itself. Heidegger, Barth, Brunner, and Gogarten shared

---

[58] Karl Barth and Rudolf Bultmann, *Briefwechsel 1911–1966*, ed. Bernd Jaspert (Zurich: Theologischer Verlag, 2nd revised and expanded edn., 1994); Rudolf Bultmann and Friedrich Gogarten, *Briefwechsel 1921–1967*, ed. Hermann Götz Göckeritz (Tübingen: Mohr Siebeck, 2002); Rudolf Bultmann and Martin Heidegger, *Briefwechsel 1925–1975*, ed. Andreas Großmann and Christof Landmesser (Frankfurt: Klostermann, 2009); Karl Barth and Emil Brunner, *Briefwechsel 1911–1966*, ed. Eberhard Busch (Zurich: Theologischer Verlag, 2000); Karl Barth and Eduard Thurneysen, *Briefwechsel 1913–1935*, 3 vols. (Zurich: Theologischer Verlag, 1973–2000).

[59] The warmth and endurance of that friendship is now documented in Bultmann and Heidegger, *Briefwechsel 1925–1975*.

[60] See e.g. Bultmann's letter to Gogarted dated 22 December 1923; in Bultmann and Gogarten, *Briefwechsel*, 53.

[61] Bultmann attended at least Heidegger's lectures on the concept of time (SS 1925) and on logic (WS 1925/6), now published as GA 20 and GA 21; see Bultmann to Gogarten, dated 21 November 1925; in Bultmann and Gogarten, *Briefwechsel*, 97.

an opposition to any 'theology of glory', whether in the shape of neo-Scholasticism or liberal theology: any assumption that human existence was continuous with transcendent reality, and that an analysis of human existence could therefore yield an uncomplicated understanding of 'transcendence', whether in the sense of the nature of God or the God-directedness of man. But this agreement of principle expressed itself in directly conflicting claims. The conflict took the initial form of a competing appropriation of sources (as discussed in Chapter 3), and the more definite one of opposing analyses of man.

Bultmann's own relationship to Heidegger, as reconstructable from the letters and memoirs of both men, had a warm but intellectually ambivalent quality. In its foreground stood their shared work at the Marburg Faculty, often as a joint front against dominant trends,[62] and their constructive joint reading of Christian sources. From 1924 until Heidegger's call to Freiburg in 1928, Heidegger and Bultmann read the Gospel of John together most Saturday afternoons with profit and enjoyment, and throughout that time, Heidegger persistently encouraged Bultmann's efforts to finish his great commentary on the book.[63] Methodologically, they shared the conviction, expressed by Bultmann to Barth in 1925, that Bultmann's task was 'to show the relation or identity of historical (exegetical) and systematic theology…and so also the identity of *critical* exegesis and systematic theology'.[64] But while Bultmann regarded this task as one inflection or aspect of a theological project also comprising a philosophical side, Heidegger saw it as an independent undertaking, dismissing Bultmann's involvement in dialectical theology almost entirely. When Erik Peterson's searing critique of Barth and Bultmann, 'What is Theology?', appeared in 1925, Bultmann wrote to Barth that he would draft a response and also try to 'mobilize Heidegger', in order to 'place phenomenology in the right spot' in the debate.[65] But Heidegger declined to get involved, and Bultmann was reduced to emphasizing in sending the galleys of

---

[62] See e.g. their exchanges between 13 and 29 March 1927; in Bultmann and Heidegger, *Briefwechsel*, 5–26.

[63] Bultmann first mentioned the joint reading to Gogarten on 19 October 1924; Bultmann and Gogarten, *Briefwechsel*, 62. Encouragement by Heidegger is found in nearly every letter he writes Bultmann during this time. Bultmann's commentary finally appeared in 1941 as *Das Evangelium des Johannes*, Meyer's Kritisch-Exegetischer Kommentar (KEK) 2 (Göttingen: Vandenhoeck & Ruprecht, 21st edn., 1986).

[64] Bultmann to Barth, 3 February 1925; in Barth and Bultmann, *Briefwechsel*, 44–5.

[65] Bultmann to Barth, 19 July 1925; in Erik Peterson, *Theologie und Theologen: Briefwechsel mit Karl Barth u.a., Reflexionen und Erinnerungen*, ed. Barbara Nichtweiß (Würzburg: Echter, 2009), 222.

his riposte to Gogarten that they had at least been 'looked through by Heidegger.'[66]

By 1927, Heidegger made his preferences more vocal, writing to Bultmann that 'your commentary must push theology back into concrete problems and make clear that something like "dialectical theology" is a mere spectre.'[67] Dismissing Barth as a 'lightweight' without enough sense even to grasp the philosophical issues at stake,[68] he expected Bultmann's agreement in describing their work as clearly segregated:

> We can only get things moving if we work radically from the most extreme positions. You from the theological side, positively-ontically..., I from the philosophical side, ontologically-critically—where the ontic in the sense of the positivity of the Christian [position] remains unthematic and question-marked.[69]

Bultmann responded evasively, and continued to try to draw Heidegger into his wider theological interests, an attempt culminating in his nomination of Heidegger as philosophy editor for *Theologische Rundschau*, a theological journal Bultmann was involved in re-launching in 1928. Heidegger declined with a renewed emphasis on the separation of theology and philosophy: 'The more I think about these things...the more it seems to me that all explicit philosophical discussion ought to disappear from theology, and all power of thought be redirected to a historical engagement with the NT, "historical" in an essential sense.' 'Your intended article about the study of the Fathers', he continued nudgingly, 'is incomparably more important than a throng of articles about Herrmann's theology and that kind of thing.'[70]

---

[66] Bultmann to Gogarten, 21 November 1925; in Bultmann and Gogarten, *Briefwechsel*, 96. Peterson's essay appeared in pamphlet form as 'Was ist Theologie?' (Bonn: Cohen, 1925) (rpt. in Peterson, *Theologische Traktate* (Würzburg: Echter, 1994 (1951), 1–22)). Bultmann's response appeared as 'Die Frage der "dialektischen" Theologie: Eine Auseinandersetzung mit Peterson' in *Zwischen den Zeiten* 4 (1926), 40–59.

[67] Letter dated 14 March 1927; in Bultmann and Heidegger, *Briefwechsel*, 19–22; p. 22.

[68] 'Für die schwelenden Probleme ist Barth sogar ein zu leicht wiegender Gegner—so leicht, daß er auf Grund [Krügers] Aufsatzes nicht einmal merken wird, worauf es ankommt'; letter dated 29 March 1927; in Bultmann and Heidegger, *Briefwechsel*, 24–6; p. 25. The essay in question is by Gerhard Krüger, a student of Heidegger. It was sent in advance copy to Heidegger and published the same year as 'Dialektische Methode und theologische Exegese: Logische Bemerkungen zu Barth's "Römerbrief"', in *Zwischen den Zeiten* 5 (1927), 116–57.

[69] Heidegger to Bultmann, 29 March 1927; in Bultmann and Heidegger, *Briefwechsel*, 24–6; p. 25.

[70] Heidegger to Bultmann, 9 April 1929; in Bultmann and Heidegger, *Briefwechsel*, 105–11; p. 108.

The fact that Heidegger is nevertheless listed as an editor of *Theologische Rundschau* on volumes 1 to 15 (1929–43) is a result partly of accident and partly of Bultmann's tenaciousness, but not one of Heidegger's practical involvement. Bultmann had already sent the first volume to print with Heidegger's name on the title page when Heidegger's negative answer came, and thought that it would be 'fatal' after that to be forced to strike it from the second volume. He attempted to persuade Heidegger to collaborate after all, arguing that his negative appraisal of theology in 'Phenomenology and Theology' did not, after all, impair his ability to be an expert adviser, and that he need not do more than contribute a few articles, something which, Bultmann prodded, Heidegger was 'keeping in view anyway'. But in effect, Heidegger never contributed to the journal.[71]

Bultmann's own appropriation of Heidegger appears somewhat naïve, perhaps even ironic, in the light of the present study. His positive experience of concrete joint work, it would seem, eclipsed the tension between their fundamental assumptions in favour of an admiring emphasis on shared methods and findings—so much so that Heidegger's eventual, systematic analysis of Dasein claimed Bultmann's allegiance more fully than his erstwhile theological colleagues. Bultmann steadfastly defended this association:

> For [Heidegger], the chief characteristic of man's Being in history is anxiety. Man exists in a permanent tension between the past and the future. At every moment he is confronted with an alternative. Either he must immerse himself in the concrete world of nature, and thus inevitably lose his individuality, or he must abandon all security and commit himself unreservedly to the future, and thus alone achieve his authentic Being. Is not that exactly the New Testament understanding of human life? Some critics have objected that I am borrowing Heidegger's categories and forcing them upon the New Testament. I am afraid this only shows that they are blinding their eyes to the real problem. I mean, one should rather be startled that philosophy is saying the same thing as the New Testament, and saying it quite independently.[72]

[71] See Heidegger to Bultmann, 23 October 1928 (in Bultmann and Heidegger, *Briefwechsel*, 62–9; pp. 62–4), Bultmann to Heidegger, 29 October 1928 (in Bultmann and Heidegger, *Briefwechsel*, 69–78; p. 70), and Heidegger to Bultmann, 9 April 1929 (in Bultmann and Heidegger, *Briefwechsel*, 105–11; p. 108).
[72] Rudolf Bultmann, 'Neues Testament und Mythologie', in Hans-Werner Bartsch (ed.), *Kerygma und Mythos*, i: *Ein theologisches Gespräch* (Hamburg: Reich & Heidrich, 1948), 15–53; translation taken from Bartsch (ed.), *Kerygma and Myth*, trans. Reginald Fuller (New York: Harper, 1961), 24–5.

It should be relatively uncontroversial, with hindsight and particularly in the context of the present study, to say that the line of influence is close to the reverse of this sketch: rather than Bultmann borrowing Heidegger's independently derived categories to illuminate the New Testament, Heidegger derived his own categories partly from a phenomenological reduction of New Testament experience ('reduction' not in the technical sense in which Husserl used the term, but in that dictated by the *lex parsimoniae*). Although Heidegger later presents his work of the late 1910s and early 1920s as one of uncovering the existential structures which made the religious experiences of the early Christian community—as well as myriad other religious and non-religious experiences—possible, I hope to have shown that this is a *post hoc* interpretation from the perspective of an already developed distinction between ontic and ontological sciences. In its initial stages, Heidegger's work on aboriginal Christian experience was the reason, not merely a laboratory, for his characteristic development of the phenomenological method. Bultmann's own reception of Heidegger requires re-evaluation in that light, though this is not a task I propose to undertake here.

The other theologians associated with dialectical theology responded to Heidegger much more critically. Karl Barth, keenly aware of the fundamental difference between Heidegger's anthropocentric and his own theocentric approaches, was careful to frame that difference not as a competition but as evidence that philosophy and theology operated on different paradigms with little mutual input. Unwilling to be pulled into a discussion he saw neither as his calling nor as his strength, he kept his distance from Heidegger from the beginning.[73] In July 1927, Barth declined Bultmann's invitation to a weekend in Marburg to meet Heidegger and attend his lecture on 'history and time' with mock self-irony: 'As a lumbering Swiss, I'm not so quick off the mark [alt.: quick with concepts] that I could grasp fast enough what Heidegger, whom I don't even know, wants' to be a useful discussion partner.[74] Bultmann urged that the belatedness of Barth's acquaintance

---

[73] 'Die Philosophie ist meine schwache (und variable!) Seite, [und ich möchte mich i]n das Handgemenge der Philosophen untereinander...grundsätzlich eigentlich *gar nicht* stürzen, 1. weil ich nicht das Zeug dazu habe, 2. weil es nicht meines Amtes ist, 3. weil mir nichts ungemütlicher wäre als das Bewußtsein, mit meiner Theologie zu stehen und zu fallen mit einer *bestimmten* Philosophie'; Barth to Brunner, 13 March 1925; in Barth and Brunner, *Briefwechsel*, 114–18; pp. 114–15.

[74] Barth to Bultmann, 15 July 1927; in Bultmann and Barth, *Briefwechsel*, 36. See also Bultmann to Barth, 4 July 1927; in Bultmann and Barth, *Briefwechsel*, 35–6.

with Heidegger made its 'necessity' all the 'more urgent', but Barth did not come.[75] Repeated invitations to lecture in Marburg were similarly persistently declined. 'Marburg is rampant with puristic adherence to Bultmann and Heidegger', Barth commentated spikily to Thurneysen. 'They keep wanting to lure me there to lecture, and I keep refusing with the explanation that I don't want anything to do with people who know it all [lit.: who've eaten the truth].'[76] In 1930, Bultmann organized a symposium on natural theology to bring together Barth, Gogarten, and Heidegger, but Barth cancelled on short notice. Bultmann, deeply disappointed, assumed that this was due to Barth's 'persistent refusal to engage with Heidegger',[77] and Barth himself confirmed his speculation by writing to Bultmann the following year that he regarded his adherence to Heidegger as a return to the 'slave house of Egypt'.[78]

Bultmann's attempts to bring together Heidegger and Gogarten were only marginally more successful. In December 1923, Bultmann wrote eagerly to Gogarten that a visit to Marburg would be most welcome, not least because it seemed 'important' that he meet Heidegger, 'who is familiar with your work and, as far as I can see, close to you'.[79] Gogarten seems not to have come;[80] a renewed invitation for winter 1924 met with similar polite refusals.[81] Bultmann's hope for reciprocal sympathy nevertheless continued through 1927, when he hastened to recommend to Gogarten upon publication of *Sein und Zeit* that he volunteer to review the book for their journal *Zwischen den*

---

[75] Bultmann to Barth, 18 July 1927; in Bultmann and Barth, *Briefwechsel*, 36–7.

[76] Barth to Thurneysen, 12 March 1928; in Barth and Thurneysen, *Briefwechsel II*, 562–67; p. 565.

[77] Letter to Ernst Fuchs, dated 17 November 1930; in Bultmann and Gogarten, *Briefwechsel*, 183–4 n. 11. See also Bultmann's exchange on the subject with Barth; Barth and Bultmann, *Briefwechsel*, 102–18. (Gogarten's cancellation had resulted from a confusion of dates and a consequent double-booking.)

[78] Barth to Bultmann, 27 May 1931; in Barth and Bultmann, *Briefwechsel*, 114–18; p. 117. The occasion is Bultmann's newly published 'Die Geschichtlichkeit des Daseins und der Glaube: Antwort an Gerhardt Kuhlmann', *Zeitschrift für Theologie und Kirche* 11 (1930), 229–64. Barth repeats his accusation in a letter of 20 June 1931; in Barth and Bultmann, *Briefwechsel*, 122–7; p. 127.

[79] Bultmann to Gogarten, 22 December 1923; in Bultmann and Gogarten, *Briefwechsel*, 54–6; p. 56.

[80] See Bultmann to Gogarten, 16 March 1924; in Bultmann and Gogarten, *Briefwechsel*, 56–7; p. 56.

[81] See Bultmann to Gogarten, 19 October 1924, and Gogarten to Bultmann, 3 November 1924; in Bultmann and Gogarten, *Briefwechsel*, 58–63 (p. 63) and 63–6 (p. 64).

Zeiten—partly to avoid a review by Heinrich Barth.[82] But Gogarten did not respond to the request, and the review eventually published was, after all, by Karl Barth's eager brother.[83] A meeting between Gogarten and Heidegger did take place in 1927 at the first of a series of symposia of (later so-called) 'Old Marburgians', but generated no warmth. The further symposium in 1930 to which Barth, too, had been unsuccessfully invited met with a short-notice cancellation by Gogarten, who had apparently confused the dates and double-booked the weekend.[84]

Emil Brunner engaged Heidegger more actively and directly. Unlike Barth, he accepted an invitation to lecture to the Marburg Theology Faculty in January 1925, choosing as his subject an attempt to ground theology in a natural perception of divine law, which reduces man to a nothingness from which he can only be raised by God's revelation in the form of forgiveness.[85] Heidegger sharply criticized the lecture, and a lengthy exchange of opinions among Brunner, Barth, Bultmann, and Gogarten followed. Bultmann immediately reported to Barth that 'Brunner spoke here yesterday... Very weak, almost embarrassing. Horribly battered by Heidegger.'[86] Brunner, in turn, complained to Barth that phenomenology and a turn to metaphysics had taken over Marburg. Wondering why Bultmann had 'behaved so uncompanionably', he hastened to warn that these views were 'not neutral ground, but enemy territory', attempting, just like 'Catholic-mystical' thinking, to 'turn into knowledge and vision what

[82] See Bultmann to Gogarten, 15 May 1927; in Bultmann and Gogarten, *Briefwechsel*, 108.
[83] 'Ontologie und Idealismus: Eine Auseinandersetzung von Heinrich Barth mit Martin Heidegger', *Zwischen den Zeiten* 7 (1929), 511–40.
[84] See Bultmann to Ernst Fuchs, 17 November 1930; in Bultmann and Gogarten, *Briefwechsel*, 183–4, n. 11.
[85] The lecture, held on 23 January 1925, was subsequently published with corrections as 'Gesetz und Offenbarung: Eine theologische Grundlegung', *Theologische Blätter* 4 (1925), cols. 53–8.
[86] Bultmann to Barth, 24 January 1925; in Barth and Bultmann, *Briefwechsel*, 40. To Gogarten, he similarly wrote on 10 March: '[Ä]rgerlich war das Auftreten Brunners, der die ganze Sache wirklich blamierte. Nachdem Heidegger und Tillich ihn scharf kritisiert hatten, sprang Bornhäuser für ihn ein!'; see Bultmann and Gogarten, *Briefwechsel*, 71–4; p. 73.
[87] 'Phänomenologie und Wendung zur Metaphysik... [sind] aus der katholisch-mystischen Vetterschaft. Es ist die alte Geschichte, daß man zum Wissen und Schauen machen will, was des Glaubens ist. Das ist für uns nicht neutraler Boden, sondern Feindesland'; Brunner to Barth, 10 March 1925; in Barth and Brunner, *Briefwechsel*, 107–13; pp. 109–10. Brunner had reported immediately after the lecture: 'In [Marburg] ging's mir... schlecht. Ich war so ermüdet, daß ich darauf verzichten mußte, den etwas pöbelhaften Anrempelungen Heideggers... zu begegnen. So schwieg ich und verlor

only belongs to faith'.[87] Barth countered that Brunner's own attempt at a quasi-Kantian foundation (*Grundlegung*) of theology, however radically theocentric, made him vulnerable to attack:

> The truly and effectively recognized law[, because it cannot be perceived outside revelation,] stands in indissoluble correlation with the gospel and vice versa. You say so yourself. But if this is so, then any 'theological groundwork' will be flimsy, inasmuch as it has to operate with a concept of law seemingly in common to theology and philosophy. Philosophy *as such* may be capable of 'noticing' something of the 'law' in its theological sense, but not of *saying* anything about it—and that's what would count.[88]

Echoed by Heidegger's own contention that 'philosophical questioning strictly "knows" nothing of sin',[89] Barth's position was, ironically, closer to that of Heidegger than was that of Brunner. Indeed, Heidegger himself encouraged Barth's and Thurneysen's insistence on a thoroughly *theo*logical rather than any philosophical grounding of theology: in 1923, he recalled Thurneysen to theology's task of calling to faith in faith.[90] In 1927, he approved the acceptance of that task by noting, in *Being and Time*, that theology was 'slowly beginning once more to understand Luther's insight that its dogmatic system rests on a "foundation" that is not rooted in... faithful [alt.: believing] questioning, and whose concepts therefore are not merely inadequate to theology's field of problems, but obscure and distort it'.[91]

---

damit die Schlacht. Ich war an diesem Ausgang insofern nicht ganz unschuldig, als ich viel zu viel in meinen Vortrag hatte hineinpacken wollen und so meine Formulierungen viel zu ungeschützt herauskamen. Etwas erstaunt hat mich, daß Bultmann nichts sagte'; Brunner to Bart, 28 January 1925; in Barth and Brunner, *Briefwechsel*, 105–7; p. 106.

[88] Barth to Brunner, 13 March 1925; in Barth and Brunner, *Briefwechsel*, 114–18; p. 116.

[89] *SZ* § 62, 306 n. 1.

[90] Recalled twice by Heidegger's student Hans-Georg Gadamer: in *Philosophische Lehrjahre*, 37, and in 'Marburger Theologie', 29. Gadamer rightly notes the ambivalence of the question: in 1977, he remembers Heidegger's 'wuchtiger Diskussionsbeitrag, der die radikalen Selbstzweifel Franz Overbecks beschwor und die Theologie—war es ihre Zurückweisung, war es ihre Bestätigung?—zu ihrer Aufgabe rief, das Wort zu finden, das es vermöchte, zum Glauben zu rufen und im Glauben zu bewahren'. In 1964, reporting the same response, he notes: 'Ein echter Heidegger-Satz, voll von Zweideutigkeit.'Thurneysen commented to Barth about the occasion that Heidegger had been generally approving of Thurneysen's lecture, but had questioned 'our relation to Kant, whom he counts with Aristotle, and whom the young Luther renounced'; Thurneysen to Barth, 21 February 1924; in Barth and Thurneysen, *Briefwechsel II*, 229. Thurneysen's lecture was published as 'Schrift und Offenbarung', *Zwischen den Zeiten* 6 (1924), 3–30.

[91] *SZ* § 3, p. 10 (emphasis removed).

Yet Heidegger's approval only exacerbated the disagreement between Brunner and Barth by posing an implicit challenge. For in separating theology and philosophy, the philosopher assigned to the task of theology a decidedly inferior role. Although he allowed, in *Being and Time*, that the Christian experience of sin, for example, 'has its own testimony, which is fundamentally inaccessible to any philosophical experience',[92] he also emphasized that 'faith and "world-view," provided they wish to make any claims to *conceptual* understanding in talking about [man's sinfulness], will have to take recourse to the existential structures we have uncovered'.[93] The second comment threatens to obviate the first, as Heidegger himself noted in a footnote: 'Strictly speaking, one cannot even say whether the ontology of Dasein *in itself* leaves open the possibility [of sin], inasmuch as philosophical questioning strictly "knows" nothing of sin'.[94]

PHILOSOPHY CONTRA THEOLOGY

'Phenomenology and Theology' (1927)

These methodological disagreements are expressed in Heidegger's now famous lecture 'Phenomenology and Theology', invited in 1927 by the Lutheran-Theological Faculty in Tübingen, and repeated a year later at the Lutheran-Theological Faculty in Marburg. Karl Heim, who was at the time Professor of Systematic Theology in Tübingen, was keenly interested in the relationship between Lutheran theology, philosophy, and science.[95] He was in the process of publishing a volume entitled *Religion and Modern Intellectual Life* (1927), and was in the first stages of preparing his *magnum opus*, *The Protestant Faith and Contemporary Thought* (1931–51). It must be assumed that it was Heim who invited Heidegger to speak on the question of how to make phenomenology

---

[92] *SZ* § 62, 306.   [93] *SZ* § 38, 180.   [94] *SZ* § 62, 306 n. 1.
[95] Heim's qualifying thesis, entitled *Das Weltbild der Zukunft. Eine Auseinandersetzung zwischen Philosophie, Naturwissenschaft und Theologie* (1907), set the tone for a very productive, if always controversial, thirty-year theological career which consistently engaged both contemporary philosophy and contemporary science in thinking through both the epistemological and the substantial foundations of faith.

fruitful for theology.[96] Why Heidegger accepted the invitation cannot be determined from the sources that survive.

The lecture, as already discussed, draws a critical distinction between ontic sciences—and these include theology—which assume the 'being' of their subjects as one of the premises of their work, and the single ontological science (philosophy) which deals with Being itself. The first guiding thesis of the lecture, accordingly, is that 'theology is a positive science and consequently as such absolutely different from philosophy.'[97] The second guiding thesis is that theology is entirely autonomous from all other ontic sciences, deriving its subject, sources, and norms not from any other science but solely from faith: 'All theological knowledge, insofar as it pertains correctly to its subject, is grounded in faith itself—it springs from faith and back into faith.'[98] Theology, in other words, is strictly secondary to faith; it cannot explain or ground faith, but only remind the faithful of the 'seriousness' of their faith by 'mak[ing it] more difficult'—a risky role, whose usefulness can never be taken for granted.[99]

Philosophy (or, more properly, phenomenology) can be helpful for theology only because it is not an ontic science, and therefore does not proffer competing material, sources, and norms. Rather, its characteristic *exitus* and *reditus* from and to 'factic life experience'[100] is merely an ontologically more basic traversal of theology's *exitus* and *reditus* from and to faith. Although faith 'overcomes' pre-Christian existence on an ontic or existentiell level, it always remains *ontologically* determined by a 'pre-Christian and therefore purely rationally graspable content.'[101] Philosophy (that is, phenomenology/ontology), consequently, functions simply as 'a formally indicative, ontological corrective to the ontic, i.e. pre-Christian content of basic theological concepts.'[102] It saves theology from pre-critically assimilating content from non-theological ontic sciences, and instead clarifies these concepts by reference to the 'understanding of being which human existence as such bears of itself, insofar as it exists at all.'[103] Philosophy itself is entirely independent of this role: it functions in its own sphere with no reference to faith or theology.[104]

---

[96] Compare Heidegger's letter to Elisabeth Blochmann dated 8 August 1928; Storck (ed.), *Heidegger/Blochmann*, 24–6; p. 24.

[97] GA 9, 49 (emphasis removed).

[98] GA 9, 61.

[99] GA 9, 56.

[100] GA 60, 9–14.

[101] GA 9, 63.

[102] GA 9, 64–5.

[103] GA 9, 63.

[104] GA 9, 66.

We will return to the substance of this claim in a moment. But first a biographical postscript. It is unclear why Heidegger accepted Heim's invitation to lecture on this subject. What is clear is that he had at least retrospective misgivings about having acceded to the request. As already noted, he wrote to Elisabeth Blochmann shortly after the Marburg reprise that the very remit of the lecture, namely to make philosophy fruitful for theology, put him 'as a philosopher in a terribly skewed light... and ma[de] the whole thing into an apology for Christian theology rather than', as it should be, 'a confrontation'.[105] It did not reflect his own commitments, but was merely meant to show '*how, given* that someone stands in the Christian Protestant faith and busies himself with theology, he ought to take philosophy, assuming that he wants it to be a help and not', as is really the case, 'a fundamental agitation'.[106] It was also not long after this experience that Heidegger wrote to his friend Bultmann that 'the more I think about these things... the more it seems to me that all explicit philosophical discussion ought to disappear from theology' in favour of concentrated textual and historical work.[107] The relationship between philosophy and theology, though abstractly explicable, was nevertheless practically deeply fraught.

'What is Metaphysics?' (1929)

The culmination of the eschatological trajectory in Heidegger's early thought is his sections on 'being-unto-death' in *Being and Time* (§§ 46–53)—the subject of Chapter 6—and his 1929 inaugural lecture at Freiburg, 'What is Metaphysics?' In that lecture, 'Being-there means: being immersed in Nothingness'.[108] Nothingness is revealed to Dasein in the experience of dread, in which the totality of that-which-is (*das Seiende im Ganzen*) 'slides' or 'slips away' from Dasein.[109] This experience, paradoxically described as 'the bright night of the Nothing of Angst',[110] is what first gives rise to 'the original openness of that which is as... something that *is*—i.e. is not nothing'.[111] By 'soliciting' or

---

[105] Letter dated 8 August 1928; Storck (ed.), *Heidegger/Blochmann*, 24–6; p. 24.
[106] Ibid., 26.
[107] Heidegger to Bultmann, 9 April 1929; in Bultmann and Heidegger, *Briefwechsel*, 105–11; p. 108.
[108] GA 9, 35.
[109] GA 9, 34.
[110] GA 9, 34.
[111] GA 9, 34.

'making tremble' that-which-is in its totality (to borrow a Derridean term[112]), the Nothing is 'the condition of possibility of the revealed-ness, to human Dasein, of that-which-is *as* being [*seiend*]'.[113] It is only by countenancing the 'solicitation' of the Nothing, and thus allowing itself to experience its own immersion into the Nothing, that Dasein 'transcends' that-which-is. But 'to transcend' (for Heidegger as for scholastic thought) means not only 'to surpass' but also 'to gather up': by acknowledging its own 'ownmost and deepest finitude',[114] Dasein also leads all other beings to themselves: 'Only in the Nothing of Dasein does that-which-is come to itself according to its ownmost possibility, i.e. in a finite way.'[115]

Christian eschatological practice as a conscious 'immersion into the night' both resembles and radically diverges from this vision. Christ unfailingly reiterates that because his listeners are chosen and called by God, dread or fear has become an inadequate gauge of their condition, and must give way to faith, hope, and love. As 'Sons of Light' and 'adopted children of God', their presence within the 'night' of corruption is a prophetic presence which identifies the darkness of the world precisely as *night*—a transient state in which the coming dawn is already implicit.[116] In this way, the vigilant faithful transcend and so 'gather up' all things—not merely in an acknowledgement of their finitude, but in a more radical acknowledgement that that fini-tude has itself been 'solicited' (here in the double sense of 'made to tremble' and 'demanded') by its Maker. In other words, they direct the world not to its own merely natural possibility, but to God's promise of renewed life, which the faithful grasp by 'partaking' of Christ in faith and hope:

> For the creation waits with eager longing for the revealing of the chil-dren of God; for the creation was subjected to futility...in hope that [it] will be set free from its bondage to decay and will obtain the freedom of the glory of the children of God.[117]

This reading of the biblical and liturgical texts, which also claims to be a reading of the phenomenological horizon of the believer, implicitly queries Heidegger's argument, in 'Phenomenology and Theology', that

---

[112] See for example Derrida, *Margins of Philosophy*, trans. Alan Bass (Brighton: Harvester, 1982), 18.
[113] GA 9, 35.   [114] GA 9, 38.   [115] GA 9, 40.
[116] Cf., for example, Ps. 57: 8; Ps. 130: 6; 1 Thess. 5: 6.
[117] Rom. 8: 18–22.   [118] See GA 9, 64.

phenomenology is logically prior to theology because it lays bare the existential structures of which specifically Christian experiences or concepts are only particular *existentiell* outworkings.[118] For what the believer asserts is precisely an ontological transformation of Dasein's relation to the Nothing or, put differently, an eschatological transformation of the Nothing itself through the divinely enabled 'transcendence' of man. Thus, Paul's First Letter to the Thessalonians does not instantiate but potentially subsumes Heidegger's interpretation of 'the night'. A fuller development of these thoughts must await the concluding chapter.

6

Death and Authenticity

Das Sein [zum Tode] läßt das Dasein verstehen, daß ihm als äußerste Möglichkeit der Existenz bevorsteht, sich selbst aufzugeben.[1]

—Martin Heidegger, *Sein und Zeit*

THE ESCHATOLOGICAL HORIZON OF *BEING AND TIME*

Heidegger's early eschatology without eschaton culminated in the account of being-unto-death in his magnum opus *Being and Time* (particularly §§ 39–40 and 46–53).[2]

The goal of *Being and Time* is a renewal of the question of the meaning of 'Being'[3]; and this means first of all the attempt not to answer a long-standing question but to find the right way of asking it. The ability to ask the question of Being, to Heidegger, has been stunted since after Plato and Aristotle by the uncritical assumption of a particular mode of being, namely 'presence' (Gk: παρουσία, Ger.: *Gegenwart* or *Vorhandensein*), as Being *per se*. This assumption, determinative of

---

[1] 'Being[-unto-death] lets Dasein understand that it faces, as its utmost existential possibility, the prospect of relinquishing itself.'

[2] *Sein und Zeit* (Tübingen: Max Niemeyer Verlag, 18th edn., 2001 (1927)). In-text and footnote citations are by section number followed by page number (e.g. *SZ* § 2, 6). All translations are my own.Both standard English translations—*Being and Time*, trans. John Macquarrie and Edward Robinson (London: SCM Press, 1962) and *Being and Time*, trans. Joan Stambaugh (New York: State University of New York Press, 1996)—reproduce the German pagination in the margins; therefore, no separate references to page numbers in an English translation are provided here.

[3] *SZ* prologue.

ontology from classical and medieval times even to the most influential philosophical projects of modernity, those of Descartes and Kant,
has made 'being' the most *general* term, neither requiring nor allowing any further definition.[4] Heidegger, instead, proposes to return to
Bonaventure's transcendental conception of being as illumination:

> Just as the eye, when it turns towards the manifold differences of the
> colours, does not see the light…, so the eye of the mind, when it
> turns towards beings in particular and in general, does not notice
> being itself,…even though it is only through being that it encounters
> everything.[5]

For Bonaventure as for Heidegger, a transcendental viewpoint, which
seeks the conditions of the possibility of all knowledge, does not discover a new entity, but asks after that which is no entity and yet makes
possible all intentionality—and this is Being itself.[6] For Heidegger,
consequently, Being cannot come into view directly at all, but only
indirectly through an analysis of the existential structure[7] of that being
'for whom its being is about that being'[8]: the human being or *Dasein*.
This analysis reveals at least two structures that are revelatory of Being
in a different way from that expected by the champion of 'presence',
Descartes: Human existence is always possibility, and it is always
being-in-a-world. Further, precisely in so far as it is temporal and relational, it is also inherently 'moral', i.e. susceptible to evaluation of the
success or failure of those relations and that development.

Also noteworthy is that if these things are true of human existence,
they also determine the dimensions that a formally accurate *description*
of that existence must have: Any attempt to describe human existence
statically, in isolation, or in a form repudiative of evaluative language

---

[4] Edith Stein's 'Martin Heideggers Existenzphilosophie' (1937), to which the preceding sentences are indebted, remains one of the most succinct synopses of *Being
and Time*. See 'Anhang: Martin Heideggers Existenzphilosophie', in Stein, *Endliches
und ewiges Sein. Versuch eines Aufstiegs zum Sinn des Seins*, ed. Andreas Uwe Müller
(Freiburg: Herder, 2006), being volume 11/12 of the Edith Stein Gesamtausgabe, gen.
ed. Hanna-Barbara Gerl-Falkovitz (Freiburg: Herder, 2000–), 445–99. [Hereafter cited
as ESGA 11/12.]

[5] Bonaventure, as quoted by Heidegger's teacher Carl Braig in his *Vom Sein*, 5–6
(no reference to the original given). Heidegger emphasizes Braig's influence on him
in GA 14, 82; see also the present Chapter 1 and (more thoroughly) Schaber, 'Der
Theologiestudent Martin Heidegger'.

[6] Cf. Schaeffler, *Frömmigkeit des Denkens*, 6–8.

[7] *SZ* § 9, 44.

[8] *SZ* § 9, 42.

already falls short of its object. What follows will make clear why this is an *eschatological* existence, requiring (and receiving in *Being and Time*) an eschatological analysis.[9]

DEATH AND POSSIBILITY

At its simplest, Heidegger's account of human existence in *Being and Time* is 'eschatological' because it envisions the possibility of authentic existence as dependent on a certain (existential) relation to one's future.

Because existence, in Heidegger's phenomenological analysis, constitutes essence, the 'essence' or identity of each person remains continually dependent on a future that she can neither fully know nor fully control.[10] 'If the being of Dasein is determined by existence, and its essence is constituted partly by its capability [lit.: possibility] of being, then Dasein must, as long as it exists... *not yet be* something.'[11] Heidegger develops this insight in two helical revolutions in Parts I and II of *Being and Time*.

Part I's interpretation of Dasein's constitutive 'not yet' begins from a formalization of the fact that how Dasein is to be the next moment, and whether it is to be the next moment, are never simple givens for it: Dasein always faces its future first and foremost as a range of possibilities, only some of which are under its control. In his 'existential analytic',[12] Heidegger is less interested in the *particular* choices a Dasein will make, events it will experience, and changes it will undergo in the future, than in the *fact* of these possibilities as a permanent structural constituent of human existence. Dasein, he specifies, is

---

[9] The first (and so far, to my knowledge, only) reading of *Being and Time* as an eschatological text was offered in Hans Urs von Balthasar's *Apokalypse der deutschen Seele*, iii: *Die Vergöttlichung des Todes* (Leipzig: Anton Pustet, 1939). This monumental three-volume work, ranging from German Idealism to Nietzsche, Heidegger, and finally Karl Barth, deserves a study of its own. Its premises, perspectives, and questions, however, are too specific and self-contained to permit a meaningful engagement within the present context.

[10] See *SZ* § 9, 42; § 45, 233.

[11] *SZ* § 45, 233.

[12] *SZ* § 4, 13.

not an independently existing thing which, in addition to existing, has possibilities—'it *is* first and foremost possibility'.[13]

'Possibility', here, must be interpreted not as a deficient form of reality ('something not yet real and never inevitable'), but as a wholly different mode of being: Dasein's 'possibility of being never remains outstanding as something not yet present, but...rather *is* with the being of Dasein (*viz*, existence) *as* essentially never present'.[14] Or, put differently: 'The being for whom its Being is about that Being engages with its Being as its ownmost possibility. Each Dasein *is* its possibility and does not merely "have" it, as if that possibility were an attribute of an [independently] existing thing'.[15] Possibility, then, is an 'existentiale'—in fact, 'the aboriginal and final positive ontological determination of Dasein'.[16]

But this understanding of possibility as a unique mode of being rather than a deficient form of reality, which pervades Part I of *Being and Time*, can be criticized on Heidegger's own terms as a 'spatialization' of Dasein's being-as-possibility. Because Dasein *is* its possibility (in the present) rather than relating to any particular possibility (in the future), no particular choice or event actually matters for its essence: Dasein always already is what it is, in the mode of possibility.

> [Although] Dasein is always 'more' than it actually is, if one would and could draw up its ontological inventory as something-at-hand, [it] is never more than it factically is, because capability [lit.: possibility] of being belongs by nature to its facticity. Neither, however, is Dasein as being-possible ever anything less, for that which, in its capability of being, it *is not yet*, it [nevertheless] *is* existentially.[17]

In thus 'spatializing' possibility, Part I retains, despite its explicit commitment to a phenomenological method, characteristics of a *philosophia perennis*: a philosophy arrogating to itself a God's-eye view from outside factic experience. As such it seems, in part, merely another security (*Sicherung*) against temporality—a tendency Heidegger rejected in favour of an authentic eschatological attitude in *Introduction to the Phenomenology of Religion*.[18]

---

[13] *SZ* § 31, 143. Heidegger goes on to specify the senses of 'possibility' as applied to *Vorhandenes* and Dasein: 'Als modale Kategorie der Vorhandenheit bedeutet Möglichkeit das *noch nicht* Wirkliche und das *nicht jemals* Notwendige. Sie charakterisiert das *nur* Mögliche. Sie ist ontologisch niedriger als Wirklichkeit und Notwendigkeit. Die Möglichkeit als Existenzial dagegen ist die ursprünglichste und letzte positive ontologische Bestimmtheit des Daseins'; *SZ* §31, 143–4.

[14] *SZ* § 9, 42.　　[15] *SZ* § 31, 144.　　[16] *SZ* § 31, 144　　[17] *SZ* § 31, 145.

[18] See GA 60, 38–54.

But this distortion is not a shortcoming, but a strategy. In Part II, Heidegger traverses the circle of Part I once more on a deeper level, revealing the eschatological perspective necessary for any proper understanding of human existence. By setting the entire subject matter of Part I against the horizon of death, Part II discloses the conditions for formulating the analysis of Part I: an existential acknowledgement that possibility is always futurity, and that that future's horizon is death. Only from such a position can Dasein authentically understand 'possibility', namely as something which (in Stanley Cavell's terminology) must be acknowledged, not known—which can only be 'possibility' when it is grasped rather than contemplated.[19]

Earlier, Heidegger had described possibility as that which, rather than 'not yet [being] real',[20] already '*is* with the being of Dasein *as* essentially never present'.[21] Now, he replaces the subject of this definition: 'Death is not something not-yet-present, not something outstanding until the last, but rather an imminence [*Bevorstand*].'[22] Death, as he follows up more explicitly, is Dasein's last and 'un-overtakable possibility'.[23] Like all possibility, it must therefore be understood as an existentiale:

> Just as Dasein always *is*, as long as it is, already its not-yet, so also it always *is* already its end. The ending meant by death is not the being-at-an-end of Dasein, but the *being-towards-the-end* of this being. Death is a way of being which Dasein assumes as soon as it is.[24]

But death, as the horizon of possibility as futurity, is also its negation. 'As long as Dasein *is* as a being', Heidegger summarizes starkly, 'it never attains its "fullness". And once it attains it, this attainment turns into the loss of being-in-the-world *per se*.'[25] Put in the constitutive ter-

---

[19] See Heidegger's important gloss on his oft-quoted statement that 'possibility is higher than reality': 'Höher als die Wirklichkeit steht die *Möglichkeit*. Das Verständnis der Phänomenologie liegt einzig im Ergreifen ihrer als Möglichkeit'; *SZ* § 7, 38 (emphasis added). Cavell's distinction between knowledge and acknowledgement is first developed in his 'Knowing and Acknowledging', in S. Cavell, *Must We Mean What We Say?* (Cambridge: Cambridge University Press, 1969), 238–66.

[20] *SZ* § 31, 143.

[21] *SZ* § 31, 144.

[22] *SZ* § 50, 250 (underlining added).

[23] *SZ* § 50, 250.

[24] *SZ* § 48, 245.

[25] *SZ* § 46, 236.

minology of possibility, Dasein's last and 'un-overtakable possibility' is that of 'no-longer-being-able-to-exist', the 'impossibility of existing'.[26]

This 'possible impossibility' demands a reformation of one's ordinary understanding of 'possibility'—a reformation which, for Heidegger, must become paradigmatic for *all* possibility. In ordinary experience, possibility tends to be understood 'teleologically', that is, by reference to its realizable content. Dasein, as Heidegger puts it, looks to the possible 'not in terms of its possibility *qua* possibility, but in such a way that it circumspectly looks *away* from the possible to the possibility-of-*what*'.[27] But death cannot be treated this way. 'Death as possibility gives Dasein nothing that it can "realize," nothing that it could, if it were real, itself *be*.'[28] Any attempt to 'realize' the possibility of death (e.g. by suicide) would merely 'dissolve the ground of Dasein's existent being-unto-death'.[29]

Rather, death must be understood as 'pure' possibility: 'Being-unto-death…, if it wants to disclose the described possibility *as such*, must robustly understand, develop and *bear* this possibility *as possibility*.'[30] In other words, Dasein must engage with death in and through its being-in-the-world; Heidegger calls the appropriate attitude the 'anticipation of' or 'running-forward to' the possibility of death.[31]

BEING-IN-THE-WORLD: THE DREAD OF HOMELESSNESS

The eschatology of Part II is a reframing not only of the programmatic statement that Dasein 'engages with its being as its ownmost possibility', i.e. '*is* its possibility',[32] but also of the other programmatic

---

[26] *SZ* § 50, 250.
[27] *SZ* § 53, 261.
[28] *SZ* § 53, 262.
[29] *SZ* § 53, 261.
[30] *SZ* § 53, 261.
[31] *SZ* § 53, 262. A fuller analysis of Heidegger's (existential) concept of *Vorlauf* in its indebtedness to Immanuel Kant's and Hermann Cohen's (epistemological) concepts of *Antizipation* exceeds the scope of this chapter. A full-scale critical analysis of 'anticipation' in Kant, Cohen, Husserl, Heidegger, and Bultmann is attempted in Lothar Kugelmann, *Antizipation: Eine begriffsgeschichtliche Untersuchung* (Göttingen: Vandenhoeck & Ruprecht, 1986), chs. 4–5.
[32] *SZ* § 9, 42.

statement that existence (*Dasein*) is always being-in-the-world (*In-der-Welt-Sein*).[33]

Early in *Being and Time*, Heidegger makes the guiding claim that 'Dasein [being-there] essentially includes being in a world. Dasein's understanding of Being is therefore equally originally an understanding of something like "world" and an understanding of the being of the beings that are accessible within the world.'[34] Dasein, in other words, always already is and knows itself as immersed in a world of *Zuhandenem* ('things that are to hand') and *Mit-Dasein* ('beings with whom it is there'). Rather than, like the (hypothetical) Cartesian *ego*, arguing its way from its own indisputable existence to the reliability of the appearance of the existence of others, the Heideggerian Dasein is shaped by and comes to know itself as among others.[35]

> Others do not come into view by first distinguishing the initially present proper subject from other existing subjects, i.e. in first looking at oneself and so determining the 'as opposed to' of a difference. Rather, they come into view from within the *world* in which care-determined Dasein essentially dwells.[36]

This existential structure of being-in-the-world is reflected in the fact that the general, in most respects, comes before the specific.[37] As Stephen Mulhall puts it, humans first find and understand themselves in socially defined and culturally inherited roles, which are defined prior to and independently of their own individuality. '[W]e relate to ourselves as practitioners—as followers of the rules, customs, and habits definitive of proper practice in any given field of endeavour. Such practices are necessarily interpersonal, and so importantly impersonal.'[38] When humans remain immersed in this 'impersonal' structure, Heidegger argues, their individuality is submerged by the crowd—the impersonal 'one' (Ger.: *man*) to which a mother or instructor appeals in initiating her ward into

---

[33] See *SZ* § 4, 13.

[34] *SZ* § 4, 13.

[35] See also §21 of *Being and Time* and § 6.b.γ of Heidegger's WS 1929/30 lecture series *Die Grundbegriffe der Metaphysik: Welt–Endlichkeit–Einsamkeit*, published under the same name as GA 29/30, ed. Friedrich-Wilhelm von Herrmann (Frankfurt: Klostermann, 3rd edn., 2004), esp. 30. For a fuller account of Heidegger *contra* Descartes, see Simon Glendinning, *On Being With Others: Heidegger–Wittgenstein–Derrida* (London: Routledge, 1998), esp. chapter 3.

[36] *SZ* § 26, 119.

[37] See esp. *SZ* § 47, 239.

[38] Mulhall, *Philosophical Myths of the Fall*, 53–4.

what 'one' does or doesn't do:[39] *Initially* there's not "I" not in the sense of a proper self, but the others in the form of the "crowd." From within this and as this, I "myself" am initially "given" to myself.[40]

But death radically reinterprets this 'essential dwelling' of Dasein in the world; indeed, to confront death is nothing other than a re-formation of that dwelling. Being-unto-death is not a theoretical or cerebral process,[41] but arises in and as a particular disposition to the world. Specifically, 'being-unto-death is by its nature *dread*.'[42] Dread, as a 'sympathetic antipathy',[43] is the only way of remaining before (*vor*) death: 'Dread of death is dread "of" [*vor*] one's ownmost, non-relational and unovertakable possibility of being.'[44] 'In it, Dasein is placed *before* [*vor*] the nothingness of the possible impossibility of its existence.'[45]

As Heidegger's play with the word *vor* suggests, dread expresses the paradox of being-unto-death. As a *Befindlichkeit*, it is by definition a way of being *in* the world, an attunement to the world.[46] (The deverbal *Befinden*, from which *Befindlichkeit* is coined, means both 'residing' or 'being situated in ...' and 'condition' or 'disposition'.[47]) But as dread *of* the world as such, it makes that world appear uncanny (lit.: 'not home-like'). If dread is paradigmatic, then this 'not-at-home-ness must existentially-ontologically be regarded as the ... original/originary phenomenon', and Dasein's ordinary, 'tranquil-familiar being-in-the-world', accordingly, as 'a mode of the uncanniness [lit.: not-at-home-ness] of Dasein, not vice versa'.[48] Dispersion in the world (i.e. fallenness) can now be defined as the 'avoidance of uncanniness, or, as we can now say, of one's ownmost being-unto-death'.[49] 'The

[39] See *SZ* § 27, 126.
[40] *SZ* § 27, 129. Edith Stein traces this Heideggerian idea back to Max Scheler; see 'Martin Heideggers Existenzphilosophie', ESGA 11/12, 466.
[41] Cf. Heidegger's disparagement of 'thinking about death': 'Solches Verhalten bedenkt die Möglichkeit, wann und wie sie sich wohl verwirklichen möchte. Dieses Grübeln über den Tod nimmt ihm zwar nicht völlig seinen Möglichkeitscharakter, er wird immer noch begrübelt als kommender, wohl aber schwächt es ihn ab durch ein berechnendes Verfügenwollen über den Tod'; *SZ* § 53, 261.
[42] *SZ* § 53, 266 (emphasis added).
[43] Kierkegaard, *Begrebet Angest*, ch. 1, § 5 (ET 41).
[44] *SZ* § 50, 251.
[45] *SZ* § 53, 266. Cf. *SZ* §29, 135.
[46] 'Attunement' is Stephen Mulhall's Cavellian translation of *Befindlichkeit*; see his *Heidegger and Being and Time*, 116.
[47] See Grimm, *Deutsches Wörterbuch*, vol. i, cols. 1259–62.
[48] *SZ* § 40, 189.
[49] *SZ* § 50, 252.

crowd' (in a typically ironic formulation) 'suppresses the courage to dread death'.[50]

But if death 'solicits' Dasein's being-in-the-world, Dasein's (ordinary) being-in-the-world is, at the same time, the necessary ground in which, though breaking through it, being-unto-death remains to grow.

> Death is the *ownmost* possibility of Dasein. Being-unto that possibility opens to Dasein its *ownmost* capability [lit.: possibility] of being, in which what is at stake is the being of Dasein as such. [Only t]hus can it become manifest to Dasein that in [this] distinguished possibility of itself, it is wrested from the crowd, i.e. can already wrest itself from the crowd in [the] anticipation [of death]. But only an understanding of this 'ability' first reveals [to Dasein] its factic lostness in the banality [alt.: everydayness] of the crowd-self.[51]

But it is precisely this 'wresting itself' from the crowd which constitutes authentic existence. Just as 'falling' (*Verfall*) is an 'ontological concept of movement',[52] so 'anticipation' (*Vorlaufen*) also is a concept of movement, an ever-renewed movement out of the crowd: Dasein, Heidegger had said earlier, 'can only fall [alt.: be corrupted] because it is concerned with an attuned and understanding being-in-the-world. Conversely, *authentic* existence does not hover above corrupt ordinariness, but is, existentially speaking, only a modified seizing of the latter.'[53] (As such, it is, to a large extent, hidden: 'authentic being[-unto-death must] in its meaning remain hidden from others'.[54])

Heidegger repeats this argument with specific reference to being-with further on. On one hand,

> Death claims [Dasein] *individually*. The non-relational character of death, grasped in anticipation, throws Dasein back on itself as individual [alt.: solitary]....It reveals that all Dasein's being-around-that-with-which-it-concerns-itself and all its being-with-others fails when the ownmost capability of being is at stake. Dasein can only *authentically* be *itself* when it enables itself from out of itself thus to be.[55]

On the other hand, this individuation is not a departure from being-with, but a mode of it:

[50] *SZ* § 51, 254 (italics omitted).
[51] *SZ* § 53, 263.
[52] *SZ* § 38, 180.
[53] *SZ* § 38, 179 (some italics omitted). Cf. Heidegger's gloss of this passage in *SZ* § 54, 267.
[54] *SZ* § 53, 260.
[55] *SZ* § 53, 263.

As essential structures of Dasein, [concern and solicitude] are part of the condition of the possibility of existence *per se*. Dasein is authentically itself only insofar as it projects itself *as* concerned being-around-...and solicitous being-with-...primarily on its ownmost capability of being, rather than on the possibilities of the crowd-self.[56]

Being-unto-death, as Heidegger puts it, 'recalls Dasein from its corruption and reveals to it authenticity and inauthenticity as possibilities of its being.'[57] But authenticity (*Eigentlichkeit*) as Dasein's grasping of itself is only possible as an ever-renewed *choice* or a *task*, and so is possible only on the enduring ground of Dasein's ordinary being-in-the-world.

BEING-UNTO-DEATH AND 'ORIGINAL SIN'

It is by now clear that *Being and Time* is 'eschatological' both in its vision and its dynamic. Human existence can only be understood in light of the 'last things', which reveal human existence as a *task*, a way of dwelling in the world as uncanny, as not-at-home.[58] Concomitantly, only from the eschatological viewpoint of Part II does *Verfall* come into view as more than merely a geometric indicator of Dasein's structure of possibility. Just as in Christian thought the *status corruptionis* is only discernible from beyond the eschatological sacrifice of Christ, so in *Being and Time*, Dasein's 'fall into' the world can only be understood as 'corrupt' or 'deviant' from the eschatological perspective of being-unto-death.

But the eschatological horizon of *Being and Time* is at once similar and radically different from its Christian counterpart. This is importantly signalled by the fact that not only Heidegger's term 'falling' or 'corruption' (*Verfall*) *but also* the positive term 'being-unto-death' are modelled on theological descriptions of original sin.[59] 'Being-unto-

---

[56] *SZ* § 53, 263.

[57] *SZ* § 40, 190–1.

[58] Compare e.g. 1 Thess. 5 and Heidegger's reading of it (discussed in Chapter 2); John 14–15.

[59] Although usually translated somewhat clumsily as 'falling', *Verfall* is simply a Germanization of the Latin *corruptio*, 'corruption'. As such, it references the Christian concept of the Fall both in appearance (*Verfall/Sündenfall*) and in meaning (cf. *status corruptionis*).

death' (*Sein zum Tode*) is coined in parallel to Kierkegaard's 'sickness-unto-death' (translated into German in 1911 as *Die Krankheit zum Tode*[60]). The alternative formulation 'anticipation of [lit.: running-forward towards] death' (*Vorlaufen zum Tode*) is an almost direct translation of Luther's *cursus ad mortem*.[61] But both theological terms describe the outworking of original sin. Can the provenance of the borrowing be accidental?

CORRUPTION AND GUILT

> Although we do not wish to call the life we live here a death, neverthe-less it surely is nothing else than a continuous journey toward death [*perpetuus cursus ad mortem*]. Just as a person infected with a plague has already started to die when the infection has begun, so—because of sin, and death, the punishment for sin—this life can no longer properly be called life after it has been infected by sin. Right from our mother's womb we begin to die.[62]

Heidegger's scepticism regarding the dogmatic framing of Luther's 'journey towards death' by ideas of sin and grace has already been dis-cussed in Chapter 3. It is repeated forcefully in his introduction of the concept *Verfall* in Part I of *Being and Time*. 'The name [*Verfall*], which does not express a negative valuation, means:...Dasein has always already fallen from itself as the possibility of authentically being itself, and fallen to the "world".'[63] This must be understood as a perma-nent structural constituent of human existence, not as 'a "fall" from a purer and higher "original state"'.[64] The postulation of such a Fall, he expounds, is philosophically empty, because Dasein, 'as existing, can

---

[60] Kierkegaard, *Die Krankheit zum Tode* (Jena: Diederichs, 1911), being volume viii of Kierkegaard, *Gesammelte Werke*, 12 vols., trans. H. Gottsched and C. Schrempf (Jena: Eugen Diederichs, 1909–22).

[61] 'Vorlaufen zum Tode' appears in *SZ* § 53, 263; § 62, 305.

[62] *In Genesin Enarrationum* (1535–8), WA 42, 146. ET: *Lectures on Genesis 1–5*, 196.

[63] *SZ* § 38, 175.

[64] *SZ* § 38, 176.

never go behind its being-thrown[-into-the-world].'[65] But philosophy is an 'analysis of existence which affixes the guiding line of philosophical questioning to the place whence it arises and whither it returns', namely that existence itself.[66] Consequently, it 'not only [does] not (ontically) have any experience of such a thing [as a primordial Fall]; [it] also do[es] not (ontologically) possess any possibilities or guidelines for interpreting it'.[67]

Heidegger therefore positions his analysis as ontologically prior to the Christian understanding of the Fall: 'This existential-ontological interpretation makes...no ontic statement about the "corruption of human nature," not because the necessary evidence is lacking, but because its set of problems occurs *before* any statement about depravity or undepravedness.'[68] 'Falling [or corruption] is an ontological movement-concept. Ontically, we are not deciding whether man "wallows in sin" (i.e. in the *status corruptionis*), walks in the *status integritatis*, or finds himself in an intermediary state, the *status gratiae*.'[69] Quite the reverse: 'faith and "world-view," in talking about Dasein as any of these and as being in the world, provided they wish to make any claims to *conceptual* understanding will have to take recourse to the existential structures we have uncovered'.[70]

However, on the deeper level of Part II, being-unto-death itself is an affirmation of 'sinfulness'. The path for this has been prepared by Heidegger's engagement with sin in the mid-1920s, resulting in his radical rejection of the horizon of grace in favour of a horizon of nothingness. This thought flows into Heidegger's analysis, in *Being and Time*, of the terms *Gewissen* (conscience) and *Schuld* (guilt/debt).

After his existential analysis of being-unto-death, Heidegger raises the question of the *existentiell* attainment of authenticity—the question not whether being-unto-death is theoretically but whether it is practically possible. For Heidegger as for Paul, this practical turn must be occasioned by the call of a voice already aware of the coming end, recalling the hearer from his or her entanglement in the world to anticipation and wakefulness. In 1 Thessalonians 5, Heidegger's source

[65] *SZ* § 58, 284.
[66] *SZ* § 7, 38 (emphasis omitted).
[67] *SZ* § 38, 176.
[68] *SZ* § 38, 179–80.
[69] *SZ* § 38, 180.
[70] *SZ* § 38, 180.

text in formulating his understanding of eschatological anticipation in 1921, Paul himself takes the role of that caller:

> Now concerning the times and the seasons [of Christ's return], brothers and sisters, you do not need to have anything written to you. For you yourselves know very well that the day of the Lord will come like a thief in the night. When they say, 'There is peace and security', then sudden destruction will come upon them, as labour pains come upon a pregnant woman, and there will be no escape! But you, beloved, are not in darkness, for that day to surprise you like a thief; for you are all children of light and children of the day; we are not of the night or of darkness. So then, let us not fall asleep as others do, but let us keep awake and sober. (1 Thess. 5: 1–5)

For Heidegger, the matter is more complicated. Because it is 'lost in the crowd', Dasein 'must be "shown" to itself in its own potential authenticity'; it 'requires testimony to its capability [lit.: possibility] of being itself, which, in potentiality, it already is'.[71] But because authenticity is Dasein's ownmost and non-relational possibility,[72] this testimony cannot be given by an external, but only by an internal voice: 'The call [cannot] come from another who is in the world with me. The call comes *from* me and yet *over* me'.[73] Heidegger finds an existentiell pointer to the possibility of such an inner voice in Dasein's ordinary understanding of conscience.[74] He now reinterprets this voice of conscience existentially as the internal, eschatological call of Dasein *as* already 'in the depth of its uncanniness'[75] to itself *as* still lost in the crowd.

The *Doppelgänger* imagery here is difficult but unignorable. Earlier, Heidegger had called death 'an imminence [*Bevorstand*]',[76] 'something *vis-à-vis* which Dasein *acts*'.[77] But the *vis-à-vis* of death, he had said, was not an other, but Dasein itself, facing itself as capable of authenticity: 'With death, Dasein stands before itself in its *ownmost* capability [lit.: possibility] of being'.[78] Dasein, as he will say further

---

[71] *SZ* § 54, 268.
[72] See e.g. *SZ* §50, 250–1.
[73] *SZ* § 57, 275.
[74] *SZ* § 54, 268.
[75] '…im Grunde seiner Unheimlichkeit sich befindend'; *SZ* § 57, 276. The nuances of the German (which obliquely draws Heidegger's key concepts *Grund* and *Befinden* into the analysis) are, as so often, lost in any English translation concerned (as it must be) with readability.
[76] *SZ* § 50, 250.
[77] *SZ* § 50, 250.
[78] *SZ* § 50, 250.

on, 'always comes towards itself'.[79] The voice of conscience is nothing other than a reification of this *Doppelgänger* imagery. As such, it offers a potent commentary on a literary motif. (One of the finest examples in this context is Charles Williams's *Descent into Hell*, whose female protagonist Pauline lives in perpetual dread of her *Doppelgänger*. Ultimately, this *Doppelgänger* turns out to be a possible but unrealized Pauline: a Pauline who has precisely faced her own dread. By personifying this possible Pauline, the *Doppelgänger* also becomes the means by which that possibility is realized—for once Pauline stops avoiding her dread of the *Doppelgänger* and faces the figure, the *Doppelgänger* disappears.[80]) However, it is notoriously unclear in what sense Heidegger regards this as a *practical* solution to the problem of the possibility of authenticity. Stephen Mulhall, in his introduction to *Being and Time*, consequently offers a Cavellian reading of the section, in which the 'friend' or 'mentor' replaces an internal conscience, as the only practically viable interpretation.[81] Simon Critchley, by contrast, criticizes Heidegger's 'autarkic' conception of conscience, and proposes its replacement by a (Freudian) conception of conscience as essentially relational.[82] We will return to this later.

Following the ordinary intuition that conscience speaks of guilt (*Schuld*),[83] Heidegger pursues his analysis of conscience through an

[79] *SZ* § 65, 325.
[80] *Descent into Hell* (London: Faber & Faber, 1937). Stanley Cavell finds a comparable *Doppelgänger* figure in *King Lear*'s Gloucester. See Cavell, 'The Avoidance of Love: A Reading of *King Lear*', in Cavell, *Disowning Knowledge: In Seven Plays of Shakespeare* (Cambridge: Cambridge University Press, 2nd expanded edn., 2003), 39–124; p. 79.
[81] See Mulhall, *Heidegger and Being and Time* (London: Routledge, 2nd edn., 2005), 143–5. Mulhall's interpretation is textually based on Heidegger's parenthetical comparison of the role of *Being and Time* to that of conscience in *SZ* § 60, 298. Stanley Cavell's Emersonian perfectionism can be read as following the interpretation that the philosopher *can*, to some extent, anticipate or fulfil the voice of conscience for another; see e.g. his *Conditions Handsome and Unhandsome: The Constitution of Emersonian Perfectionism* (Chicago: University of Chicago Press, 1990) and *Cities of Words: Pedagogical Letters on a Register of the Moral Life* (Cambridge, Mass.: Harvard University Press, 2004).
[82] See Critchley, 'Originary Inauthenticity—on Heidegger's *Sein und Zeit*', in Simon Critchley and Reiner Schürmann, *On Heidegger's Being and Time*, ed. Steven Levine (London: Routledge, 2008), 132–51; pp. 145–7.
[83] The translation of Heidegger's *Schuld* is notoriously difficult. Like the cognate Old English *scyld*, German *Schuld* acquired its theological (and by Heidegger's time dominant) meaning 'guilt' from its primary, economical meaning 'debt', and retains a strong etymological association with that root. English 'guilt' has no similar etymology, although it is sometimes falsely traced to the Old Teutonic root *geld-, gald-, guld-*, 'to pay' or 'yield'. See Grimm, *Deutsches Wörterbuch*, vol. xv, col. 1870, and John Simpson and Edmund Weiner (eds.), *The Oxford English Dictionary* (Oxford: Oxford University Press, 2nd edn., 1989), 'guilt'.

ontological analysis of guilt, i.e. one that reveals the existential ground of ordinary sensations and postulations of guilt: 'Being-guilty', is his guiding assumption, 'does not first result from having incurred guilt [alt.: an indebtedness]; on the contrary: this incurrence is only possible "on the basis of" an original/originary being-guilty'.[84] Such existential guilt cannot be understood as a 'lack' in the sense of 'the absence of a mandatory something'[85] any more than Dasein's perpetual 'unfinishedness' can be understood as a 'something yet outstanding'.[86] These senses of incompleteness accrue only to modes of being—being-to-hand or being-at-hand—that are not defined from out of themselves, but by reference to a pre-defined use or essence. Rather, Dasein's guilt, like its unfinishedness, is a distinguishing mark of Dasein's *existential* finitude.

As inescapably 'thrown into the world', Dasein is always 'in debt' for its existence: to parents and shaping influences too numerous and diffuse to count; to the world as a whole.

> Being [namely, existing], Dasein is thrown, not brought into existence [lit.: into its 'there' (*Da*)] by itself. Being, it is defined as a capability-of-being that belongs to itself yet has *not* given itself as itself. Existing, it can never go behind its being-thrown, so that it might dismiss this 'that it is and is called to be' from *its being*-itself into the There....*As this entity*, committed to which it can only exist as the entity that it is, *it is, existing*, the ground of its capability of being.[87]

The primary import of this difficult quote is this: The existentiell possibility of being-unto-death is grounded precisely in the fact Heidegger had claimed earlier, namely that Dasein is shaped and comes to know itself from within a 'world'. The call of *conscience* is the summons to acknowledge this fact as a *task* rather than a puzzle that does or even could have an answer. Dasein's origin in the world is not a defined 'there' onto which, as the causal 'explanation' of its existence, Dasein can slough off responsibility for that existence. Rather, that ungraspable origin functions precisely as the bar to any belief that existence can be *known* rather than or before it is lived, any belief that existence is explicable by a 'ground': Dasein itself *in existing* is the 'null ground' of its own being.

---

[84] *SZ* § 58, 284. For conscience as speaking of guilt, see *SZ* § 57, 279.
[85] *SZ* § 58, 283.
[86] *SZ* § 48, 242.
[87] *SZ* § 58, 284.

But to shoulder that existence is not to redress that nullity. On the contrary, authentic existence consists, practically, in a perpetual series of choices, each of which rejects or makes impossible other choices: 'Not only is the projection always, as thrown, determined by the nullity of its being-[its-own-]ground; it is also, *as projection*, itself essentially null.'[88] The determination of life by death only acuminates this point: The final ground and purpose, the uttermost depth of Dasein (the German *Grund* carries all three meanings) is its thrownness into death: 'The nothingness before which dread brings us reveals the nullity that determines life in its *ground* [depth/essence/purpose], namely thrownness into death'.[89]

The entire being of Dasein as a 'thrown projection' (*geworfener Entwurf*), then, is 'the null ground of a nullity'.[90] The call of conscience, although away from 'corruption' as dispersion in the world, is therefore not away from 'being guilty', but *towards* it: it is a call to accept the 'heaviness' or 'difficulty' (*Schwere*)[91] of being the 'null ground' of an existence pervaded by nullity. The voice of conscience is 'a summons to be guilty'.[92]

> Does not the being of Dasein [being-there] become more mysterious with the explication of the existential constitution of the being of its 'there' as thrown projection? Indeed. We must first allow the full mysteriousness of this being to become apparent, if only to be able truly to fail in [alt.: be shipwrecked against] its 'solution' and begin to ask the question of the being of the thrown-projecting being-in-the-world anew.[93]

AUTHENTICITY AND THE (IM)POSSIBILITY OF WHOLENESS

However, Heidegger's understanding of guilt and conscience, with its startling formulation of Dasein's being as 'the null ground of a nullity', is predicated on the unspoken assumption that the *wish* for a ground and a goal

[88] *SZ* § 58, 285.
[89] *SZ* § 62, 308.
[90] *SZ* § 58, 285.
[91] *SZ* § 58, 284.
[92] *SZ* § 58, 287.
[93] *SZ* § 32, 148.

remains constitutive of Dasein. To become oneself, indeed, is to accept that one is *neither* grounded in a definite origin (or even able coherently to express what such a ground would be), *nor* able to escape the desire for a ground; neither moving towards fulfilment (or even able coherently to express what such fulfilment would be), nor able to escape that desire. To become oneself, in other words, is to accept as a *task* rather than a mere refutation of one's desire the fact that one cannot access such a beginning or end. The crowd is a temptation because it provides either a distraction from the question of wholeness, or an illusion that Dasein is already part of a whole that is unproblematically and already 'there'. Being-guilty and being-unto-death, by contrast, arise from the wish for wholeness coupled with an acknowledgement of the fact that beginning and end are onto-logically inaccessible: that we *must* but cannot be whole.

This is Heidegger's eschatological reformulation, against the horizon of Nothingness, of Kierkegaard's definition of faith as relating oneself absolutely to the absolute precisely by relating relatively to all relative things.[94] As Heidegger writes,

> The anticipating becoming-free *for* its own death liberates [Dasein] from its lostness in possibilities arbitrarily crowding in by allowing it, for the first time, to authentically understand and choose the factic possibilities that precede the unovertakable [one]. Anticipation opens up to exist-ence, as its uttermost possibility, [the possibility of] self-surrender, and so breaks every stiff focus on the existence already achieved.... [Dasein becomes] free for its ownmost possibilities, defined from their *end*, that is, understood as *finite*.[95]

In Heidegger's re-analysis of Kierkegaard, in other words, things appear as finite not by contrast to the infinite, but as illuminated from the horizon of the end or *finis*. We can now understand bet-ter Heidegger's position, two years later, in *What is Metaphysics?* (1929). Here, *Dasein* 'transcends' that-which-is. But 'to transcend' (for Heidegger as for Scholastic thought) means not only 'to surpass' but also 'to gather up': by acknowledging its own 'ownmost and deepest finitude',[96] Dasein also leads all other beings to themselves: 'Only in the Nothing of Dasein does that-which-is come to itself according to its ownmost possibility, i.e. in a finite way'.[97]

[94] Cf. Mulhall, *Heidegger and Being and Time*, 137.
[95] *SZ* § 53, 264.
[96] GA 9, 38.
[97] GA 9, 40.

The meaning of Dasein, then, is care,[98] the meaning of care is temporality,[99] and the meaning of temporality is finitude.[100] This is not an intellectual but an existential 'meaning', one that cannot be known, but only lived—in that sense, too, it is eschatological. Heidegger summarizes starkly:

> Only a being that is essentially, in its being, *futural*, i.e. able, available for its death, to let itself be shattered against that death and thrown back on its factic 'there'—only a being, in other words, which, as futural, is equally originally/originarily *past* [alt.: has been]—can assume its own thrownness by passing on to itself its inherited possibility, and so be [alt.: exist] for 'its time' *in the moment*. Only authentic temporality, which is at the same time finite, makes destiny, that is, authentic historicality, possible.[101]

AN ESCHATOLOGY WITHOUT ESCHATON?

Speaking on a more general level, Heidegger's project in *Being and Time* can be viewed as an ethical inflection of the Kantian problem of metaphysics, centring on a morally charged description of 'the human' as most vitally defined by the tension between ineluctable finitude and the equally persistent desire to transcend it. The aim of both speculative and moral philosophy is here no longer to aspire to a transcendent ideal, but to sustain an 'authentic' human existence by refusing to collapse this constitutive tension into either a metaphysical meta-narrative or an (apathetic or 'sceptical') denial of its allure.

But while Heidegger's analysis is a virtuoso *plaidoyer* for the ineluctable finitude of human existence, its pathos depends on the assumption of a desire to transcend finitude which the analysis itself cannot and does not attempt to account for. The passionate acts of 'shattering oneself against death' or bearing its 'affliction' which characterize authentic human existence are predicated on a contrary longing which is as consistently assumed as it is obfuscated by Heidegger's analysis.

---

[98] See e.g. *SZ* § 39, 182.
[99] See e.g. *SZ* § 65, 326.
[100] See e.g. *SZ* § 65, 331.
[101] *SZ* § 74, 385. Compare Karl Barth's assertion that man 'shatters himself' on God (*The Epistle to the Romans*, trans. E. C. Hoskyns (Oxford: Oxford University Press, 1965), 43).

A pressure point is the analysis of the experienceability of death in *Sein und Zeit*, § 47. Heidegger claims that an existential experience of death can only be gained by anticipating one's own death, never by witnessing another's. But as both Edith Stein and more recently Simon Critchley have countered from different perspectives, it is not one's own death but the death of others—specifically, that of loved ones—which is most immediately disclosive of finitude.[102] In an inversion of Heidegger's assertion, Nothing can only show up against the horizon of Being. If Being can only appear 'as' threatened by Nothing, then at the same time, Nothing can appear only *as* a threat. But only what is valued can be threatened, and if the threat makes the value amply clear, it does not in itself create it. To love, as Heidegger himself realized in analysing his love for Hannah Arendt, is to say '*volo ut sis* ('I want you to be')'.[103] Only in one's love for another can death appear as the horrendous negation it is. But this implies that the apprehension of being which is always already constitutive of Dasein includes a *desire* that being should be infinite which is not easily dismissed as a mere misanalysis of our finitude.

The experience of Christian eschatology takes seriously that desire as well as that impossibility. The problem with theology, from Heidegger's perspective, is one of two things: Either, like Roman Catholic 'theologies of glory', it assumes an uncomplicated continuity between earthly existence and heavenly—an assumption that must be deconstructed by reminders of the ultimacy of death (ontological critique). Or, like a Lutheran 'theology of the cross', it assumes a complete break between this life and the next—an assumption that must be deconstructed by an analysis of how constitutive *this* life is for anything we might mean by 'human' (grammatical critique). Those are formidable challenges; nevertheless, Heidegger's own configuration cannot escape the

---

[102] See Critchley, 'Originary Inauthenticity', 143–5; Stein, 'Martin Heideggers Existenzphilosophie', ESGA 11/12, 475–6. Despite some fine observations, Critchley's account of Heidegger's 'authenticity' is too distorting, and his own suggested 'inauthenticity' too polemical and ambiguous, to constitute a formidable overall critique of Heidegger.
[103] Letters to Hannah Arendt, 13 May 1925 and 7 December 1927. In Ludz (ed.), *Hannah Arendt/Martin Heidegger*, 31 and 59.

constitutive significance of desire, which he assumes from his escha-tological sources, but never successfully re-situates.[104]

If human existence teaches us that we can never attain fulfilment but also that we seek it, that we can never find our ground but also that we crave it, then the phenomenological conclusion cannot *simply* be a denial of the object. C. S. Lewis gives a perhaps more accurate phenomenological summary:

> [I]f a man diligently follow[s]...desire, pursuing the false objects until their falsity appear[s] and then resolutely abandoning them, he must come out at last into the clear knowledge that the human soul was made to enjoy some object that is never fully given—nay, cannot even be imag-ined as given—in our present mode of subjective and spatio-temporal experience.[105]

The final chapter of this book, after giving an account of the contem-poraneous theological reception of *Being and Time*, is concerned with following out that suggestion.

---

[104] A full exploration of this problem in Heidegger requires much more detailed anal-ysis of both the text and its inheritance. My work-in-progress develops the claim of an irreducible ambiguity in Heidegger's account of authentic *Dasein* by reading the opposing accounts of 'the ordinary' given by Jacques Derrida and Stanley Cavell as developments of two possible (but conflicting) interpretations of that account. Derrida's exposure of the continual 'solicitation' of the ordinary by 'iterability'—by the opposite of authenticity or even existence—is a variation on Heidegger's claim, here taken as primary, that death 'solicits' life in its entirety. Cavell's vision of authentic human exist-ence as forged in open and vulnerable community with others, by contrast, confirms and develops Heidegger's account of *Mitsein*. These accounts are mutually critiquing: Derrida's deconstructive method poses an effective challenge to Cavell's claim that the ordinary is irreducible by further philosophical analysis, while, conversely, Cavell's val-orization of the human draws attention to a residual humanity in Derrida's text which Derrida cannot account for. These approaches are, in fact, predicated on each other like the famous *Gestalt* image of a vase and two faces: they cannot come into focus at the same time, but one cannot appear without the other to furnish its background.
[105] C. S. Lewis, *The Pilgrim's Regress* (London: J. M. Dent, 3rd edn., 1943), preface.

Conclusion: Theological Responses

The essence of man consists in his being more than merely
human.

—Martin Heidegger, *Letter on Humanism*

This concluding chapter returns to explicitly theological concerns. It
deals with theological responses both actual and possible: the earliest
reception of *Being and Time* by Protestant and Roman Catholic thinkers, and the potential for a contemporary response arising both from
these earliest reactions and from the reading of Heidegger's development offered in this book.

In 1931, Gerhardt Kuhlmann, in trying to define the task of
Protestant theology *vis-à-vis* Heidegger's ontology, dismisses the
Catholic position as a priori useless for the Protestant, because it is
incapable of even acknowledging the problem:

> For Catholicism, the relation between philosophy and theology presents
> no problem. For Catholic theology is essentially natural theology. The
> God of the Catholic doctrine of revelation is exactly and assuredly the
> God whom natural man can know as his Creator, indeed because of
> his *imago dei*-quality *must* know as his Creator unless he maliciously
> closes himself off from a true understanding of his Being.... Catholic
> theology degrades philosophy to mere conceptual analysis and logical
> statistics, and then takes it into its service as a 'handmaid'. This is not
> merely its right, but its obligation. For Catholic dogma proclaims the
> identity of the Christian Saviour-God with the Creator-God of natural
> reason.[1]

---

[1] Kuhlmann, 'Krisis der Theologie', *Zeitschrift für Theologie und Kirche* 12 (1931),
123–46; p. 144. Kuhlmann, a forceful and lucid voice in the debate about theology and
philosophy conducted in the late 1920s and early 1930s, is nowadays almost entirely
forgotten, and very little can be ascertained about him. He is likely to have been a
student of Eberhard Grisebach in Jena, where he earned his doctorate with a thesis
on Friedrich Brunstäd and Paul Tillich (*Brunstäd und Tillich: Zum Problem einer
Theonomie der Kultur* (Tübingen: Mohr Siebeck, 1928)). He later resided in Berlin,
but whether or not he was attached to the university there is not clear. His last extant
publications date from 1935.

This is a deft sketch of the rift between the Catholic and the Protestant response to Heidegger in the late 1920s and early 1930s. The Catholic response is premised on repudiating altogether the epistemological question that motivates the philosopher, namely how the question of Being is to be raised. Instead, Catholics welcome Heidegger's 'ret-rogression' to the traditional primacy of Being as the subject of phi-losophy, construing his analyses as metaphysical claims that stand to be either refuted or harnessed for the superior enterprise of Roman Catholic metaphysics. This construction is at once problematic and thought-provoking. On one hand, it falls short of the problematization of metaphysics that is at the heart of Heidegger's (as of Kierkegaard's and Barth's) work.[2] But on the other, it raises the counter-question whether it really is (as Heidegger wishes) possible to extract oneself from metaphysical commitment. The Catholic claim is precisely that Heidegger's deconstruction of metaphysics is itself based on a dog-matically assumed 'metaphysics of immanence'. Disagreement among Catholic commentators arises in their assessment of whether this metaphysics lends itself to supplementation or correction, or whether it must be combated.

The Protestant reaction to Heidegger, by contrast, is marked by a shared question and sharply diverging answers. For his Protestant critics, as for Heidegger himself, the question how to know what it is to be human is central. What Bultmann, Brunner, Barth, and their col-leagues argue about is the question whether the challenge implicit in Heidegger's project of a fundamental description of man must be met, or whether to fight on the turf staked out by the philosopher is already to cede victory. Bultmann and Brunner feel strongly that Heidegger's challenge cannot be ignored without risking forfeiture of theology's claim to be relevant, indeed necessary, to both knowing and forming human existence in its full depth. Barth, on the other hand, is con-vinced that because only revelation can disclose anything of import about man, philosophy is precisely irrelevant, and to engage it at all is already to have distorted both subject and object of any enquiry into what it is to be human.

---

[2] Stephen Mulhall's *Faith and Reason* (London: Duckworth, 1994) remains one of the most incisive accounts of Kierkegaard's problematization of the language of meta-physics in the context of faith.

HEIDEGGER AND DIALECTICAL THEOLOGY

The dominant Protestant response to Heidegger's fundamental ontology came from those within or in direct engagement with dialectical theology, and assumed the contours of the debate within and around that movement: Rudolf Bultmann attempted a valorization of Heidegger's philosophy for dialectical theology; Friedrich Gogarten and Emil Brunner, at least in the 1920s, rejected his philosophy as incompatible with dialectical theology; Erik Peterson and Gerhardt Kuhlmann censured Heidegger's philosophy and dialectical theology for one and the same reason; and Karl Barth maintained principled silence.

These Protestant interlocutors sympathize with Heidegger's metaphysical reticence for intrinsically theological reasons: reasons related to original sin and salvation.[3] In Roman Catholic teaching, the Fall has stained but not obliterated the image of God in humans; in other words, sin has weakened but not paralysed their natural ability to discern their supernatural origin and end, and to orient themselves towards it. In Protestant thought, by contrast, the Fall into sin has wrought a radical ontological change in man, manifest in the mortality of human life and the radical limitation of the human will and intellect: Man is no longer naturally capable of knowing or following God or the good, but is wholly dependent on the power of supernaturally infused grace to do so. An urgent question therefore arises for Protestant theologians how to delimit the spheres of natural humanity and divinely infused grace: Are humans 'naturally' capable of receiving grace (even if they cannot naturally replicate its effects), or is its infusion unanticipated and unprepared? Does grace work a radical ontological change in believers, or does God merely impute righteousness to persons who remain ontologically unchanged at least until the Last Judgement?[4] It is in the context of these questions that Protestant theologians, particularly exponents and critics of dialectical theology, engage Heidegger's phenomenology.

[3] It is in this context that Erich Przywara SJ describes Heidegger's account of being-unto-death as 'a metaphysics of sin and salvation—concretely...the religious metaphysics of Kierkegaard and Barth'; in 'Drei Richtungen der Phänomenologie', *Stimmen der Zeit* 115 (1928), 252–64; pp. 260–1.

[4] Eduard Thurneysen, for example, maintains that man is 'reconciled but not yet saved', i.e. the ontological change only takes place after the Last Judgement. Thurneysen, 'Christus und seine Zukunft: Ein Beitrag zur Eschatologie', *Zwischen den Zeiten* 9 (1931), 187–211; p. 210.

Emil Brunner first attempts to engage these questions *vis-à-vis* Heidegger in a 1925 article entitled 'Law and Revelation: A Theological Groundwork'—a revised version of the lecture he presented with such unhappy results in Marburg.[5] In that article, Brunner, following Augustine, presents the law as an antithetical preparation for the gospel: It brings man face to face with his own nothingness, from which only grace can raise him.[6] This is a dynamic initiated by God, in so far as the law is divinely decreed; but it is a realization arrived at by man when he is still in his sinful state. In this way, the law—inscribed in the Scriptures, in church teaching, and in the human heart—drives man to radically question himself, and call on God for help.

After the publication of *Being and Time*, Gerhardt Kuhlmann tries to leverage this Brunnerian idea against Heidegger's analysis.[7] In a 1931 article entitled 'The Crisis of Theology', he argues that '[t]he self-knowledge of the creature can only ever be knowledge of its transgressions against God's law, i.e. knowledge of sin'. The voice of conscience, which 'makes the depth of its own existence transparent' to the creature, at the same stroke also places that creature 'before God its Lord'.[8] Knowledge of self, in other words, always implies knowledge of God. For Kuhlmann, this analysis is apposite to Heidegger's because of the role that 'nothingness' plays in each. For Kuhlmann as for Brunner, *lex redigit ad nihilum*: it reduces man to his nullity before God.[9] But this nullity or nothingness is precisely a nullity *vis-à-vis* God, and so a function of the 'law of the Creator': 'Only the Creator...can call the creature into question in such a way that it is struck to the depths of its being.'[10] In Heidegger's work, by contrast, 'man arrogates to himself the right and the ability to inquire after his nature so radically...that he himself, with the essence of his being, is called into question.'[11]

---

[5] Brunner, 'Gesetz und Offenbarung: Eine theologische Grundlegung', *Theologische Blätter* 4 (1925), cols. 53–8; on his presentation of this material in Marburg, see Chapter 5.

[6] Brunner, 'Gesetz und Offenbarung'; cf. Augustine, 'In eumdem Psalmum 118: Sermo 24', on verse 118. Cf. also Erik Peterson, 'Was ist Theologie?' (1925), in Peterson, *Theologische Traktate* (Würzburg: Echter, 1994 [1951]), 1–22; p. 8.

[7] Gerhardt Kuhlmann, 'Krisis der Theologie', *Zeitschrift für Theologie und Kirche* 12 (1931), 123–46.

[8] Ibid., 140.

[9] Kotaro Okoyama, *Zur Grundlegung christlicher Ethik* (Berlin: De Gruyter, 1976), 43.

[10] Kuhlmann, 'Krisis der Theologie', 140.

[11] Ibid., 139.

For Kuhlmann, this can never be authentic self-knowledge: It always remains a pose, a flinching from the true nature of human depravity.

Kuhlmann's article is complemented by a companion piece by Emil Brunner in the same issue of the *Journal of Theology and the Church*. Like Kuhlmann, Brunner argues that Heidegger's claim to an analysis of human existence that is neutral with regard to states of sin and grace must be rejected on both ontological and epistemological grounds.[12] Ontologically, the (divinely created) nature of man has been obscured by the Fall to such an extent that there can be no such thing as an analysis of 'existential structures' that are neutral *vis-à-vis* states of sin and grace: There is no 'neutral humanity', as Heidegger claims, but only 'unbelieving' and 'believing' man.[13] Epistemologically, human nature, quite regardless of its branding by sin and faith, cannot be understood at all except theologically: 'The paradox', Brunner writes, 'is already in the concept of man, because man is a being made through God's word, i.e. a being whose nature can be known only in revelation, only in Christ.'[14]

Kuhlmann and Brunner may be justified in pressing their theological charges, but their case risks dismissal for inadmissible evidence. Their methodology, as it stands, is too confused. Their choice to introduce the claim that the divine law reduces man to his nullity before God as a fact of experience makes that claim liable to phenomenological analysis; but such analysis is nowhere attempted, and there is a sense that it may be impossible. Kuhlmann and Brunner thus exemplify precisely what Heidegger criticizes about the Protestant tradition, namely a conflation of appeals to experience and dogmatic assertions which cannot be unravelled without setting aside their dogmatic component.

Karl Barth registers this problem through principled silence. Though in substantial agreement with the content of Brunner's description of man, Barth vigorously repudiates the attempt to set it into any kind of relation to philosophy, even that of a contestation. Already in 1925, Barth had disdained the attempt of a theological 'groundwork'. However radically theocentric, he wrote to Brunner, such an endeavour must

---

[12] Emil Brunner, 'Theologie und Ontologie', *Zeitschrift für Theologie und Kirche* 12 (1931), 111–22.

[13] Ibid., 113.

[14] Ibid., 119. Cf. Karl Barth, 'Ludwig Feuerbach: Mit einem polemischen Nachwort', *Zwischen den Zeiten* 5 (1927), 10–40; p. 40n.

always 'operate with a concept of law seemingly in common to theology and philosophy', when in fact, philosophy is incapable of 'saying anything about it' at all.[15] Now, in 1930, in a heated letter to his friend Thurneysen, Barth anticipates his 1934 *No!*:

> I find the whole business by which we're so closely surrounded abhorrent, and I don't know whether I won't someday erupt in a big article of repudiation and valediction to Emil [Brunner], Paul [Tillich], Friedrich [Gogarten], Rudolf [Bultmann] *e tutti quanti*. ... The problem is not that one cannot honourably have some kind of philosophy in mind, much less that it mustn't ... be Heidegger's. It's that those people all want to run for shelter from philosophy; that, rather than from God, they want to start from some kind of 'possibility'; [that they want to] avoid the scandal of theology by means of some kind of 'pre-apprehension' or some trick to lead the pagans *ad absurdum* and look good. And then they boast to me about the clarity of their concepts, as if that were an art if one takes those concepts from anywhere except from within the matter itself.[16]

Barth's declaration bears a superficial resemblance to Heidegger's statement that faith 'has its own testimony, which is fundamentally inaccessible to any philosophical experience'.[17] But this similarity conceals a wholesale rejection, on Barth's part, of the distinction between ontic and ontological levels of existence and discourse within which Heidegger situates his statement. This position, like Brunner's, has a theological rationale. Both Barth and Brunner assume an ontological rift (here in the traditional rather than the Heideggerian sense of 'ontological') between ungraced and graced existence. But whereas Brunner wants to bridge this gap by a natural recognition of sinfulness and consequent appeal for grace, Barth regards the sinful state as one of complete anosognosia: the unsaved cannot know God or themselves even to the extent of discerning their sinfulness and God's judgement over them.[18] Brunner, consequently, comes into direct conflict with Heidegger, because he must construe Heidegger's 'fundamental analytic' as either vacuous (because it purports to describe what does not exist, namely a 'neutral' humanity) or downright dangerous (because what it describes—accurately—is humanity in its fallen state,

---

[15] Barth to Brunner, 13 March 1925; in Barth and Brunner, *Briefwechsel*, 114–18; p. 116.
[16] Barth to Thurneysen, 26 January 1930; in Barth and Thurneysen, *Briefwechsel II*, 699–706; pp. 701–2.
[17] *SZ* § 62, 306.
[18] See e.g. Barth's letter to Brunner of 13 March 1925; in Barth and Brunner, *Briefwechsel*, 114–18; p. 116 (quoted in Chapter 5).

and the authenticity it counsels, because it does not acknowledge God or his grace, is merely a further entangling in that fallenness). Barth's work, by contrast, is not so much in conflict as incommensurable with Heidegger's. Heidegger, registering Barth's disregard for the elementary distinction between ontic and ontological, dismisses Barth as an 'opponent who weighs too little—so little that he [does] not even notice what matters'.[19] Barth, conversely, contends that philosophy is precisely irrelevant to 'what matters', and to engage it at all is already to have lost any chance of success.

The dispute between Heidegger, Brunner, and Barth is to some extent recapitulated and transformed by Rudolf Bultmann, who engages Heidegger more intensely than any other theologian of his circle. In a series of publications between 1926 and 1929, Bultmann develops a theological reading of Johannine eschatology that deliberately relies on Heidegger's existential analytic as a conceptual and ontological framework. In 1930, he elaborates and defends this method against critical questions posed by Gerhardt Kuhlmann. While it seems at first sight as if Bultmann unquestioningly adopts Heidegger's (perhaps somewhat disingenuous) 1927 explication of the relationship between phenomenology and theology, his 1930 essay in fact proposes a substantial reconfiguration of the relationship between 'ontic' and 'ontological' levels of enquiry, and therefore also of theology and phenomenology.

The first fruits of Bultmann's five-year working partnership with Heidegger at Marburg were a series of studies on the Johannine corpus, most importantly 'The Eschatology of the Gospel of John' (1928). In this essay, Bultmann identifies as the central impetus of John's Gospel an eschatological dynamic that eschews the dramatic, other-worldly apocalypticism of other New Testament texts in favour of an 'eschatological now' which opens up—every moment anew—the future as possibility: as the advent of the genuinely new.[20]

Bultmann sets the stage by a broad assimilation of the Johannine '*kosmos*'[21] to Heidegger's '*Welt*' ('world' or 'worldhood'), of which

---

[19] Letter to Bultmann dated 29 March 1927; in Bultmann and Heidegger, *Briefwechsel*, 24–6; p. 25.

[20] 'Die Eschatologie des Johannes-Evangeliums', *Zwischen den Zeiten* 6 (1928), 4–22; p. 14. Elements of 'the old dramatic eschatology', as they appear e.g. in John 5: 28f. and 6: 54, are ascribed to a later redactor. See 'Eschatologie des Johannes-Evangeliums', 4–5.

[21] A representative list of references is given in 'Eschatologie des Johannes-Evangeliums', 5n.

humans are always already part. But he tacitly superimposes on this existential description a theological dimension:

> Man does not *face* the world, he *is* world; i.e. the world is not an object present at hand 'in itself', which man confronts in theoretical contemplation. (Rather, such contemplation would itself be part of the world, itself be 'world'.) But being [part of the] world means first of all being created; and that man *is* world—that is, created—includes, according to the Prologue [of John's Gospel], that man is capable of *understanding* himself in this his creatureliness.[22]

Bultmann does not defend or theorize the identification of 'being world' and 'being created', or substantiate man's capacity for creaturely self-understanding beyond the offhand remark, 'according to the Prologue'. This failure to clarify the relation between phenomenological and biblical or dogmatic insights introduces a deleterious ambiguity into his account, which becomes evident in the following two steps of his argument.

In a first step, Bultmann makes his emphasis on the creatureliness of the world into the linchpin of an interpretation of the disjunctive force of John's Gospel as a Heideggerian tension between authenticity and inauthenticity. 'Precisely because it is created', he writes, the world 'has the possibility of misunderstanding itself, of setting itself against God'.[23] At the same time, 'in the possibility of knowing oneself a creature, the world has always already had the possibility of accepting the Word'.[24] This 'Word'—the proclamation of the gospel—in this scheme only 'activates' or 'actualizes' antecedent existential possibilities: By bringing man face to face with his Creator, it elicits either an acknowledgement of his own creatureliness or its denial.

In a second step, Bultmann tries to resolve this existential possibility into the Christian concepts of sin and salvation: for the denial of creatureliness, when it is maintained in the face of a direct revelation, is no longer mere misunderstanding but downright sin.[25] At this point, Bultmann reverts to a specifically biblical use of the term 'world' which he never explicitly delineates against the first: 'In the face of revelation, which calls the world in its worldhood into question, it is sin to cleave to worldhood'.[26] Conversely, for those who believe, 'the world is, in

---

[22] Bultmann, 'Eschatologie des Johannes-Evangeliums', 6.
[23] Ibid., 6.
[24] Ibid., 8.
[25] Ibid., 8–9.
[26] Ibid., 8.

some sense, at an end'.[27] Here, the term 'world' is reduced to denoting an obstinately immanent realm, barring itself against the irruption of the Word and thereby forfeiting any genuine possibility of change or growth. Just this irruption of the Word creates 'the eschatological now' in which 'the decision between death and life is made':

> [L]ife is nothing provable or present-at-hand, no inwardness or set of experiences, but rather the determination of the present moment by the Word, in so far as it is heard in faith; in so far, in other words, as the now is understood as the ever-new possibility of my being as capable of being, as having a future. Life is no state, no stable possession of things present or eternal, but rather existence in the moment as a true present determined by the future.[28]

The emotionally compelling rhetoric of this paragraph cannot conceal the inconsistency of Bultmann's account: If 'worldhood' is an existential feature of Dasein, which may be engaged authentically or inauthentically, then 'worldhood' cannot at the same time be an existentiell condition that can be avoided by accepting a particular proclamation, or contracted by its rejection. In a response to Bultmann published the following year (1929), Gerhardt Kuhlmann sets this problem in a larger context.[29] There are, Kuhlmann argues, two alternative ways in which a theologian wishing to appropriate Heidegger might interpret the philosopher's 'existentialia': either as purely formal analyses, which span Christian and non-Christian existence alike; or as specific descriptions of sinful existence, which cannot encompass the new life of faith. Bultmann risks incoherence by drawing indiscriminately on both interpretations. What is worse, Kuhlmann continues, both are ultimately self-subversive. In the first case, the Christian terms introduced by the theologian are merely mythologizations of philosophical ones, and so at best superfluous; in the second, the theologian must disregard the most basic guiding intentions of the philosopher he is trying to appropriate, and is therefore prima facie untrustworthy in his construal of that thought.[30] Bultmann's case seems to collapse under the combined weight of these problems.

But Kuhlmann's critique elicits from Bultmann a response that is both more critical and more substantial than his original contribution.

[27] Bultmann, 'Eschatologie des Johannes-Evangeliums', 9.
[28] Ibid., 17.
[29] Gerhardt Kuhlmann, 'Zum theologischen Problem der Existenz: Fragen an Rudolf Bultmann', *Zeitschrift für Theologie und Kirche* 10 (1929), 28–57.
[30] Ibid., 47–52.

In his rejoinder, 'The Historicity of Dasein and Faith' (1930), Bultmann reiterates his conviction that the theologian, in order to speak scientifically (*wissenschaftlich*), must draw on the phenomenological work of the philosopher.[31] 'If the Christian event that takes place in faith and "rebirth" is not a magical transformation that lifts the believer right out of human existence', Bultmann argues, then the theologian can and must come to grips with the existential structures that are receptive to redemption.[32]

The question that necessarily follows is whether an atheist philosopher, who knows nothing of redeemed human existence, is equipped to identify these enduring existential structures. Bultmann's answer is ambivalent. He initially responds by way of an analogy of Christian faith with friendship that 'a friendless man who consciously or unconsciously longs for friendship *knows* what "friendship" is' every bit as well as a man who has experienced it.[33] A lived friendship adds no conceptual knowledge about the phenomenon 'friendship', but only an ever new 'qualification' of one's own life—'in work, joy, struggle and pain'—by the concrete relationship.[34] In the same way, Bultmann polemically argues, 'no believer can say more precisely or fully what "revelation" is than any unbeliever', because every being that knows death is also capable of knowing, and longing for, 'revelation and life, grace and forgiveness'.[35]

This is a problematic but also intriguing statement, both as an independent argument and as an interpretation of Heidegger. Its problems are obvious. First, Bultmann's claim that the friendless man knows all there is to know about friendship does not carry the force he intends; for that man's knowledge is likely to rest on the cultural and personal testimony of those who have experienced friendship (including such seminal figures as Cicero and Augustine) rather than on pure intuition. Bultmann's analogous claim about revelation is liable to the same problem. Furthermore, his claim about the unbeliever's knowledge of revelation sits uneasily as an interpretation of Heidegger, since far from projecting a longing for life, grace, and forgiveness, authentic existence,

---

[31] Rudolf Bultmann, 'Die Geschichtlichkeit des Daseins und der Glaube: Antwort an Gerhardt Kuhlmann', *Zeitschrift für Theologie und Kirche* 11 (1930), 329–64.

[32] Ibid., 346.

[33] Ibid., 351; emphasis added.

[34] Ibid., 351.

[35] Ibid., 351–2.

for Heidegger, is premised precisely on an unflinching acceptance of the ultimacy of death and the immovability of guilt.

Nevertheless, Bultmann's discussion of knowledge is worth probing a little more fully. The claim that the friend gains not conceptual knowledge but a 'qualification of life' may reiterate a Kierkegaardian dismissal of the rational content of Christian faith in favour of its existential dynamic.[36] But equally or more so, I would argue, it registers the need to distinguish between knowledge and what Stanley Cavell later comes to call 'acknowledgement'.[37] In his seminal essay 'Knowing and Acknowledging' (1969), Cavell engages traditional sceptical arguments against the possibility of knowing other minds. Unlike most philosophers, however, Cavell does not attempt to repudiate the sceptic's concerns by devising a proof of the existence of other minds or a method for knowing them with certainty. Any such proof, he argues, would merely perpetuate the sceptic's fundamental mistake that it is indeed *knowledge* which is called for in this context. But the sceptic is absolutely right in complaining that we cannot know other minds; his error lies in analysing this problem as an 'intellectual lack' rather than as what it really is, namely a 'metaphysical finitude': the fact that humans are irremediably separate.[38] In Cavell's analysis, the sceptic's wish to cast this separation as a limitation of *knowledge* is a symptom of the more general human wish to escape the full impact of human finitude: the unbridgeable gap between us and those we love, the inability to hold the world as a stable possession. It is to register this difference between intellectual and existential or 'metaphysical' limitation that Cavell introduces the concept of 'acknowledgement' as the form or inflection of knowledge proper to the case of knowing other minds. It underscores two things: One, knowledge of others is not automatic, but involves an element of openness and choice, and so also of inavertible risk: it is always susceptible to dissembling, misunderstanding, and loss. Two, because every person is already situated within the human community, a refusal to 'know' others is never an autonomous and therefore authoritative decision, but a failure to

---

[36] See e.g. Søren Kierkegaard, *Eighteen Upbuilding Discourses*, trans. H. and E. Hong (Princeton: Princeton University Press, 1990).

[37] Stanley Cavell, 'Knowing and Acknowledging', in *Must We Mean What We Say?* (Cambridge: Cambridge University Press, 1969), 238–66.

[38] Ibid., 263; cf. Ludwig Wittgenstein, *Philosophical Investigations*, ed. and trans. G. E. M. Anscombe (Cambridge: Cambridge University Press, 1953), §287.

fulfil one's responsibility towards others—in other words, a denial of acknowledgement.[39]

It seems that what Bultmann tries to register in his discussion of friendship is just such a distinction between knowledge and acknowledgement. The relevance of this distinction to a theological response to Heidegger is already partially apparent. Heidegger's ontological account of being-with, because it seeks to uncover the existential structures within each individual that make phenomena such as community possible in the first place, bars itself by that very principle from making an ontologically significant distinction between the capability for relationship and its achievement. Real others are bracketed from the analysis; the ontological concept of *being-with* is called upon to explicate, univocally, both the attainment and the failure of actual community. One consequence is that being-with (*Mitsein*) as an existential structure of Dasein is always in tension (if not outright contradiction) with being-unto-death. The inescapable solitariness of death as the ultimate criterion of authenticity implies a deep rift within Dasein: even if a form of authentic community can be found by and among 'self-owning' (*eigentlich*) individuals, it will be rooted in mutual recognition of the ultimate isolation of each.[40] While such distance can take salutary forms in practice, its necessity nevertheless queries Heidegger's claim of the existential, i.e. constitutive, relationality of Dasein. These are the pressure points that Bultmann addresses in the remainder of his essay, through a juxtaposition of Heidegger's 'being-unto-death' and Friedrich Gogarten's 'being-towards-the-other' (love).

While for Heidegger, it is being-unto-death that defines the historicity of human existence, for Gogarten, history—in the sense of 'something happening'—takes place only 'when a Thou faces an I and is acknowledged [*anerkannt*] in its claims by the I'. These two analyses, Bultmann argues, are not in direct conflict, but reflect the two thinkers' different disciplinary spheres: 'Heidegger speaks as an ontologist and therefore has neither the occasion nor the right to speak of love.

[39] See Cavell, 'Knowing and Acknowledging', 263. For a much fuller philosophical-theological assessment of Cavell's concepts of acknowledgement and scepticism, see Judith (Tonning) Wolfe, 'Acknowledging a Hidden God: A Theological Critique of Stanley Cavell on Scepticism', *Heythrop Journal* 48, no. 3 (2007), 384–405.

[40] This recognition—or acknowledgement—is salutary when framed in a Cavellian way, i.e. when the primacy of neighbourliness is assumed, and the threat is, rather, the denial of separateness and the arrogation of complete knowledge of the other; see e.g. Cavell, *Disowning Knowledge*, particularly chapters 2 and 6. But the premises of Heidegger's analysis are very different.

Gogarten, on the other hand, speaks as a theologian of the ontic; and it is in this sphere alone that love, in the radical sense in which he understands it, is to be found.'[41] In other words, fundamental ontology can only ever speak of internal human structures ('existentialia'); it cannot, by its nature, include in its analysis any actual relationships. But it is precisely such actual relationships which, for Gogarten (and Bultmann following him), alone make possible the authentic actualization of human historicity.

Bultmann expresses this idea and its implications in a paragraph of dense theological-philosophical prose:

> Love is only possible in Christ. What does that mean? To answer this, we must recall that on one hand, love is not the concrete purpose of a resolution which Dasein can simply take, but is rather the 'how' of resolution, which first reveals its purpose; on the other hand, love is not (like historicity) a characteristic of Dasein as such (an existentiale) but rather an ontic determination of resolution. Since these things are the case, I can only appropriate my own factic thereness [*Da*] as someone who loves if I am already loved, i.e. already immersed in love, and if the fact that I am always already loved is promised me by the proclamation of Christ and appropriated in faith.[42]

In other words, authentic resolution (of the kind that grasps its own historicity) is only possible when motivated by love. But loving is only possible if one is already loved, and it is this 'already' which is revealed and received in faith. What is more, it is only from this standpoint of knowing oneself to have always already been loved by God that one is capable of seeing natural existence (the 'world' of Bultmann's earlier article) as always already graced, '*as creation*'.[43]

This means that the theologian cannot ultimately accept the philosopher's analysis as final. For from the perspective gained by faith, the resolution to face death in solitude must appear not authentic but inauthentic, because death is *not* in fact solitary: It is always shared with Christ. And yet this cannot be known in advance of the proclamation of the gospel. This perspective also entails a critique of Heidegger's central term 'possibility'. For ultimately, Bultmann argues, Heidegger's analysis neutralizes this term by disallowing anything genuinely *new* ever to happen to Dasein. Possibility must indeed, as Heidegger

---

[41] Bultmann, 'Die Geschichtlichkeit des Daseins und der Glaube', 358.
[42] Ibid., 359.
[43] Ibid., 353.

implicitly argues in Part II of *Being and Time*, be defined eschatologically: but eschatology must be allowed to retain its irruptive character, its promise of the advent of something new and unanticipated.

This brings Bultmann surprisingly close to Thomas Aquinas's contention that 'man by his nature is ordained to beatitude'—that is, communion with God—'as his end', but that he is ordained to *attain* this end 'not by his own strength, but by the help of grace'.[44] The strict separation here between capability and attainment is not arbitrary, but entailed by the kind of vocation of which the Christian faith speaks, namely a vocation to transcend both self and death. The self cannot effect this transcendence of its own boundaries with its own resources; rather, it is the Incarnation—God's human birth, death, and resurrection from the dead—that enables humans to participate in God's life. Death, which once was final, is now transformed from within into a means of sharing in the action and life of Christ, and so of moving towards that life with God which is the innermost human calling. The implications of this convergence with Thomist ideas will be followed out in the final section of this chapter.

PHENOMENOLOGY AND NEO-SCHOLASTICISM

The thinkers who most shaped the earliest Roman Catholic responses to Heidegger were theologians with neo-Scholastic sympathies and varying degrees of phenomenological training: Erich Przywara (1889–1972), Edith Stein (1891–1942), Romano Guardini (1886–1968), and, from the periphery of the movement, Hans Urs von Balthasar (1905–88).[45] Their responses were shaped by certain expectations established (intentionally or unintentionally) by Heidegger himself. His last published work, eleven years earlier, had been a quasi-neo-Scholastic treatise on Duns Scotus (or rather, Thomas of Erfurt). His new work signalled a radical return, within secular modern philosophy, to Scholastic or scholastically derived

---

[44] *Summa Theologiae* 1–2. 114. 2. The identification of beatitude and communion with God (deification) is most explicitly made in 1. 12. 2 and 3. 9. 3 ad 3.

[45] A second wave of Catholic responses from those who had studied with Heidegger—particularly Karl Rahner (1904–84), Gustav Siewerth (1903–63), Bernhard Welte (1906–83), and Max Müller (1906–94)—goes beyond the historical and systematic scope of this book.

language, particularly 'being' and 'essence'. To the neo-Scholastics, consequently, Heidegger's project presented itself as a key for re-establishing the philosophical primacy of Being repudiated by Kant. Their main critique, accordingly, was that this project frustrated its own potential through a wilful obfuscation of the Scholastic categories it employed, amounting to a dogmatic and/or incoherent denial of the transcendence of (divine) Being and of the analogical nature of human existence and discourse.[46]

Erich Przywara, a leading editor of the Jesuit journal *Stimmen der Zeit*, was at the forefront of a larger endeavour to harness the insights of Husserlian, Schelerian, and Heideggerian phenomenology for a renewal of neo-Scholasticism. He was influenced by his encounters with Edith Stein, and himself exercised a decisive influence on Hans Urs von Balthasar, particularly through his *magnum opus, Analogia Entis*.[47] In his essay 'Three Directions of Phenomenology' (1928), Przywara succinctly expresses the neo-Scholastics' ambivalence regarding Heidegger's project:

> The work [*Being and Time*] seems, on the one hand, a most incisive 'regression towards tradition', since, in sharpest opposition to the entirety of modern philosophy, it traces knowledge (theoretical reason) and action and obligation (practical reason) back to the concept of Being and thereby establishes the Aristotelian-Thomist doctrine of Being as foundational *prima philosophia* (see pp. 1ff, 436). And yet it frames the concept of Being in such a way that, perhaps more axiomatically than anywhere else in modern philosophy, the immanent [lit.: inner-worldly] is closed and locked in on itself, since Being as Being is in its essence 'in the world'. At the same time, the transcendent [lit.: super-worldly] falls away by itself or must at least be traced back to the immanent (cf. pp. 180, 313, 427).[48]

Catholic critics develop this basic position variously. Alfred Delp SJ, in his extremely influential *Tragic Existence: On the Philosophy of*

---

[46] Heidegger's Marburg student Hans-Georg Gadamer notes in his 1977 memoir that a 'newly acquired edition of Thomas' was the 'symbol of Heidegger's entrance at the Protestant Marburg'; *Philosophische Lehrjahre*, 19–20.Some notable recent interpretations of the relation of Heidegger's fundamental ontology to Scholastic philosophy are John D. Caputo, *Heidegger and Aquinas: An Essay on Overcoming Metaphysics* (New York: Fordham University Press, 1982), and McGrath, *The Early Heidegger & Medieval Philosophy*.

[47] Munich: Kösel & Pustet, 1932.

[48] Przywara, 'Drei Richtungen der Phänomenologie', 252. Hedwig Conrad-Martius offers a similar analysis in 'Sein und Zeit' (review), *Philosophischer Anzeiger* 8 (1933), 185.

Martin Heidegger (1931)—the first book-length study of Heidegger's existential ontology—accuses the philosopher of aspiring to a 'self-divinization of man' by distorting the Scholastic use of *analogia*.[49] Following Aquinas, Delp regards human existence as explicable only by an *analogia attributionis*: an analogical use of the term 'being' in reference to God (*analogans*) and man (*analogatum*), warranted by the fact that man's being is causally dependent on God's being, which is the first and proper referent of the term. In J. A. Quenstedt's formulation of Aquinas, made famous by Barth: *'Deus substantia est absoluta et independenter, creatura vero dependenter et per participationem.'*[50] In other words, man exists by participation, and his finite being therefore intrinsically points beyond itself to the infinite being of God. Heidegger, Delp argues, presents a skewed *analogia attributionis* in which not God but Nothingness functions as the analogans of man's being.[51] What Delp finds interesting here is that Heidegger derives not a weary nihilism but a tragic heroism from this fact—a heroism that requires but also contradicts man's constitutive 'immersion in Nothingness'.[52] 'The resolution, the heroism of [man in the face of] nothing', Delp maintains, 'is nothing other than a denial of the finitude that has just been asserted with such pathos.'[53] Heidegger's narrative is an intoxicating but ultimately incoherent myth.[54]

Przywara is more optimistic. Rather than requiring debunking, Heidegger's work, in his estimation, invites supplementation by the theologian. Przywara takes Heidegger's 'misprision' of Aquinas to consist

---

[49] Alfred Delp, *Tragische Existenz: Zur Philosophie Martin Heideggers* (Freiburg: Herder, 1931). 'Tragic existence' became a popular term and a convenient shortcut in critically describing Heidegger's philosophy, well beyond the borders of the German language. See e.g. H. Thielemans SJ's 'Existence tragique: la métaphysique du Nazisme', *Nouvelle Revue théologique*, vol. 63, no. 6 (1936), 561–79.

[50] Karl Barth, *Church Dogmatics*, ii/1: *The Doctrine of God*, trans. G. W. Bromiley and T. F. Torrance (Edinburgh: T. & T. Clark, 1957), 237, summarizing the presentation of the Thomistic use of *analogia* in Johannes Andreas Quenstedt, *Theologia didactico-polemica sive systema theologicum* (Wittenberg, 1685), I. 8. 2. 1; cf. Aquinas, *ST* 1. 13. 3.

[51] Similar arguments are reiterated by many contemporaneous critics, perhaps most famously Karl Löwith; see e.g. his 'Les Implications politiques de la philosophie de l'existence chez Heidegger', *Les Temps modernes* 14 (1946), 343–60; p. 345.

[52] GA 9, 35.

[53] Delp, *Tragische Existenz*, 114.

[54] Note C. S. Lewis's similar, though more appreciative, analysis of the 'cultural myth' (as opposed to the scientific theory) of evolution in 'The Funeral of a Great Myth', *Christian Reflections*, ed. Walter Hooper (Grand Rapids, Mich.: Eerdmans, 1967), 82–93.

not in a misidentification of the analogans of man's being, but in deny-
ing the contingency of human existence altogether. Heidegger's ontology, he argues, posits an absolutized existence as the 'essence' of Dasein;
in other words, it claims the exclusively divine identity of existence
and essence for the creature, rejecting the ontological difference which
characterizes all created beings in Patristic and Scholastic thought.[55]
But, Przywara goes on, 'Heidegger's ontology... is forced back into the
Patristic-Scholastic doctrine... by the course of its own investigation':
the Scholastic difference between Being and essence merely resurfaces
in Heidegger's 'doctrine of the difference between being there [*Dasein*]
and being thus [*Sosein*]'.[56] This, Przywara argues, inescapably opens his
analysis to a theological dimension: 'Phenomenology here transcends
itself towards the essential doctrine of Scholasticism: the existential
openness [*seinshafte Aufgebrochenheit*] of the creature towards God
lodged in the inner difference between being thus and being there', i.e.
between essence and existence.[57]

At first sight, Delp and Przywara's criticisms seem to demonstrate merely that Scholastic ontology is a Procrustean bed unfit
for Heidegger's existential analytic. Rather than trying to tune
into Heidegger's methodological and terminological innovations,
they transpose his terms back into the metaphysical system that
Heidegger seeks to expose as inadequate. It is clear, for example,
that Heidegger does not in fact try to deny an ontological difference;
indeed, his work is premised on it. Rather, he seeks to problematize
what we can know and how we can speak of Being from our inescapably localized and temporal perspective. The dictum 'The "essence"
of Dasein lies in its existence'[58] is deliberately unsettling: an 'out-
rageous send-up' (L. P. Hemming[59]) of the Scholastic definition of
God as the necessary being, rather than merely the transposition
of a definition of God onto man. Delp's pre-critical assimilation of
Heideggerian to Scholastic terms is similarly inadequate, as Edith
Stein already notes.[60] And yet for all that, their counter-question
whether Heidegger really can extract himself from metaphysical
commitment as easily as he would like commands attention. If neither Delp nor Przywara succeeds in formulating this question in a

---

[55] Przywara, 'Drei Richtungen', 262. On the unity of being and essence in God, see e.g.
Thomas Aquinas, *ST* 1. 2. 1.
[56] Przywara, 'Drei Richtungen', 262.   [57] Ibid., 264.
[58] *SZ* § 9, 42.   [59] In private correspondence with the author.
[60] See ESGA 11/12, 483.

manner adequate to Heidegger's analysis, their colleague Edith Stein comes considerably closer to doing so.

Stein had known Heidegger personally since 1916 through their respective work with Husserl. To her friend and colleague Roman Ingarden, she recounted a memorable 'religion-philosophical walk' in 1918 with Husserl and 'little Heidegger',[61] and continued to report on Heidegger's development in subsequent years, noting in particular the 'decisive' differences between him and Husserl.[62] She read *Being and Time* 'soon after it was published, being left with a strong impression',[63] and grappled with the work first in an unpublished manuscript entitled 'Die weltanschauliche Bedeutung der Phänomenologie' (*c.*1932)[64] and then in a 50-page précis and appraisal of 'Heidegger's existential philosophy' (1935–7) presented as an appendix to her own *magnum opus*, *Finite and Eternal Being*.[65] In 1931, Heidegger in turn read the manuscript of Stein's *Potency and Act*—an early version of *Finite and Eternal Being*, prepared as a qualifying thesis (*Habilitation*) for Freiburg—and invited Stein to what she described as a 'very stimulating and fruitful' discussion about it at his Freiburg home.[66]

Stein praises the 'richness and force of the often truly illuminating analysis' in Heidegger's 'great fragment', which seems to her the contemporary book that has 'most strongly influenced the philosophical

[61] 'Wir machten...zu dritt einen—übrigens sehr hübschen—religionsphilosophischen Spaziergang, der sich bis eben (3/4 12) hinzog'; Edith Stein to Roman Ingarden, 8 June 1918; in ESGA 4, 85–6; p. 85.

[62] Stein to Ingarden, 9 October 1926; in ESGA 4, 172. See also her letters of 15 October 1921 (ESGA 4, 144), 24 October 1926 (ESGA 4, 174), and 2 October 1927 (ESGA 4, 185). The substance of Stein's analysis, collected as 'Gegensatz von Husserl und Heidegger' (1932), was published posthumously in Stein, *Die weltanschauliche Bedeutung der Phänomenologie* (Freiburg: Herder, 1962), 1–17.

[63] ESGA 11/12, 7. Cf. Stein's more informal comment to Ingarden, as early as 2 October 1927, that reading *Being and Time* has made clear to her that Heidegger 'etwas Großes ist und daß er uns alle in die Tasche stecken kann' (ESGA 4, 185).

[64] See ESGA 11/12, xx (preface).

[65] *Endliches und ewiges Sein: Versuch eines Aufstiegs zum Sinn des Seins*, though written for publication and completed in 1938, could not be published during Stein's lifetime because of National Socialist restrictions on Jewish publications. It was published posthumously, with the Heidegger appendix, as volume i of *Edith Steins Werke*, ed. Lucy Gelber and Romaeus Leuven (Freiburg: Herder, 1951). The appendix was dropped from subsequent reprints, and first re-inserted in 2006 as 'Anhang: Martin Heideggers Existenzphilosophie' in ESGA 11/12, 445–99. (See n. 5 of Chapter 6.)

[66] Stein to Ingarden, 15 December 1931; ESGA 4, 225–26. Stein reports being grateful to Heidegger for working through the manuscript despite knowing that any attempt to submit it for *Habilitation* would be 'hopeless' (*aussichtslos*) in the current political climate.

thought of today'.[67] However, Stein also thinks that this vibrancy and depth defies (rather than springs from) the assumption that 'guides and dominates the whole work', namely of the human as at once *solus ipse* and radically temporal.[68] With her friend and colleague Hedwig Conrad-Martius (whom she cites at length), Stein locates the greatest strength of Heidegger's work in his circumvention of 'all subjectivizing, relativizing and idealizing spectres' of modern philosophy towards a renewed, direct access to Being by means of an 'inimitably sharp and energetically developed conception of the human I' as a being that conducts itself *vis-à-vis* Being.[69] This Heideggerian 'I', as Stein reads it, is capable precisely of grasping 'not only its own Being, but also the Being of the world and the divine Being which grounds all created Being'.[70] Heidegger's own descriptions of human existence as 'thrown', as 'with others', and as 'fallen', in particular, inherently point beyond themselves to an ungrasped and ungraspable origin which, she concludes, is only revealed in Catholic dogma.[71] Heidegger's own refusal of the question of this origin, by contrast, is in Stein's estimation entirely dogmatic, motivated not by unbiased enquiry but rather by the 'axiomatic attempt to prove the temporality of Being', which leads him to 'bar any unfolding perspective on eternity' in his analyses.[72]

This dogmatism is particularly evident, for Stein, in Heidegger's discussion of death. This discussion, though in many ways the most profound aspect of *Being and Time*, must be queried both regarding its self-positioning *vis-à-vis* religious belief and regarding its own analysis. On the former, Heidegger contends that the ontological analysis of death as the end of human life implies no judgement on the question whether or not there is a life after death—indeed, that the 'ontic' question of life after death can only be asked after the 'full ontological essence' of death has been grasped.[73] But Heidegger's analysis cannot be said to leave open the possibility of life after death (except in an extremely attenuated sense of life) if it is already defined as the end of existence or Dasein. Consequently, Stein points out, the decisive question regarding the meaning of death, and therefore of Dasein, is precisely whether it is indeed the end of existence or merely the transition

---

[67] ESGA 11/12, 445.   [68] Ibid., 471.

[69] Ibid., 481, quoting Hedwig Conrad-Martius, 'Sein und Zeit' (review), *Philosophischer Anzeiger* 8 (1933), 185.

[70] Ibid., 481.

[71] Ibid., 465–70.   [72] Ibid., 482.   [73] *SZ* § 49, 247–8.

from one form of being to another. 'If it should turn out to be the case that the analysis of Dasein cannot provide an answer to this question', she concludes, 'then this would show precisely that the analysis of Dasein is not capable of resolving the question of the meaning of death, and therefore also cannot give sufficient information about the meaning of Dasein.'[74]

Such inadequacy is made likelier by the internal problems of Heidegger's analysis of death. One of these—relating to the possibility of a genuine engagement with death in the experience of the death of a loved one—has already been mentioned: in Heidegger's phenomenology, anticipation of death must fulfil a role that, even on his own admission elsewhere, only love can fulfil, namely the *valorization* of the life threatened by death.[75] A similar perspective can be brought to bear on Heidegger's analysis of dread (*Angst*). Heidegger describes dread as at once dread *of* and dread *for* one's own being. Stein regards this as a sleight of hand, concealing two very different senses of 'one's own being':

> Is it the same aspect of being *of* which and *for* which one is afraid? That of which one is afraid is the possibility of not being attested by dread: It is the experience of the *nullity of our being*. That for which one is afraid— i.e. that with which man is concerned in his being—is being as *plenitude that one wants to preserve and not let go*. This goes unmentioned in Heidegger's entire analysis, and yet alone would be able to ground it.... Dread *of* not-being-able-to-be and dread *for* being-able-to-be [are] possible only because human existence [lit.: being] is participation in a plenitude which always slips through our fingers and is always being gained: life and death at the same time.[76]

Stein's critique is more sensitive than Delp's or Przywara's to Heidegger's method: Rather than faulting him for altering the traditional sense of 'being' or failing to adhere to a dogmatically assumed doctrine of analogy, her criticisms arise from phenomenological observation and conceptual analysis. Stein's conclusion is that Heidegger's analyses, in so far as they are phenomenologically correct, point beyond themselves to realities that exceed the grasp of phenomenology, but must nevertheless be acknowledged as conditions of the possibility of the phenomena at hand. This line of thought is not wholly alien to Heidegger:

[74] ESGA 11/12, 472.
[75] See Chapter 6. [76] ESGA 11/12, 473.

after all, for him death is just such a reality systematically exceeding the grasp of phenomenology.[77] What Stein seeks to show is that 'death' or 'nothing' can fulfil their function in his analysis only by a systematic ambiguity, which must be exposed.

For Stein, it is at this point that an appeal to revelation or dogma as a supplementary source of knowledge legitimately comes into play. If (Stein reasons) phenomenology requires a grounding it cannot encompass, and if an available set of (religious) teachings both accurately predicts the results of phenomenological enquiry and proffers such grounding, then the theologian is justified in heeding the metaphysical claims of that teaching.[78] This does not render phenomenological analysis superfluous within a theological enterprise. Rather, it tasks phenomenology with providing a 'grammar' (in the late Wittgensteinian sense) of certain things that Christian doctrine asserts but does not describe. Thus, for example, Heidegger offers a grammatical analysis of 'life', and so also delineates what characteristics must be posited of the Christian idea of life after death if that life is to count as 'life' in any recognizably human sense. The most significant of these characteristics, on a Steinian reading, are relationality and orientation towards possibility. We will return to this in the final section of this chapter.

To some extent, Stein's theological project is a return to Heidegger's own earliest use of phenomenology as a method adequate to describing religious experience. But must not her project therefore eventually bend to Heidegger's own realization, in the mid-1920s, that a rigorous pursuit of the phenomenological method ultimately does not support but exposes the inadequacy of a dogmatic insistence on the 'basic' (or, in his terminology, ontological) nature of specifically *religious* experience? Though attractive, to answer in the affirmative would be to absolutize Heidegger's highly specific theological path, forgetting the extent to which his reasoning was tied to his progressively Protestant reading and sensibilities. But whereas Heidegger was a cradle Catholic directly confronted by the authoritarian and restrictive measures of the Anti-Modernist Oath and the *Doctoris Angelici*, Stein did not convert to Catholicism until 1922, when the Thomist tradition was being reinvigorated by thinkers such as Réginald Garrigou-Lagrange and

---

[77] See esp. Mulhall, *Heidegger and Being and Time*, ch. 4.
[78] There is an interesting similarity between this claim and G. K. Chesterton's description of the Church as 'a truth-telling thing' in *Orthodoxy* (London: John Lane, 1909), 291 ('Authority and the Adventurer').

Jacques Maritain. Thus, whereas Heidegger experienced the Church as a source of academic constraint, Stein felt restrained in her work not by the Roman magisterium but by the German academy, which barred her from qualifying as a professor on the grounds of her sex. Partly for these biographical reasons, Heidegger rejected the Scholastic tradition from the outset of his career as incapable of accommodating the questioning attitude and temporal openness that seemed to him definitive of true human experience and its description. Stein, by contrast, pursued her phenomenological investigations within the Scholastic tradition, which seemed to her a framework capable of accommodating and contextualizing them.

One of the most relevant differences between Stein's Thomist and Heidegger's Lutheran sensibilities in relation to their shared commitment to phenomenology is the Catholic affirmation—rejected or disregarded by much of the Lutheran tradition—of God's continual presence within man. Responding to the question whether God is in all things, Aquinas argues that God, who is 'very Being by His own essence', is indeed not only present but 'innermost in each thing'; for to be is nothing other than to be continually preserved in being by God, 'as light is caused in the air by the sun as long as the air remains illuminated'.[79] Thus, whereas the Lutheran tradition has always stressed what Kierkegaard calls the 'infinite qualitative difference' between man and God—the immeasurable rift both between created and uncreated being and between human depravity and divine holiness—the Thomist tradition has tended to emphasize the God who is '*magis intimum cuilibet*'. While this idea remained in the background of late-nineteenth-century neo-Scholasticism, it regained its central position in the Thomist revival of Maritain, Gilson, and Stein herself.

But this means that for a Thomist thinker like Stein, a phenomenological analysis of human existence risks not merely incompleteness but incoherence by bracketing the divine. This is the implicit argument running through *Finite and Eternal Being*, in which she seeks to show—beginning from Aquinas's *De Ente et Essentia* ('Of Being and Essence') and proceeding by way of phenomenological analysis—that 'the "I am" of the person only finds its fullness, its ultimate meaning and grounding in the "I am" of the Eternal One'.[80] What Heidegger contributes, from this perspective, are certain correctives and emphases latent in the Thomist tradition, but buried by the Vatican I emphasis on a

---

[79] *Summa Theologiae* 1. 8. 1 (see also 1. 4. 1 ad 3).   [80] ESGA 11/12, xviii.

'perennial philosophy'. In particular, Heidegger can be interpreted as suggesting an eschatological account of the ontological difference postulated by Aquinas. Where in neo-Scholastic thought, the creature is statically poised between 'is' and 'is not'—a middle position correlative with the difference between its being and its essence—in Heidegger, this ontological difference is not a question of being and essence but of eschatological diastasis. Some of the implications of such a shift of emphasis are sketched in the final section of this chapter.

FUTURE DIRECTIONS

As the preceding chapters have shown, Heidegger's eschatology without eschaton seems compelling partly because it uncovers the weaknesses of two competing theological approaches. On one hand, it exposes the *philosophia perennis* of Catholic neo-Scholasticism as inadequate to the human spirit, which is inherently temporal, and so can neither speak nor be spoken about from a spuriously assumed God's-eye view. Call this Roman Catholicism's denial of eschatology. On the other hand, Heidegger shows up a split within the eschatologies of Protestant thinkers from Luther to Thurneysen—a split between, first, their avowedly *experiential* insight into a constitutive human dread, affliction, or care in the face of one's own sinful existence, lived in anticipation of death, and, second, their dogmatic framing of this affliction by the anticipation of externally declared justification on the coming Day of Judgement. Call this Lutheranism's divided eschatology. As this chapter has begun to show, a theological response to Heidegger capable of responding to these challenges without relinquishing a specifically Christian perspective needs to integrate aspects of both a 'Catholic' and a 'Protestant' perspective. Specifically, such a response needs to display a dialectical attitude grounded not primarily in the depravity but in the incompleteness of man, and focused on Christ's Incarnation as occasioned not principally by man's Fall, but by God's eternal purpose of human participation in divine life—of *theosis*. I can here do no more than outline some aspects of such an eschatological perspective as they emerge from the Christian source texts and the responses to Heidegger of Bultmann, Stein, and others.

Heidegger describes death as 'an imminence [*Bevorstand*]', 'something *vis-à-vis which* Dasein *acts*'.[81] But this imminent death, he has

---

[81] SZ § 50, 250.

said earlier, is not an other, but Dasein itself, facing itself as capable of authenticity: 'With death, Dasein stands before itself in its *ownmost* capability [lit.: possibility] of being.'[82] In other words, death, as Helmut Echternach pointedly formulates it, 'is the mirror, itself unseen, in which Dasein beholds itself; it becomes real only in the function of making Dasein its ownmost by concerning it ownmostly.'[83] Differently formulated, humans are essentially self-reflective; and according to Heidegger, death is the condition of the possibility of that self-reflexion. This means both that we could not see ourselves if we were not mortal and that, conversely, we cannot see ourselves truly except as mortal.

'Onto-theology', seen from this critical Heideggerian perspective, is an escape mechanism (*Sicherungstendenz*) that substitutes God for death (or Nothing). It constructs God as the 'mirror' in which humans see themselves: a mirror of their own making, projecting their desire for infinity onto the deity. It is this structural distortion, related to the Christian inability to 'ask questions',[84] which Heidegger calls, in a 1929 letter to Elisabeth Blochmann, an 'abhorrence'.[85]

But a reading of the earliest Christian sources that is sensitive to Heidegger's analysis reveals an eschatological vision that reverses this structure altogether. For in the New Testament epistles and related texts, it is not God but humans who are, in some sense, 'mirrors'. Now that Christ has been revealed, Paul writes, 'we, who with unveiled faces all reflect the Lord's glory, are being transformed into his likeness with ever-increasing glory, which comes from the Lord, who is the Spirit.'[86] This process will not be complete until the eschaton. As St John exhorts his community, 'Beloved, now are we the sons of God, and it doth not yet appear what we shall be: but we know that, when he shall appear, we shall be like him; for we shall see him as he is.'[87] And in that most celebrated of Pauline visions, 'we now see in a mirror, dimly, but then we will see face to face. Now I know only in part; then I will know fully, even as I have been

---

[82] *SZ* § 50, 250.

[83] Helmut Echternach, 'Die Auferstehungshoffnung als Voraussetzung der Todeswirklichkeit: Zur Auseinandersetzung über das Todesproblem mit Heidegger, Nietzsche und anderen', *Christentum und Wissenschaft* 6 (1930), 241–9; p. 243.

[84] GA 40, 9.

[85] Letter dated 12 September 1929; in Storck (ed.), *Martin Heidegger/Elisabeth Blochmann*, 33.

[86] 2 Cor. 3: 18.   [87] 1 John 3: 2. See also Col. 3: 3–4.

fully known.'[88] Eschatological reflection here exposes a firm demarcation of the limits of human knowledge, including knowledge of self: humans cannot fathom their own identity in advance of the Resurrection because they cannot, in advance of that End, see the God in whose image they are made.

This understanding of humans as being themselves in reflecting God is also fundamental to Augustine's *Confessions*. What Heidegger regards as an importation of Neo-Platonist *visio* is in fact deeply Christian. For Augustine, one central aspect of the discovery that the memory exceeds the human grasp is that it contains an implicit knowledge of 'the happy life' (*vitam beatam*): 'Is not the happy life that which all desire, which indeed no one fails to desire? But how have they known about it so as to want it? Where did they see it to love it?'[89] To turn to Christ is to recognize this *anamnesis* as the presence of God in the human soul; for the happy life is nothing other than enjoyment of God, the *summum bonum*.[90]

However, this presence in a sense does not alleviate but only concentrates the restlessness of the human heart, because it is not the presence-at-hand of an object, but the presence '*magis intimum cuilibet*' of the One who is both Maker and Other, at a depth of the believer's heart which (as Augustine has just emphasized) is beyond his or her own grasp.[91] In other words, it is a perpetual reminder that the believer is not 'self-contained', but made in the image of, and in relation to, God: '*fecisti nos ad te*'. This implies that he or she is not even tendentially self-identical, but can only come to him- or herself in the enjoyment of another—'*et inquietum est cor nostrum, donec requiescat in te*'. Augustine's eschatology, in other words, is not a Neo-Platonic import, but distinctively Christian—an eschatology in which the human being is ultimately not self-reflective but 'God-reflective', and therefore can never find rest in him- or herself, but only in an eternal, 'face to face' encounter with God.

This theological principle, derived from Christian sources under the pressure of Heidegger's investigations, shares with its Protestant interlocutors a valorization of the finite and temporal perspective of human beings, and with its Catholic interlocutors an emphasis on

---

[88] 1 Cor. 13: 12.
[89] *Confessiones* X. xx (29).
[90] 'Gaudere de te, ad te, propter te'; *Confessiones* X. xxii (32); see also X. xxvii (38).
[91] Cf. Thomas Aquinas, *Summa Theologiae* 1. 8. 1; *Confessiones* X. xx (29).

Christ's death and resurrection as occasioned not primarily by the severity of human sin (and consequent need for restoration) but by the incompleteness of their nature, which is to be fulfilled in communion with God. This theological starting point differs markedly from the premises on which Heidegger himself began to test the relation between religious experience and the phenomenological method. To test this relation anew is one of the joyful tasks Heidegger has bequeathed to theology.

Bibliography

Works by Heidegger

Volumes of the Gesamtausgabe:

GA 1 *Frühe Schriften* (1912–16), ed. Friedrich-Wilhelm von Herrmann (Frankfurt: Klostermann, 1978).

GA 4 *Erläuterungen zu Hölderlins Dichtung* (1936–68), ed. Friedrich-Wilhelm von Herrmann (Frankfurt: Klostermann, 2nd edn., 1996).

GA 5 *Holzwege* (1935–46), ed. Friedrich-Wilhelm von Herrmann (Frankfurt: Klostermann, 2nd edn., 2003).

GA 9 *Wegmarken* (1919–61), ed. Friedrich-Wilhelm von Herrmann (Frankfurt: Klostermann, 2nd edn., 1996).

GA 12 *Unterwegs zur Sprache* (1950-9), ed. Friedrich-Wilhelm von Herrmann (Frankfurt: Klostermann, 1985).

GA 13 *Aus der Erfahrung des Denkens* (1910–76), ed. Hermann Heidegger (Frankfurt: Klostermann, 2nd edn., 2002).

GA 14 *Zur Sache des Denkens* (1962-4), ed. Friedrich-Wilhelm von Herrmann. Frankfurt: Klostermann, 2007.

GA 16 *Reden und andere Zeugnisse eines Lebensweges* (1910–76), ed. Hermann (Heidegger Frankfurt: Klostermann, 2000).

GA 18 *Grundbegriffe der aristotelischen Philosophie* (SS 1924), ed. Mark Michalski Frankfurt: (Klostermann, 2002).

GA 20 *Prolegomena zur Geschichte des Zeitbegriffs* (SS 1925), ed. Petra Jaeger. (Frankfurt: Klostermann, 2nd edn., 1988).

GA 21 *Logik: Die Frage nach der Wahrheit* (WS 1925/6), ed. Walter Biemel. (Frankfurt: Klostermann, 2nd edn., 1995).

GA 29/30 *Die Grundbegriffe der Metaphysik: Welt–Endlichkeit–Einsamkeit* (WS 1929/30), ed. Friedrich-Wilhelm von Herrmann (Frankfurt: Klostermann, 3rd edn., 2004).

GA 40 *Einführung in die Metaphysik* (SS 1935), ed. Petra Jaeger (Frankfurt: Klostermann, 1983).

GA 56/57 *Zur Bestimmung der Philosophie* (KNS 1919 and SS 1919), ed. Bernd Heimbüchel (Frankfurt: Klostermann, 2nd edn., 1999).

GA 58 *Grundprobleme der Phänomenologie* (WS 1919/20), ed. Hans-Helmuth Gander (Frankfurt: Klostermann, 1992).

GA 60 *Phänomenologie des religiösen Lebens* (1918/19, WS 1920/1 and SS 1921), ed. Matthias Jung, Thomas Regehly, and Claudius Strube (Frankfurt: Klostermann, 1995).

GA 61 *Phänomenologische Interpretationen zu Aristoteles: Einführung in die phänomenologische Forschung* (WS 1921/2), ed. Walter Bröcker and Käte Bröcker-Oltmanns (Frankfurt: Klostermann, 2nd edn., 1994).

GA 62 *Phänomenologische Interpretationen ausgewählter Abhandlungen des Aristoteles zu Ontologie und Logik* (1922 and SS 1922), ed. Günther Neumann (Frankfurt: Klostermann, 2005).

GA 63 *Ontologie. Hermeneutik der Faktizität* (SS 1923), ed. Käte Bröcker-Oltmanns (Frankfurt: Klostermann, 2nd edn., 1995).

GA 64 *Der Begriff der Zeit* (1924), ed. Friedrich-Wilhelm von Herrmann (Frankfurt: Klostermann, 2004).

GA 66 *Besinnung* (1938–9), ed. Friedrich-Wilhelm von Herrmann (Frankfurt: Klostermann, 1997).

Single works:
'Das Problem der Sünde bei Martin Luther' (1924). In Bernd Jaspert (ed.), *Sachgemäße Exegese: Die Protokolle aus Rudolf Bultmanns Neutestamentlichen Seminaren 1921–1951.* (Marburg: Elwert, 1996), 28–33.

'"Nur noch ein Gott kann uns retten": *Spiegel*-Gespräch mit Martin Heidegger am 23. September 1966', *Der Spiegel* 30, no. 23 (31 May 1976), 193–219.

Sein und Zeit. (Tübingen: Max Niemeyer Verlag, 18th edn., 2001 [1927]).

'Wilhelm Diltheys Forschungsarbeit und der gegenwärtige Kampf um eine historische Weltanschauung (Kasseler Vorträge)', ed. Walter Bröcker and Frithjof Rodi. *Dilthey-Jahrbuch* 8 (1992–3), 143–80.

Correspondences:
Denker, Alfred (ed.), *Martin Heidegger/Heinrich Rickert: Briefe 1912–1933* (Frankfurt: Klostermann, 2002).

Großmann, Andreas, and Christof Landmesser (eds.), *Rudolf Bultmann/ Martin Heidegger: Briefwechsel 1925–1975* (Frankfurt: Klostermann, 2009).

Heidegger, Gertrud (ed.), *'Mein liebes Seelchen!': Briefe Martin Heideggers an seine Frau Elfride, 1915–1970* (Munich: Deutsche Verlags-Anstalt, 2005).

Ludz, Ursula (ed.), *Hannah Arendt/Martin Heidegger: Briefe 1925–1975* (Frankfurt: Klostermann, 2nd edn., 1999).

Storck, Joachim (ed.), *Martin Heidegger/Elisabeth Blochmann: Briefwechsel 1918–1969* (Marbach: Deutsches Literaturarchiv, 2nd edn., 1990).

Tietjen, Hartmut (ed.), 'Drei Briefe Martin Heideggers an Karl Löwith', in Dietrich Papenfuss and Otto Pöggeler (eds.), *Zur philosophischen Aktualität Heideggers.* 2 vols (Frankfurt: Klostermann, 1990. Vol. ii), 27–38.

Early Responses to Being and Time:

Barth, Hans, 'Zur Philosophie unserer Zeit', *Neue Schweizer Rundschau,* 22 (1929), 912–17.

_____ 'Ontologie und Idealismus: Eine Auseinandersetzung von Heinrich Barth mit Martin Heidegger', *Zwischen den Zeiten,* 7 (1929), 511–40.

Beck, Maximilian (ed.), *Philosophische Hefte* 1: *Sonderheft über Martin Heidegger* (1928).

Brunner, Emil, 'Theologie und Ontologie, oder: Die Theologie am Scheidewege', *Zeitschrift für Theologie und Kirche,* 12 (1931), 111–22.

Bultmann, Rudolf, 'Martin Heidegger', in Hermann Gunkel and Leopold Zscharnack (eds.), *Religion in Geschichte und Gegenwart* (Tübingen: Mohr Siebeck, 2nd edn., 1927–31). Vol. ii, cols. 1687–8.

Conrad-Martius, Hedwig, 'Sein und Zeit'. Review. *Philosophischer Anzeiger,* 8 (1933), 185.

_____ 'Sein und Zeit'. Review. *Deutsche Kunstwissenschaft,* 46 (1933), 246–51.

Delp, Alfred, *Tragische Existenz: Zur Philosophie Martin Heideggers* (Freiburg: Herder, 1931).

Dr. –b. 'Tragische Existenz. Auseinandersetzung mit der Philosophie Martin Heideggers,' *Germania: Zeitung für das deutsche Volk,* 65, no. 361 (29 December 1935).

Echternach, Helmut, 'Die Auferstehungshoffnung als Voraussetzung der Todeswirklichkeit: Zur Auseinandersetzung über das Todesproblem mit Heidegger, Nietzsche und anderen,' *Christentum und Wissenschaft,* 6 (1930), 241–9.

Ernst, F, 'Moderne Versuche zur Gewinnung eines neuen Lebensverständnisses in Philosophie und Theologie: M. Heidegger und dialektische Theologie', *Zeitschrift für systematische Theologie,* 9 (1931), 25–46.

Fondane, Benjamin, 'Sur la route de Dostoyewski: Martin Heidegger', *Cahiers du sud,* 19 (1932), 378–92.

Löwith, Karl, 'Grundzüge der Entwicklung der Phänomenologie zur Philosophie und ihr Verhältnis zur protestantischen Theologie', *Theologische Rundschau,* 2 (1930), 26–64 and 333–61.

_____ 'Phänomenologische Ontologie und protestantische Theologie', *Zeitschrift für Theologie und Kirche,* 11 (1930), 365–99.

_____ 'Les Implications politiques de la philosophie de l'existence chez Heidegger', *Les Temps modernes,* 14 (1946), 343–60.

Przywara, Erich, 'Drei Richtungen der Phänomenologie', *Stimmen der Zeit,* 115 (1928), 252–64.

Other Primary Works

Acta Apostolicae Sedis (Vatican City: Typis Polyglottis Vaticanis, 1909–).

Althaus, Paul, *Die letzten Dinge: Lehrbuch der Eschatologie* (Gütersloh: Mohn, 9th edn., 1964 [1922]).

Aquinas, Thomas, *Summa Theologiae: Latin Text and English Translation, Introductions, Notes, Appendices, and Glossaries*. 61 vols., ed. Thomas Gilby et al. (London: Blackfriars in conjunction with Eyre & Spottiswoode, 1964–81).

Arendt, Hannah, *Der Liebesbegriff bei Augustin: Versuch einer philosophischen Interpretation* (Berlin: Springer, 1929). ET: *Love and Saint Augustine*, ed. Joanna Vecchiarelli Scott and Judith Chelius Stark (Chicago: University of Chicago Press, 1996).

Athanasius of Alexandria, *De Incarnatione Verbi* (Patrologia Graeca 25).

Augustine, Bishop of Hippo, *Confessions*, trans. and (ed.), Henry Chadwick (Oxford: Oxford University Press, 1991).

von Balthasar, Hans Urs, *Apokalypse der deutschen Seele*, 3 vols. (Salzburg: Pustet, 1937–9).

———— *Eschatologie in unserer Zeit: Die letzten Dinge des Menschen und das Christentum* (1954/5), ed. Jan-Heiner Tück (Einsiedeln: Johannes Verlag, 2005).

———— 'Eschatologie', in Johannes Feiner, Josef Trütsch, and Franz Böckle (eds.), *Fragen der Theologie heute* (Einsiedeln: Benziger Verlag, 2nd edn., 1957), 403–21.

Barth, Karl, *Der Römerbrief* (Munich: Chr. Kaiser, 1919 [2nd fully revised edn., 1922]).

———— 'Unerledigte Anfragen an die heutige Theologie', In Karl Barth and Eduard Thurneysen *Zur inneren Lage des Christentums* (Munich: Chr. Kaiser, 1920), 1–14.

———— 'Das Wort Gottes als Aufgabe der Theologie', *Christliche Welt*, 36 (1922), 858–73.

———— 'Ludwig Feuerbach: Mit einem polemischen Nachwort', *Zwischen den Zeiten*, 5 (1927), 10–40.

———— 'Verheißung, Zeit—Erfüllung', *Zwischen den Zeiten*, 9 (1931), 457–63.

———— *Kirchliche Dogmatik*, 4 vols. (Zurich: Evangelischer Verlag, 1932–70). ET: *Church Dogmatics*, ed. G. W. Bromiley and T. F. Torrance, trans. H. Knight et al. (Edinburgh: T. & T. Clark, 1936–77).

———— and Emil Brunner, *Briefwechsel 1911–1966*, ed. Eberhard Busch (Zurich: Theologischer Verlag, 2000).

———— and Rudolf Bultmann, *Briefwechsel 1911–1966*, ed. Bernd Jaspert. (Zurich: Theologischer Verlag, 2nd revised and expanded edn., 1994).

———— and Eduard Thurneysen, *Briefwechsel 1913–1935*, 3 vols. (Zurich: Theologischer Verlag, 1973–2000).

Bousset, Wilhelm, *Der Antichrist in der Überlieferung des Judentums, des Neuen Testaments und der alten Kirche* (Göttingen: Vandenhoeck & Ruprecht, 1895).

———— *Die jüdische Apokalyptik: Ihre religionsgeschichtliche Herkunft und ihre Bedeutung für das neue Testament* (Berlin, 1903).

———— *Die Offenbarung Johannis: Kritisch-exegetischer Kommentar über das Neue Testament* (Göttingen: Vandenhoeck & Ruprecht, 3rd edn., 1906).

Braig, Carl, *Vom Sein: Abriß der Ontologie* (Freiburg: Herder, 1896).

———— *Vom Denken: Abriß der Logik* (Freiburg: Herder, 1896).

———— *Vom Erkennen: Abriß der Noetik*. Freiburg: Herder, 1897.

Brunner, Emil, 'Gesetz und Offenbarung: Eine theologische Grundlegung', *Theologische Blätter*, 4 (1925), cols. 53–8.

Bultmann, Rudolf, 'Die Frage der "dialektischen" Theologie: Eine Auseinandersetzung mit Erik Peterson', *Zwischen den Zeiten*, 4 (1926), 40–59.

———— 'Martin Heidegger' in Hermann Gunkel and Leopold Zscharnack (eds.), *Religion in Geschichte und Gegenwart* (Tübingen: Mohr Siebeck, 2nd edn., 1927–31), vol. ii, cols. 1687–8.

———— 'Die Eschatologie des Johannes-Evangeliums', *Zwischen den Zeiten*, 6 (1928), 4–22.

———— 'Die Geschichtlichkeit des Daseins und der Glaube: Antwort an Gerhardt Kuhlmann', *Zeitschrift für Theologie und Kirche*, 11 (1930), 339–64.

———— *Das Evangelium des Johannes*. Meyer's Kritisch-Exegetischer Kommentar 2. (Göttingen: Vandenhoeck & Ruprecht, 21st edn., 1986 [1941]).

———— 'Neues Testament und Mythologie', in Hans-Werner Bartsch (ed.), *Kerygma und Mythos*, i: *Ein theologisches Gespräch* (Hamburg: Reich & Heidrich, 1948), 15–53.

———— *History and Eschatology* (Edinburgh: Edinburgh University Press, 1957).

———— and Friedrich Gogarten, *Briefwechsel 1921–1967*, ed. Hermann Götz Göckeritz (Tübingen: Mohr Siebeck, 2002).

Bultmann Lemke, Antje, 'Der unveröffentlichte Nachlaß von Rudolf Bultmann—Ausschnitte aus dem biographischen Quellenmaterial', in *Rudolf Bultmanns Werk und Wirkung*, ed. Bernd Jaspert (Darmstadt: Wissenschaftliche Buchgesellschaft, 1984), 194–210.

Cavell, Stanley, *Must We Mean What We Say?* (Cambridge: Cambridge University Press, 1976).

———— *The Claim of Reason* (Oxford: Oxford University Press, 1979).

———— *In Quest of the Ordinary: Lines of Skepticism and Romanticism* (Chicago: University of Chicago Press, 1988).

———— *Conditions Handsome and Unhandsome: The Constitution of Emersonian Perfectionism* (Chicago: University of Chicago Press, 1990).

———— *Disowning Knowledge: In Seven Plays of Shakespeare* (Cambridge: Cambridge University Press, 2nd expanded edn., 2003).

———— *Cities of Words: Pedagogical Letters on a Register of the Moral Life* (Cambridge, Mass.: Harvard University Press, 2004).

Chesterton, G. K., *Orthodoxy* (London: John Lane, 1909).

Derrida, Jacques, *Margins of Philosophy*, trans. Alan Bass (Brighton: Harvester, 1982).

Dilthey, Wilhelm, *Leben Schleiermachers* (1870), Gesammelte Schriften 13–14, ed. Martin Redeker (Stuttgart: B. G. Teubner, 1966 and 1985).

_____*Einleitung in die Geisteswissenschaften* (1883), Gesammelte Schriften 1, ed. Bernhard Groethuysen (Stuttgart: B. G. Teubner, 10th edn., 2008).

_____ *Der Aufbau der geschichtlichen Welt in den Geisteswissenschaften* (1910), Gesammelte Schriften 7, ed. Bernhard Groethuysen (Stuttgart: B. G. Teubner, 8th edn., 1992).

_____ *Weltanschauung und Analyse des Menschen seit Renaissance und Reformation* (1914), Gesammelte Schriften 2, ed. Georg Misch (Stuttgart: B. G. Teubner, 11th edn., 1991).

_____ *Weltanschauungslehre: Abhandlungen zur Philosophie der Philosophie* (1931), Gesammelte Schriften 8, ed. Bernhard Groethuysen (Stuttgart: B. G. Teubner, 6th edn., 1991).

Dostojewski, Fjodor, *Sämtliche Werke*, 22 vols., trans. Dmitri Mereschkowski (Munich: Piper, 1908–14).

Ebbinghaus, Julius, *Interpretation und Kritik*, ed. Hariolf Oberer and Georg Geismann (Bonn: Bouvier, 1981).

Gadamer, Hans-Georg, *Philosophische Lehrjahre: Eine Rückschau* (Frankfurt: Klostermann, 1977).

_____*Heideggers Wege: Studien zum Spätwerk* (Tübingen: Mohr Siebeck, 1983).

_____ 'Selbstdarstellung 1975', in *Gadamer Lesebuch*, ed. Jean Grondin (Tübingen: Mohr Siebeck, 1997), 1–30.

Gogarten, Friedrich, *Gehören und Verstehen: Ausgewählte Aufsätze* (1928–66), ed. Hermann Götz Göckeritz (Tübingen: Mohr Siebeck, 1988).

Gunkel, Hermann, *Schöpfung und Chaos in Urzeit und Endzeit: Eine religionsgeschichtliche Untersuchung über Gen 1 und Apk Joh 21* (Göttingen: Vandenhoeck & Ruprecht, 1895).

Heim, Karl, 'Ontologie und Theologie', *Zeitschrift für Theologie und Kirche*, 11 (1930), 325–38.

_____ *Der evangelische Glaube und das Denken der Gegenwart: Grundzüge einer christlichen Lebensanschauung*, 6 vols. (Hamburg: Furche, 1931–51).

Hölderlin, Friedrich, *Sämtliche Werke und Briefe*, 3 vols, ed. Jochen Schmidt. (Frankfurt: Deutsche Klassiker Verlag, 1992–4).

_____*Gedichte* (ed.), Gerhard Kurz (Stuttgart: Reclam, 2003).

Husserl, Edmund, *Logische Untersuchungen*, 2 vols. (Halle: Max Niemeyer, 1907).

_____ *Briefwechsel*, 10 vols, ed. Karl Schuhmann (The Hague: Kluwer Academic Publishers, 1994).

Jaspers, Karl, *Psychologie der Weltanschauungen* (Berlin: Springer, 1919).

Kierkegaard, Søren, *Begrebet Angest: En simpel psychologisk-paapegende Overveielse i Retning af det dogmatiske*. Attributed to Vigilius Haufniensis. Copenhagen, 1844. ET: *The Concept of Anxiety*, trans. and ed., Reidar Thomte (Princeton: Princeton University Press, 1980).

_____*Sygdommen til Døden: En christelig psychologisk Udvikling til Opbyggelse og Opvækkelse*. Attributed to Anti-Climacus. Copenhagen, 1849. ET: *The*

Sickness unto Death, trans. and ed., Edna H. Hong and Howard V. Hong (Princeton: Princeton University Press, 1983).

——— *Gesammelte Werke*, 12 vols, trans. H. Gottsched and C. Schrempf (Jena: Eugen Diederichs, 1909–22 [Heidegger's edition]).

Krüger, Gerhard, 'Dialektische Methode und theologische Exegese: Logische Bemerkungen zu Barth's "Römerbrief"', *Zwischen den Zeiten*, 5 (1927), 116–57.

Kuhlmann, Gerhard, *Brunstäd und Tillich: Zum Problem einer Theonomie der Kultur* (Tübingen: Mohr Siebeck, 1928).

——— 'Zum theologischen Problem der Existenz: Fragen an Rudolf Bultmann', *Zeitschrift für Theologie und Kirche*, 10 (1929), 28–57.

——— 'Krisis der Theologie', *Zeitschrift für Theologie und Kirche*, 12 (1931), 123–46.

——— *Theologische Anthropologie im Abriß* (Tübingen: Mohr, 1935).

——— *Die Theologie am Scheidewege* (Tübingen: Mohr, 1935).

Lewis, C. S., *The Pilgrim's Regress* (London: J. M. Dent, 3rd edn., 1943).

——— *Christian Reflections*, ed. Walter Hooper (Grand Rapids, Mich.: Eerdmans, 1967).

——— *Essay Collection: Literature, Philosophy and Short Stories*, ed. Lesley Walmsley (London: HarperCollins, 2000).

Löwith, Karl, *Das Individuum in der Rolle des Mitmenschen* (Munich: Drei Masken-Verlag, 1928).

——— 'Les Implications politiques de la philosophie de l'existence chez Heidegger', *Les Temps modernes*, 2 (1946), 343–60.

——— *Weltgeschichte und Heilsgeschehen: Die theologischen Voraussetzungen der Geschichtsphilosophie* (Stuttgart: W. Kohlhammer Verlag, 1953).

——— *Mein Leben in Deutschland vor und nach 1933. Ein Bericht* (Stuttgart: J. B. Metzler, 1986).

Luther, Martin, *Exegetica opera latina* (Erlangen: C. Heyder, 1829–61).

——— *D. Martin Luthers Werke: Kritische Gesammtausgabe*, 120 vols. (Weimar: Hermann Böhlaus, 1883–2009).

——— *Luther's Works*, ed. Jaroslav Pelikan and Helmut T. Lehmann (St Louis, Mo.: Concordia Publishing House, 1958–86).

Meinong, Alexius, *Untersuchungen zur Gegenstandstheorie und Psychologie* (Leipzig: Barth, 1904).

Möhler, Johann Adam, *Symbolik*, 2 vols, ed. Josef Rupert Geiselmann (Cologne: Jakob Hegner, 1960).

Nietzsche, Friedrich, *Unzeitgemäße Betrachtungen*, ed. Peter Pütz (Munich: Goldmann, 1999).

Overbeck, Franz, *Über die Christlichkeit unserer heutigen Theologie* (Leipzig: C. G. Naumann, 1873).

——— *Über die Anfänge der patristischen Literatur* (Basle: Benno Schwabe & Co., 2nd edn., n.d. [first published 1882]).

—— *Das Johannes-Evangelium*, ed. C. A. Bernoulli (Tübingen: Mohr, 1911).

—— *Christentum und Kultur: Gedanken und Anmerkungen zur modernen Theologie*, ed. C. A. Bernoulli (Darmstadt: Wissenschaftliche Buchgesellschaft, 1919).

—— *Selbstbekenntnisse* (ed.), Eberhard Vischer. Basle: Benno Schwabe & Co., 1941.

Peterson, Erik, *Theologische Traktate* (Würzburg: Echter, 1994 [1951]).

—— *Theologie und Theologen: Briefwechsel mit Karl Barth u.a., Reflexionen und Erinnerungen*, ed. Barbara Nichtweiß (Würzburg: Echter, 2009).

Przywara, Erich, *Analogia entis* (Munich: Kösel & Pustet, 1932).

Reinach, Adolf, *Sämtliche Werke*, ed. Karl Schuhmann (Munich: Philosophia, 1989).

Rilke, Rainer Maria, *Neue Gedichte* (Leipzig: Insel-Verlag, 1907).

—— *Duineser Elegien* (Leipzig: Insel-Verlag, 1923).

Sartre, Jean Paul, *L'Être et le néant: essai d'ontologie phénoménologique*, ed. Arlette Elkaïm-Sartre (Paris: Gallimard, 1996 [1943]). ET: *Being and Nothingness: An Essay on Phenomenological Ontology*, trans. Hazel E. Barnes (London: Methuen, 1957).

Scheler, Max, *Abhandlungen und Aufsätze* (Leipzig: Weisse Bücher, 1915).

—— *Vom Ewigen im Menschen* (Leipzig: Der Neue Geist-Verlag, 1921).

Schell, Herman, *Katholische Dogmatik*, 3 vols. (Paderborn: Schöningh, 1889–93).

—— *Apologie des Christentums*, 2 vols. (Paderborn: Schöningh, 1902–5).

Schleiermacher, Friedrich, *Reden über die Religion: An die Gebildeten unter ihren Verächtern*, ed. Günter Meckenstock (Berlin: Walter de Gruyter, 2001 [1799]).

—— *Der christliche Glaube nach den Grundsätzen der evangelischen Kirche im Zusammenhang dargestellt*, ed. Rolf Schäfer (Berlin: Walter de Gruyter, 2008 [1830/1]).

Schweitzer, Albert, *Leben-Jesu-Forschung: Von Reimarum zu Wrede* (Tübingen: J. C. B. Mohr, 1906).

Stein, Edith, 'Husserls Phänomenologie und die Philosophie des Hl. Thomas von Aquino', in Martin Heidegger (ed.), *Festschrift, Edmund Husserl zum 70. Geburtstag gewidmet* (Halle: Niemeyer, 1929), 315–38.

—— *Die weltanschauliche Bedeutung der Phänomenologie* (Freiburg: Herder, 1962).

—— *Selbstbildnis in Briefen III: Briefe an Roman Ingarden*, ed. Maria Amata Neyer (Freiburg: Herder, 2nd edn., 2005). (Edith Stein Gesamtausgabe 4.)

—— *Endliches und Ewiges Sein: Versuch eines Aufstiegs zum Sinn des Seins,* ed. Andreas Uwe Müller (Freiburg: Herder, 2006). (Edith Stein Gesamtausgabe 11/12.)

Thielemans, H., 'Existence tragique: La métaphysique du nazisme', *Nouvelle Revue théologique,* 63 (1936), 561–79.

Thurneysen, Eduard, *Dostojewski* (Munich: Chr. Kaiser, 1921).
_____ 'Schrift und Offenbarung', *Zwischen den Zeiten*, 6 (1924), 3–30.
_____ 'Christus und seine Zukunft: Ein Beitrag zur Eschatologie', *Zwischen den Zeiten*, 9 (1931), 187–211.
Walther, Gerda, *Phänomenologie der Mystik* (Freiburg: Otto Walter, 2nd edn., 1955).
Williams, Charles, *Descent into Hell* (London: Faber & Faber, 1937).
Wittgenstein, Ludwig, *Philosophical Investigations/Philosophische Untersuchungen*, trans. G. E. M. Anscombe (Oxford: Blackwell, 1953).

Secondary Works
ANONYMOUS, *Il programma dei modernisti: Riposta all' Enciclica di Pio X, 'Pascendi Dominici gregis'* (Rome: Soc. Interna Scientifico-Religiosi, 1908).
Apel, Friedmar, *Himmelssehnsucht: Die Sichtbarkeit der Engel in der romantischen Literatur und Kunst sowie bei Klee, Rilke und Benjamin* (Paderborn: Igel Verlag, 1994).
Aulén, Gustaf, *Christus Victor: An Historical Study of the Three Main Types of the Idea of Atonement*, trans. A. G. Herber (London: SPCK, 1931).
Bautz, Wilhelm Friedrich, (ed.) *Biographisch-bibliographisches Kirchenlexikon*, 18 vols. (Hamm: Traugott Bautz Verlag, 1970–).
Beniston, Judith, *Welttheater: Hofmannsthal, Richard von Kralik, and the Revival of Catholic Drama in Austria, 1890–1934* (London: Maney & Son, 1998).
van, Buren, John, 'The Young Heidegger: Rumor of a Hidden King (1919–1926)', *Philosophy Today*, 33 (1989), 99–109.
_____ *The Young Heidegger: Rumor of the Hidden King* (Bloomington, Ind.: Indiana University Press, 1994).
_____ (ed. and trans.) *Supplements: From the Earliest Essays to Being and Time and Beyond* (Albany, NY: SUNY Press, 2002).
Capelle, Philippe, *Philosophie et théologie dans la pensée de M. Heidegger* (Paris: Cerf, 2nd edn., 2001).
_____ '"Katholizismus", "Protestantismus", "Christentum" und "Religion" im Denken Martin Heideggers: Tragweite und Abgrenzungen', in Alfred Denker, Hans-Helmuth Gander, and Holger Zaborowski (eds.), *Heidegger und die Anfänge seines Denkens* (Freiburg: Karl Alber Verlag, 2004), 346–71.
Caputo, John D., *Heidegger and Aquinas: An Essay on Overcoming Metaphysics* (New York: Fordham University Press, 1982).
_____ 'Heidegger and Theology', In Charles Guignon (ed.), *The Cambridge Companion to Heidegger* (Cambridge: Cambridge University Press, 1993), 270–88.
Carman, Taylor, *Heidegger's Analytic* (Cambridge: Cambridge University Press, 2003).
Casper, Bernhard, 'Martin Heidegger und die Katholische Fakultät Freiburg 1909–1923', *Freiburger Diözesan-Archiv* 100 (1980), 534–41.

Coriando, Paola-Ludovica (ed.), *'Herkunft aber bleibt stets Zukunft'*: *Martin Heidegger und die Gottesfrage* (Frankfurt: Klostermann, 1998).

Corvez, Maurice. *L'Être et la conscience morale* (Louvain: Éditions Nauwelaerts, 1968).

Critchley, Simon, and Schürmann Reiner, *On Heidegger's Being and Time* (London: Routledge, 2008).

Crowe, Benjamin, *Heidegger's Religious Origins* (Indianapolis: Indiana University Press, 2006).

_____ *Heidegger's Phenomenology of Religion: Realism and Cultural Criticism* (Indianapolis: Indiana University Press, 2007).

Deissmann, G. A., *Paulus: Eine kultur- und religionsgeschichtliche Skizze* (Tübingen: Mohr, 1911).

Dell, August, 'Ontologische Daseinsanalyse und theologisches Daseinsverständnis', in Heinrich Bornkamm (ed.), *Imago Dei: Beiträge zur theologischen Anthropologie* (Giessen: Töpelmann, 1932), 215–32.

Denker, Alfr(ed.), 'Heideggers Lebens- und Denkweg 1909–1919', in Alfred Denker, Hans-Helmuth Gander, and Holger Zaborowski (eds.), *Heidegger und die Anfänge seines Denkens* (Freiburg: Karl Alber Verlag, 2004), 97–122.

_____ and Büchin, Elsbeth, *Martin Heidegger und seine Heimat* (Stuttgart: Klett-Cotta, 2005).

_____ Gander, Hans-Helmuth, and Zaborowski, Holger (eds.), *Heidegger und die Anfänge seines Denkens* (Heidegger-Jahrbuch I.) (Freiburg: Karl Alber Verlag, 2004).

Dreyfus, Hubert L., 'Foreword', in Carol White (ed.), *Time and Death: Heidegger's Analysis of Finitude* (London: Ashgate, 2005), ix–xxxvi.

Feick, Hildegard, and Ziegler, Susanne (eds.) *Index zu Heideggers Sein und Zeit* (Tübingen: Max Niemeyer Verlag, 4th edn., 1991).

van Fleteren, Frederick (ed.), *Martin Heidegger's Interpretations of Saint Augustine* (Lewiston, NY: Edwin Mellen Press, 2005).

Glendinning, Simon, *On Being With Others: Heidegger–Wittgenstein–Derrida* (London: Routledge, 1998).

Glomsrud, Ryan, 'The Cat-Eyed Theologians: Franz Overbeck and Karl Barth', *Journal for the History of Modern Theology/Zeitschrift für neuere Theologiegeschichte*, 16 (2009), 37–57.

Greisch, Jean, 'The Eschatology of Being and the God of Time in Heidegger', *International Journal of Philosophical Studies*, 4, no. 1 (1996), 17–43.

Grimm, Jacob and Wilhelm, *Deutsches Wörterbuch*, 33 vols. (Leipzig: S. Hirzel, 1854–1971).

Han, Sang-Youn, 'Schleiermachers Religionsbegriff und die Philosophie des jungen Heideggers', unpublished Ph.D. dissertation (Universität Bochum, 2005).

Haugeland, John, 'Truth and Finitude: Heidegger's Transcendental Existentialism', in Mark Wrathall and Jeff Malpas (eds.), *Heidegger,*

Authenticity, and Modernity: Essays in Honor of Hubert L. Dreyfus. (Cambridge, Mass.: MIT Press, 2000), 43–77.

Hemming, Laurence Paul, *Heidegger's Atheism* (Notre Dame, Ind.: University of Notre Dame Press, 2002).

_____ 'Are We Still in Time to Know God? Apocalyptic, Sempiternity, and the Purposes of Experience', in L. Boeve, Y. de Maeseneer, and S. van den Bossche (eds.), *Religious Experience and Contemporary Theological Epistemology* (Leuven: Leuven University Press, 2003), 159–76.

Herbermann, C. G. (gen ed.), *The Catholic Encyclopedia*, 15 vols. (New York: Robert Appleton, 1907–14).

von Herrmann, Friedrich-Wilhelm, 'Gottsuche und Selbstauslegung. Das 10. Buch der Confessiones des heiligen Augustinus im Horizont von Heideggers hermeneutischer Phänomenologie des faktischen Lebens', *Studia Phænomenologica*, 1, nos. 3–4 (2001), 201–20.

Irlenborn, Bernd, *Der Ingrimm des Aufruhrs: Heidegger und das Problem des Bösen* (Vienna: Passagen Verlag, 2000).

Jüngel, Eberhard, *Gott als Geheimnis der Welt* (Tübingen: Paul Siebeck Verlag, 3rd edn., 1977).

_____ *Barth-Studien* (Gütersloh: Mohn, 1982).

Kerr, Fergus, *Immortal Longings: Versions of Transcending Humanity* (London: SPCK, 1997).

Kisiel, Theodore, *The Genesis of Heidegger's Being and Time* (Berkeley and Los Angeles: University of California Press, 1995).

_____ 'Why Students of Heidegger Will Have to Read Emil Lask', in Theodore Kisiel, *Heidegger's Way of Thought: Critical and Interpretative Signposts*, ed. Alfred Denker and Marion Heinz (London: Continuum, 2nd edn., 2002), 101–36.

_____ and van Buren, John (eds.), *Reading Heidegger from the Start: Essays in his Earliest Thought* (Albany, NY: State University of New York Press, 1994).

von Kralik, Richard, *Die katholische Literaturbewegung der Gegenwart: Ein Beitrag zu ihrer Geschichte* (Regensburg: Habbel, 1909).

_____ *Ein Jahr katholischer Literaturbewegung* (Regensburg: Habbel, 1910).

Kugelmann, Lothar, *Antizipation: Eine begriffsgeschichtliche Untersuchung.* (Göttingen: Vandenhoeck & Ruprecht, 1986).

Kümmel, W. G., *Das Neue Testament: Geschichte der Erforschung seiner Probleme* (Freiburg: Karl Alber Verlag, 1958).

Lairns, Dorion, *Conversations with Husserl and Fink,* ed. Richard M. Zaner (The Hague: Martinus Nijhoff, 1976).

Lehmann-Dronke, Richard, *Die Herrlichkeit Gottes auf dem Antlitz des Menschen: Ein Beitrag zur theologischen Deutung des menschlichen Antlitzes* (St Ottilien: EOS, 1997).

Love, Damian, 'Samuel Beckett and the Art of Madness', unpublished D.Phil. dissertation (University of Oxford, 2004).

de Lubac, Henri, *Surnaturel: Études historiques* (Paris: Aubier, 1946).

McCormack, Bruce, *Karl Barth's Critically Realistic Dialectical Theology: Its Genesis and Development, 1909–1936* (Oxford: Oxford University Press, 1997).

McGrath, Sean, 'The Facticity of Being God-Forsaken: The Young Heidegger and Luther's Theology of the Cross', *American Catholic Philosophical Quarterly*, 79, no. 2 (2005), 273–90.

_____ *The Early Heidegger & Medieval Philosophy: Phenomenology for the Godforsaken* (Washington: Catholic University of America Press, 2006).

_____ *Heidegger: A (Very) Critical Introduction* (Grand Rapids, Mich.: Eerdmans, 2008).

MacIntyre, Alasdair, *Edith Stein: A Philosophical Prologue* (London: Continuum, 2006).

Macquarrie, John, *An Existentialist Theology: A Comparison of Heidegger and Bultmann* (London: SCM Press, 1965).

_____ *Heidegger and Christianity*. London: SCM Press, 1994.

Meuffels, Otmar, and Dvorak, Rainer (eds.), *Wahrheit Gottes—Freiheit des Denkens: Herman Schell als Impulsgeber für Theologie und Kirche* (Würzburg: Schöningh, 2001).

Meyer, Hans, *Martin Heidegger und Thomas von Aquin* (Munich: Schöningh, 1964).

Morgan, Ben, 'Heidegger and the Mysticism of Everyday Life', in George Pattison (ed.), *Heidegger and Religion 1: Heidegger and the Theology of Crisis* (Oxford: Oxford Research Archive, 2008), 10–24.

Mulert, Hermann, *Antimodernismuseid, freie Forschung und theologische Fakultäten* (Halle: Verlag des Evangelischen Bundes, 1911).

Mulhall, Stephen, *On Being in the World: Wittgenstein and Heidegger on Seeing Aspects* (London: Routledge, 1990).

_____ *Faith and Reason* (London: Duckworth, 1994).

_____ *Philosophical Myths of the Fall* (Princeton: Princeton University Press, 2005).

_____ *Heidegger and Being and Time* (London: Routledge, 2nd edn., 2005).

Neske, Günther (ed.), *Erinnerungen an Martin Heidegger* (Pfullingen: Neske, 1977).

New Jerusalem Bible, ed. Henry Wansborough (London: Darton, Longman & Todd, 1994).

Okoyama, Kotaro, *Zur Grundlegung christlicher Ethik* (Berlin: De Gruyter, 1976).

Ott, Hugo, 'Der Habilitand Martin Heidegger und das von Schaezler'sche Stipendium: Ein Beitrag zur Wissenschaftsförderung der katholischen Kirche', *Freiburger Diözesan-Archiv*, 106 (1986), 142–4.

_____ *Martin Heidegger: Unterwegs zu seiner Biographie* (Frankfurt: Campus, 1988).

_____ 'Martin Heidegger's Catholic Origins', *American Catholic Philosophical Quarterly*, 69, no. 2 (Spring 1995), 137–56.

_____ 'Martin Heidegger und seine Beziehungen zur Görres-Gesellschaft zur Pflege der Wissenschaft im katholischen Deutschland', in Alfred Denker, Hans-Helmuth Gander, and Holger Zaborowski (eds.), *Heidegger und die Anfänge seines Denkens* (Freiburg: Karl Alber Verlag, 2004) 197–200.

Pfeiffer, Arnold, *Franz Overbecks Kritik des Christentums* (Göttingen: Vandenhoeck & Ruprecht, 1975).

Philipse, Herman, *Heidegger's Philosophy of Being: A Critical Interpretation*. (Princeton: Princeton University Press, 1998).

Pöggeler, Otto, 'Heideggers Begegnung mit Hölderlin', *Man and World* 10, no. 1 (1977), 13–61.

_____ 'Heidegger und Bultmann: Philosophie und Theologie', in Markus Happel (ed.), *Heidegger—neu gelesen* (Würzburg: Königshausen & Neumann, 1997), 41–53.

_____ 'Heideggers Luther-Lektüre im Freiburger Theologenkonvikt', in Alfred Denker, Hans-Helmuth Gander, and Holger Zaborowski (eds.), *Heidegger und die Anfänge seines Denkens* (Freiburg: Karl Alber Verlag, 2004), 185–96.

Reynolds, Stephen, 'Heidegger's Introduction to the Phenomenology of Religion', unpublished D.Phil. dissertation (University of Oxford, 2008).

Safranski, Rüdiger, *Ein Meister aus Deutschland: Heidegger und seine Zeit*. (Frankfurt am Main: Fischer Verlag, 2001).

Schaber, Johannes, 'Te lucis ante terminum: Martin Heidegger und das benediktinische Mönchtum', in Sánchez de Murillo (ed.), *Edith Stein Jahrbuch 8: Das Mönchtum* (Würzburg: Echter Verlag, 2002), 281–94.

_____ 'Martin Heideggers "Herkunft" im Spiegel der Theologie- und Kirchengeschichte des 19. und beginnenden 20. Jahrhunderts', in Alfred Denker, Hans-Helmuth Gander, and Zaborowski, Holger (eds.), *Heidegger und die Anfänge seines Denkens* (Freiburg: Karl Alber Verlag, 2004). 159–84.

_____ 'Der Theologiestudent Martin Heidegger und sein Dogmatikprofessor Carl Braig', *Freiburger Diözesanarchiv*, 125 (2005), 332–47.

Schaeffler, Richard, *Frömmigkeit des Denkens? Martin Heidegger und die katholische Theologie* (Darmstadt: Wissenschaftliche Buchgesellschaft, 1978).

Schindler, D. C., *Hans Urs von Balthasar and the Dramatic Structure of Truth: A Philosophical Investigation* (New York: Fordham University Press, 2004).

Schindler, Hans, *Barth und Overbeck* (Gotha: Leopold Klotz Verlag, 1936).

Schwöbel, Christoph, 'Wolfhart Pannenberg', in David Ford (ed.), *The Modern Theologians* (Oxford: Blackwell, 2nd edn., 1997), 180–208.

Sheehan, Thomas, 'Heidegger's *Lehrjahre*', in John Sallis et al. (eds.), *The Collegium Phaenomenologicum* (Dordrecht: Kluwer, 1988), 77–137.

———— 'Reading a Life: Heidegger and Hard Times', in Charles Guignon (ed.), *The Cambridge Companion to Heidegger* (Cambridge: Cambridge University Press, 1993), 70–96.

———— 'Husserl and Heidegger: The Making and Unmaking of a Relationship', in *Edmund Husserl: Psychological and Transcendental Phenomenology and the Confrontation with Heidegger (1927–1931)*, ed. and trans. Thomas Sheehan and R. E. Palmer (The Hague: Kluwer Academic Publishers, 1997), 1–40.

Simmons, J. Aaron, and Nathan, Kerr, 'From Necessity to Hope: A Continental Perspective on Eschatology without *Telos*', *Heythrop Journal*, 50, no. 6 (2009), 948–65.

Simpson, John, and Edmund, Weiner (eds.), *The Oxford English Dictionary* (Oxford: Oxford University Press, 2nd edn., 1989).

Vigliotti, Robert, 'The Young Heidegger's Ambitions for the Chair of Catholic Philosophy and Hugo Ott's Charge of Opportunism', *Studia Phænomenologica*, 1, nos. 3–4 (2001), 323–50.

Weber, Edwin Ernst (ed.), *Renitenz und Genie: Meßkirch und der badische Seekreis zwischen 1848/49 und dem Kulturkampf* (Konstanz: Gesellschaft Oberschwaben, 2003).

Weber, Simon, *Theologie als freie Wissenschaft und die wahren Feinde wissenschaftlicher Freiheit. Ein Wort zum Streit um den Antimodernisteneid* (Freiburg: Herder, 1912).

Wehrli, Rudolf, *Alter und Tod des Christentums bei Franz Overbeck* (Zurich: Theologischer Verlag, 1977).

Weiß, Otto, *Der Modernismus in Deutschland: Ein Beitrag zur Theologiegeschichte* (Regensburg: Pustet, 2001).

Westphal, Merold, *Overcoming Onto-Theology: Toward a Postmodern Christian Faith* (New York: Fordham, 2001).

White, Carol, *Time and Death: Heidegger's Analysis of Finitude* (London: Ashgate, 2005).

Wolf, Hubert (ed.), *Antimodernismus und Modernismus in der katholischen Kirche: Beiträge zum theologiegeschichtlichen Vorfeld des II. Vatikanums* (Paderborn: Schöningh, 1998).

Wolfe, Judith, 'Acknowledging a Hidden God: A Theological Critique of Stanley Cavell on Scepticism', *Heythrop Journal*, 48, no. 3 (2007), 384–405.

———— 'Messianism', in Nick Adams, George Pattison, and Graham Ward (eds.), *The Oxford Handbook of Theology and Modern European Thought* (Oxford: Oxford University Press, 2013).

———— *Heidegger and Theology* (London: Continuum, 2013).

Wright, Kathleen, 'Heidegger and the Authorization of Hölderlin's Poetry', in Karsten Harries and Christoph Jamme (eds.), *Martin Heidegger: Politics, Art, Technology* (New York: Holmes and Meier, 1994), 164–74.

Zaborowski, Holger, '"Herkunft aber bleibt stets Zukunft." Anmerkungen zur religiösen und theologischen Dimension des Denkweges Martin Heideggers bis 1919', in Alfred Denker, Hans-Helmuth Gander, and Holger Zaborowski (eds.), *Heidegger und die Anfänge seines Denkens* (Freiburg: Karl Alber Verlag, 2004), 123–58.

Index